**Positive Approaches To Healthy Sexuality
Presents**

Counselor Training Program Manual

Assisting Those with Same-Sex Attraction (SSA) and Their Loved Ones

Richard Cohen, M.A.

PATH Press

© Richard Cohen, M.A. 2008, Revised edition 2023

All rights reserved. No part of this book may be reproduced or transmitted in any form or by any means, electronic or mechanical, including photocopying, recording, or by information storage and retrieval systems, without the written permission of the author and publisher.

The author and publisher hereby grant the right only to the purchaser of this manual to reproduce some of the material contained herein only for his or her own exclusive, personal, professional, and non-commercial use.

ISBN: 979-8-9870260-5-2

Library of Congress Control Number: 2023916779

Layout Design: Lisa De Spain / www.book2bestseller.com
Cover Design: Katarina / fiverr.com

Publisher:
Richard Cohen, M.A.
Positive Approaches To Healthy Sexuality
P.O. Box 2315
Bowie, MD 20718

Tel. (301) 805-5155
Email: pathinfo@pathinfo.org
Website: www.pathinfo.org
Counselor Training Program film series: https://www.pathinfo.org/counselortrainingprogramfilmseries

The author and publisher of this material make no medical claims for its use. This material is not intended to substitute for effective psychotherapy. Please see a professional therapist or certified sexual orientation coach for individual help. If you would like a referral, please contact our office.

Dedication

This *Counselor Training Program Manual* is dedicated to my loving God who called me into ministry in 1987. Faithfully I have followed His calling, and faithfully He has led me each step of the way. This is my gift to you, oh Lord, and your gift to the world through me. May it serve to help set many free.

Special Thanks

I would like to thank my beautiful wife Jae Sook and our three remarkable children for their loving support throughout my career. Thanks to my incomparable editors and friends: Mary Hamm, Phillip Schanker, and Lily Oliveri.

Thanks to my beloved pastors and friends: John & Trina Jenkins, Keith & Vicki Battle, Ron & Brenda Crawford, Alfred & Susie Owens, and Anthony & Cynthia Moore. I love you all so very much.

Endorsements

I am so blessed to have participated in the first course for certification as a Sexual Orientation Coach with the Positive Approaches To Healthy Sexuality. I feel it has thoroughly prepared me to deal with clients in this sensitive area. Comprehensive in scope, sensitive in approach, and detailed in methodology this course will untangle the nuances of counseling the struggler with unwanted SSA. As more therapists become familiar with this course, many SSA strugglers who have been disappointed with traditional therapeutic approaches will obtain the help they need to progress in the difficult journey towards personal wholeness and heterosexuality.

Keith Vennum, M.D., LMHC,
Former President of The Alliance for
Therapeutic Choice and Scientific Integrity

No one today has more practical, real-life experience helping individuals process and explore unwanted same-sex attraction than Richard Cohen. I have applied techniques and ideas that I've learned from Richard with great success as I've worked with life-coaching clients and groups over the years. His instruction and mentoring have been invaluable.

Rich Wyler
Founder and Director, Brothers Road

Richard Cohen's Counselor Training Program really speaks to me. In fact, I believe his new, lucid approach to understanding SSA will be considered nothing less than groundbreaking. Addressing therapists, Mr. Cohen definitely broadens our vision, explaining a very clear route to follow in helping individuals heal complex inner wounds and thus live happier, more fulfilled lives. I therefore thoroughly recommend this course.

Mtra. Elena Barrero
Dean of Psychology Department
Universidad Anahuac Mexico Sur

The Counselor Training Program was a tremendous help to me. It was a refreshing approach to learning the many facets of healing SSA. Cohen's hands-on approach and interpersonal training skills made for a relaxed, non-threatening learning environment. The opportunities acquired in the program were priceless. I recommend this to anyone at any level—seasoned therapist, new counselor, counseling student, pastor, mentor, or coach.

James E. Phelan, Psy.D, LCSW

Richard Cohen, with his keen sensitivity and ability to empower and transform lives, is just phenomenal. Being a part of the training, responding to, and helping persons with same-sex attractions has revolutionized and empowered my ministry tremendously. I now have a relentless passion to minister in a broader context in an effort to reach all. The content of this training was consistent with the Word, a courageous Work, and challenged my Will.

Pastor Anthony Moore
Carolina Church

It was my distinct honor and privilege to have attended ten of Richard's classes on SSA. Not only did the classes enlighten me on the many emotional and mental issues surrounding that lifestyle, but it provoked a greater understanding for those who desire to be set free. I highly recommend Richard's classes and teaching materials to anyone who ministers to persons with SSA or any other type of emotional wounds. I not only found the course to be beneficial for understanding SSA, but much of the material can be used in other areas of ministry. I thank God for Richard's courage to continue to reach out to those who are in need. And I thank God for the many who have been healed, and who will be healed as a result of his ministry.

Rev. Dr. Paulette L. Scott
Christ CornerStone Healing Ministries

I highly recommend the Counselor Training Program to all parish pastors. It will help and instruct any pastor so that they can be sensitive to those who choose to change as well as those who choose to live the lifestyle.

Wenda Fry, Pastor

Thank You. It would have taken me a lifetime to come to this wisdom. I would attend this seminar again and encourage others to attend as well. It helped me to understand the causes of SSA. It gave me valuable training to minister to those struggling with SSA. It allowed me to get in touch with my own wounding and to learn steps for healing. I want to bring this program to my church.

Pastor Robin Wright
Mt. Holy Church

Contents

Endorsements ... 4
Introduction ... 11
Day One: Syllabus ... 14
Day Two: Syllabus ... 15
Day Three: Syllabus ... 16
Day Four: Syllabus ... 17
Day Five: Syllabus ... 18
Table of Contents for the Counselor Training Program MP3 Series ... 19
Counselor Training Program Questionnaire ... 22
Day One: Syllabus ... 23
Terminology used to describe the phenomenon of Same-Sex Attraction (SSA) in our culture ... 24
Scripture on Homosexuality* ... 25
What We Believe ... 26
Biological and Genetic Studies of Homosexuality ... 27
200 Participants Reporting a Change from Homosexual to Heterosexual Orientation ... 28
People Are Not Essentially Born with SSA ... 29
Meaning Behind Same-Sex Attraction (SSA) ... 32
Potential Variables Creating Same-Sex Attraction (SSA) ... 37
Causes of SSA ... 43
The Heart of Female Same-Sex Attraction ... 44
Process of Healing Unwanted SSA ... 45
Four Stages of Resolving Unwanted Same-Sex Attraction ... 46

How to Assist Those Who Experience Unwanted SSA	47
Family History Questionnaire	49
Resources for Resolving Unwanted SSA	54
Bibliography	55
Initial Client Intake	56
Example of an Evaluation/Content Analysis and Treatment Plan for a Male Client	57
Example of a Treatment Plan	62
Example of a Liability and Release Form	69
Therapeutic Relationship Between Therapist / Coach and Client	71
Components of Session	72
Day Two: Syllabus	73
Stage One: Transitioning (Behavioral Therapy)	74
Masturbation	76
Sexual Fantasies	79
Support Network	83
Creating Healthy Same-Gender Relationships	84
How to Tell a Straight Friend	86
Additional Tips for SSA Strugglers Sharing with Straight Friends	88
Mentorship of Men Who Struggle with Same-Sex Attraction	89
Affirmations	94
Group Process Protocol	97
Feelings Wheel	98
Stage Two: Grounding (Cognitive Therapy)	99
Cognitive Therapy	100
Communication Skills – Effective Listening & Sharing	101
Journaling	107
Inner Child Healing	108
Seven Stages of Development	109
Three Stages of Healing Your Inner Child	110
Day Three: Syllabus	111

- Stage Three: Healing Homo-Emotional/Social Wounds ... 112
- Therapeutic Approaches to Healing ... 114
- Focusing ... 116
- Voice Dialogue ... 117
- Shame and Attachment Loss: The Practical Work of Reparative Therapy ... 119
- Body-Centered Therapy Protocol ... 120
- Healing Body Image Wounds ... 122
- Healing Body Image Wounds—Mirror Exercise ... 123
- Healthy Touch in the Healing Process ... 124
- Bioenergetics ... 132
- Role Play / Healing Prayer (Theophostic) / EMDR ... 133
- Process Training Protocol ... 135
- Day Four: Syllabus ... 147
- Alcohol and High-Stress Family System ... 148
- Sexual Abuse ... 149
- Stage Four: Healing Hetero-Emotional / Social Wounds ... 150
- Dating and Mating for Former SSA Men and Women ... 151
- Five Love Languages ... 152
- Developing Heterosexual Attractions ... 154
- Conscious Dating MP3 ... 156
- Conscious Dating: Finding the Love of Your Life in Today's World ... 161
- Summary: Preparing Men and Women for Dating and Mating ... 166
- Day Five: Syllabus ... 167
- Protocol for Family and Friends Who Have SSA Loved Ones ... 168
- Summary of the Key Points from *Gay Children, Straight Parents* ... 171
- Syllabus for a Parents Support Group ... 173
- Two stories from parents who participated in our classes: ... 178
- Counter-Transference ... 183
- Taking Care of the Therapist/Coach/Counselor: Preventing Burnout ... 185
- Continued Growth into Manhood / Womanhood ... 187

Political Aspects of SSA in the World	188
After the Ball	189
Major Gay Rights Organizations / Religion / Mental Health Profession	206
Solution	207
How to Meet the Press: A Survival Guide	208
Media Prep	217
Family Healing Session (FHS) Protocol Manual	219
About the Author	253

Introduction

Same-Sex Attraction (SSA) is not about SSA. Ultimately, it is about hurts in the heart that have not healed, and legitimate needs for love that have never been experienced in the critical ages and stages of child development. Therefore, SSA is not about sex but the psyche's attempt to heal and grow into the fullness of one's masculinity or femininity.

From the 1970s to the mid-1980s, I was the client who desperately sought help to resolve my unwanted same-sex attraction (SSA). Most therapists had no clue how to help me. After my breakthrough in 1987, I went back to graduate school for a Master of Art's degree in counseling psychology. From 1989, I became the psychotherapist helping hundreds of men and women find freedom from unwanted SSA, ultimately fulfilling their heterosexual dreams. I know personally and professionally that change *is* possible.

"Dear God. Please take away my homosexual feelings. I never asked for them. Why won't you take them away?"

I prayed this prayer day after day, month after month, and year after year from elementary school to my undergraduate years at Boston University. But God never took them away. At the same time, I had a dream to marry a woman and create a beautiful family.

In 1970 I came out as a gay man in my senior year of High School. My parents swiftly sent me to a psychiatrist who had absolutely no idea how to help me. Off to Boston University I went. There I had several boyfriends in my freshman year, and a partner for the next three years. I grew up outside of Philadelphia in a Jewish family. My boyfriend Kurt loved Jesus. Because I loved Kurt, I wanted to understand about this Jesus, so I read the New Testament for the first time in my life. It was amazing. I fell in love with Christ. He was congruent on the inside and outside, and he offered grace, forgiveness and love.

I became a believer and prayed to the Lord, "Please take away my unwanted same-sex attractions," but still they persisted. While reading Scripture, Kurt and I realized that we were not supposed to be having sex, and we broke off our relationship.

For the next nine years I lived as a celibate man. During this time, I met my wife-to-be, Jae Sook, who hails from Korea. I told her about my past. She was completely loving and accepting. And yet, after we married my homosexual feelings returned. It became a living nightmare.

I hit the floor in prayer: "Why didn't you take these desires away? I did everything you asked of me. I was a good Christian man." Back into therapy I went and one-by-one the causes of my SSA were revealed:

1) Lack of bonding with my father
2) Overattachment to my mother
3) Physical abuse by my older brother
4) Sexual abuse by my Uncle Phil when I was five years old

As I began to work through the pains of my past, my same-sex attractions diminished. Finally, in the arms of a dear friend, who just happened to also be named Phillip, I grieved the core pain of my sexual abuse and the hurts I incurred from my father and older brother. There I discovered the secret to freedom—when my broken heart was heard and healed while being held by a healthy heterosexual man, my homosexual feelings no longer had a purpose in my life.

After my breakthrough, I prayed to God, "What would you have me do now?" In 1987 I received my calling: help others who experience unwanted SSA, assist their family members and friends, and teach the world the truth about homosexuality. I went to graduate school and received my Master of Arts (M.A.) degree in counseling psychology, and for the past 35 years as a psychotherapist, I have had the honor of assisting thousands worldwide who experience unwanted SSA in fulfilling their heterosexual dreams, helped hundreds of parents in reconciling with their LGBTQ+ loved ones, and trained over 6,000 professional therapists and ministry leaders how to love and understand those who wrestle with their sexual orientation and gender identity.

I am neither homophobic nor anti-gay. I love the entire LGBTQ+ community and respect each individual's right to choose his or her own path. Today my beautiful wife and I have been married for 43 years, and we have three amazing adult children. My dream came true. I know personally, professionally and scientifically that people are not essentially born with same-sex attraction, that no one chooses to have SSA, and that change *is* possible!

Many of your clients are looking to you for help, hope, and a path that will allow them to resolve their unwanted Same-Sex Attraction (SSA). It is essential that you educate yourself about the basic causes of SSA as well as a plan for healing/resolving their unwanted desires. Additionally, their family members and friends will also seek your guidance. I will offer you practical tools to assist both of these populations.

- First, I have developed a four-stage protocol for assisting those who experience unwanted SSA as detailed in *Being Gay: Nature, Nurture or Both?*
- Second, I have authored a 12-step protocol for parents, family members, friends, and the religious community as outlined in *Gay Children, Straight Parents: A Plan for Family Healing.*
- Third, I have created a protocol for therapists, counselors, coaches and ministry leaders detailed in our *Counselor Training Program Manual and Film Series.*

The majority of SSA strugglers, those who have LGBTQ+ loved ones, therapists and ministry leaders are ignorant about these solutions and the potential for real and lasting change. I therefore want to share with you in this book (and further detailed in the other three publications) the truth, the gold that I have mined from my personal and professional journey:

- Struggler: I experienced unwanted SSA from the time I was in elementary school. It was extremely painful not understanding why I experienced homosexual desires or how to resolve them.
- Overcomer: It was a long and painful journey to figure out why I experienced SSA, and it took even longer to heal the wounds that created those desires in the first place. Today, I stand as a victor of love. I have been married to my wonderful wife Jae Sook since 1980, and we have three incredible adult children.
- Healer: For thirty-five years as a psychotherapist and sexual orientation and gender identity specialist, I have helped hundreds of men and women who experienced unwanted SSA fulfill their heterosexual potential, helped hundreds of parents restore relationships with their SSA children, and helped thousands of others through our healing seminars and online classes.
- Educator: I have taught thousands of therapists, counselors, coaches, ministry leaders and the general public about the causes of SSA and a successful treatment plan for change.

I have had the privilege of being on both sides of the therapist's couch—first as a client and now as a counselor. As in all professions, we bring our life experiences to our work. I am a healing artist. I know the slings and arrows of outrageous fortune that burden those living with unwanted same-sex attraction. I am a worthy journeyman. I can talk the talk because I have walked the walk. And it certainly was a "road less traveled."

My greatest desire is to shed light upon the truth of SSA, how to help those who seek change, and how to assist their loved ones.

Counselor Training Program Film Series:

https://www.pathinfo.org/counselortrainingprogramfilmseries

I am also including two other manuals:

1 – **Process Training Protocols** (various therapeutic tools for individual and group therapy).
2 – **Family Healing Session (FHS) Protocol** (how to facilitate a two-day family healing session). This is part of our FHS Film Series:

https://www.pathinfo.org/fhs-film-series-manual

> Throughout this training manual and MP3/MP4 series, sometimes I address the professional directly, and other times I address the SSA strugglers and/or their loved ones. In this way, the coach, therapist, or ministry leader will know how to share with the strugglers, as you may use the same language in your practice.

Day One: Syllabus

1. Read *Being Gay* Chapters Two, Four, and Six

Class Syllabus:

1. Introduction
2. Terminology
3. Meaning and Causes of Same-Sex Attractions (SSA)
4. Four Stages of Healing Unwanted SSA (Therapeutic Framework)

Break

5. Resources for Those who Experience Unwanted SSA and Their Loved Ones
6. Consultation/Evaluation/Treatment Plan
    a. Review History: Based on Family History Questionnaire (FHQ)
    b. Content Analysis/Evaluation: Causes of SSA
    c. Treatment Plan: Four Stages of Healing
7. Therapeutic Relationship between Therapist/Clergy/Ministry Leader/Coach and Client
8. Components of a Session

PROGRAM OVERVIEW

Day Two: Syllabus

1. Continue reading *Being Gay* Chapters Four and Six
2. Read and do the exercises in *Ten Days to Self-Esteem* by David Burns
3. Read and do the exercises in *Recovery of Your Inner Child* by Lucia Capacchione

Class Syllabus:

Stage One: Transitioning (Behavioral Therapy)

1. Cut Off from 3 Ps (Playgrounds, Playmates, and Playthings)
    a. Masturbation and Sexual Fantasies

2. Develop a Support Network
    a. Healthy Same-Gender Relationships
    b. How to Share with Heterosexual Friends and Mentors
    c. Mentoring Relationships

Break

3. Relationship with God
    a. Spend Time in Prayer and Meditation
    b. Not Gay, Bisexual, Lesbian, Transgender, Non-Binary, etc.: Child of God (Son or Daughter); Man or Woman
    c. Affirmations

4. Group Process Protocol

Stage Two: Grounding (Cognitive/Affective Therapies)

1. Cognitive Therapy: *Ten Days to Self-Esteem* by David Burns
   Your Perfect Right by Alberti and Emmons

2. Communication Skills: Sharing and Listening

3. Journaling

4. Affective Therapy: *Recovery of Your Inner Child* by Lucia Capacchione

Day Three: Syllabus

1. Read *Being Gay* Chapters Six, Eight, Ten, and Twelve
2. Read *Focusing* by Eugene Gendlin
3. Read *Embracing Ourselves* by Hal and Sidra Stone
4. Read *Door of Hope* by Jan Frank
5. Read *Unwanted* by Jay Stringer

Class Syllabus:

Stage Three: Healing Homo-Emotional and Homo-Social Wounds (Psychodynamic Therapy)

1. Root Causes: Process of Grieving, Forgiving, and Taking Responsibility
2. Therapeutic Approaches to Healing
3. Attend Healing Seminars
4. Focusing Protocol and Practice
5. Voice Dialogue Protocol and Practice

Break

6. Body-Centered Therapy Protocol
7. Healthy Touch in the Healing Process
8. Bioenergetics – Use of Anger in the Healing Process, *Bioenergetics*, by Alexander Lowen
9. Role Play
10. Healing Prayer
11. *EMDR: Eye Movement Desensitization Reprocessing* by Francine Shapiro
12. Process Training Program Manual

Day Four: Syllabus

1. Read *Getting the Love You Want* by Harville Hendrix
2. Read *How to Get a Date Worth Keeping* by Henry Cloud
3. Read *Five Love Languages* by Gary Chapman
4. Read *Bioenergetics* by Alexander Lowen

Class Syllabus:

Stage Three: Healing Homo-Emotional and Homo-Social Wounds (Psychodynamic Therapy)

1. Alcoholic and High-Stress Family Systems
2. Sexual Abuse Issues

Break

Stage Four: Healing Hetero-Emotional and Hetero-Social Wounds (Psychodynamic Therapy)

3. Healing Mother-Son/Father-Daughter Relationships and Hetero-Social Wounds
4. Process of Grieving, Forgiving, and Taking Responsibility
5. Five Love Languages
6. Understanding Healthy Male-Female Relationships
7. Preparing Former SSA Men and Women for Dating and Mating

COUNSELOR TRAINING PROGRAM MANUAL

Day Five: Syllabus

1. Read *Gay Children, Straight Parents* by Richard Cohen
2. Read *After the Ball* Summary
3. Read *How to Meet the Press* Summary

Class Syllabus:

1. Twelve-Step Protocol for Parents/Families with SSA Children: Assisting Parents, Family Members, and Friends Whose Loved Ones experience SSA

2. Parents Support Group Protocol

3. Counter-Transference: Therapist's Shadow Work

Break

4. Taking Care of the Therapist/Ministry Leader/Clergy/Coach: Preventing Burnout

5. Socio-Political Issues and the Gay Rights Movement: Their Impact Upon Our Religious Institutions, Schools, Children, and Therapeutic Practices

6. Media Training: How to Meet the Press – TV, Radio, and Newsprint

7. Family Healing Session Protocol Manual

Instructor and Facilitator:
Richard Cohen, M.A., Executive Director
Positive Approaches To Healthy Sexuality (PATH)

Tel. (301) 805-5155
Web: www.pathinfo.org
Email: PATHinfo@pathinfo.org

Counselor Training Program Film Series:
https://www.pathinfo.org/counselortrainingprogramfilmseries

Family Healing Session (FHS) Protocol:
https://www.pathinfo.org/fhs-film-series-manual

PROGRAM OVERVIEW

Table of Contents for the Counselor Training Program MP3 Series

Disc One

Introduction Part I – 4:44
Introduction Part II: Justin's Story – 15:10
Introduction Part III: Requirements/Syllabus – 13:24
Meaning and Causes of SSA Part I – 32:42   Total Time: 66:08

Disc Two

Richard Cohen's Story – 14:21
Meaning and Causes Part II – 4:39
Meaning and Causes Part III: Ten Causes of SSA – 35:56
Four Stages of Healing Part I: Keys to Healing – 3:51
Four Stages of Healing Part II – 20:07   Total Time: 79:03

Disc Three

Bob Abbott's Story – 36:33
National Organizations and Bibliography – 19:24   Total Time: 55:59

Disc Four

Evaluations and Treatment Plans – 58:11
Therapeutic Relationship – 6:24
Components of a Session – 5:33   Total Time: 70:13

Disc Five

Stage One: Overview and Masturbation – 19:34
Stage One: Sexual Fantasies – 30:39
Stage One: Developing a Support Network – 29:38   Total Time: 79:55

Disc Six

Stage One: Relationship with God – 11:27
Stage One: Group Process Protocol – 10:00
Bob's Story – 20:22
Stage Two: Cognitive Therapy – 17:22
Stage Two: Communication Skills – 15:30
Stage Two: Journaling – 1:27   Total Time: 76:21

Disc Seven
    Stage Two: Inner Child Healing – 21:04
    Tom's Story – 46:12   Total Time: 67:18

Disc Eight
    Stage Three: Healing Homo-Emotional/Social Wounds – 19:42
    Stage Three: Focusing – 15:53
    Stage Three: Voice Dialogue – 23:47
    Stage Three: Healing Body Image Wounds – 5:11
    Stage Three: Healthy Touch – 14:27   Total Time: 79:09

Disc Nine
    Stage Three: Bioenergetics – 10:00
    Stage Three: Family Constellations – 5:21
    Stage Three: EMDR – 9:24
    Lee Brundidge's Story – 27:24
    Stage Three: Alcohol and High Stress Family Systems – 10:28
    Stage Three: Sexual Abuse – 15:40   Total Time: 78:30

Disc Ten
    Stage Four: Healing Hetero-Emotional/Social Wounds – 4:14
    Stage Four: Dating and Marriage – 8:01
    Stage Four: Five Love Languages – 8:20
    Stage Four: Conscious Dating Part I – 17:02
    Stage Four: Conscious Dating Part II – 10:43
    Review of the Four Stages of Healing – 10:49
    Joseph's Story Part I – 18:02   Total Time: 77:25

Disc Eleven
    Joseph's Story Part II – 18:45
    Protocol for Families with SSA Children Part I – 37:03
    Protocol for Families with SSA Children Part II – 6:53
    Protocol for Families with SSA Children Part III – 6:10   Total Time: 68:58

Disc Twelve
    Michael and Elizabeth's Story – 35:49
    Protocol for Families with SSA Children Part IV – 2:36
    Mark and Wenda's Story – 31:21
    Protocol for Families with SSA Children Part V – 2:41   Total Time: 72:35

PROGRAM OVERVIEW

Disc Thirteen
    Sue's Story – 22:09
    Dad and Mom's Letters – 33:08
    Protocol for Families with SSA Children Part VI – 2:47
    Lee's Story – 15:43   Total Time: 73:54

Disc Fourteen
    Protocol for Families with SSA Children Part VII – 4:10
    Bonnie's Story – 21:29
    Protocol for Families with SSA Children Part VIII – 2:25
    Jarish's Story – 22:14
    Taking Care of the Caregiver – 23:23   Total Time: 73:51

Disc Fifteen
    Socio-Political Aspects of SSA – 59:56   Total Time: 59:56

Disc Sixteen
    Media Training – 46:07   Total Time: 46:07

Total Listening Time (MP3): 18 hours 42 minutes

Counselor Training Program Questionnaire

PLEASE ANSWER THE FOLLOWING QUESTIONS:

1. What are three things you would like us to know about you, should you die today?

2. Why do you want to be (or why are you) a therapist, clergy, ministry leader, or coach working with the Same-Sex Attracted population and their loved ones?

3. Who loves you?

4. What do you want to get from this training program?

5. What are your passions in life?

Day One

Homework

1. Read *Being Gay* Chapters Two, Four, and Six

Class Syllabus:

1. Introduction
2. Terminology
3. Meaning and Causes of Same-Sex Attractions (SSA)
4. Four Stages of Healing Unwanted SSA (Therapeutic Framework)

Break

5. Resources for Those Who Experience Unwanted SSA and Their Loved Ones
6. Consultation/Evaluation/Treatment Plan
    a. Review History: Based on Family History Questionnaire (FHQ)
    b. Content Analysis/Evaluation: Causes of SSA
    c. Treatment Plan: Four Stages of Healing
7. Therapeutic Relationship between Therapist/Clergy/Ministry Leader/Coach and Client
8. Components of a Session

The terminology used to describe the phenomenon of Same-Sex Attraction (SSA) in our culture.*

Homosexual: Adj. Of, relating to, or having a sexual orientation to persons of the same sex; N. A homosexual person; a gay man or a lesbian.

Homosexuality: N. Sexual orientation to persons of the same sex; N. Sexual activity with another of the same sex.

Gay: Adj. Of, relating to, or having a sexual orientation to persons of the same sex; N. A person whose sexual orientation is to persons of the same sex. A man whose sexual orientation is to men: *an alliance of gays and lesbians.*

Lesbian: N. A woman whose sexual orientation is to women.

Bisexual: Adj. Of or relating to both sexes; Adj. Of, relating to, or having a sexual orientation to persons of either sex.

Transvestite: N. A person who dresses and acts in a style or manner traditionally associated with the opposite sex.

Transgender: Adj. Appearing as, wishing to be considered as, or having undergone surgery to become a member of the opposite sex; N. A person appearing or attempting to be a member of the opposite sex, as a transsexual or habitual cross-dresser.

Non-Binary: Adj. 1. Not binary; not consisting of or relating to two parts or components. 2. Of or relating to a person whose gender identity is other than conventionally male or female.

Unwanted SSA: [Defined by Richard Cohen, M.A.] Those who experience same-sex attraction and are not identified as "gay," "lesbian," "bisexual," etc. They desire to be heterosexual and/or live in compatibility with their spiritual beliefs concerning this issue.

* All definitions are taken from the American Heritage Dictionary (2007). Additionally, there are more than 70 definitions of sexual orientation and gender identity on Facebook as of 2023.

DAY ONE

Scripture on Homosexuality*

Old Testament

- Genesis 1:27
- Genesis 19:4-8
- Leviticus 18:22
- Leviticus 20:13
- Judges 19:22-26

New Testament

- Matthew 15:18-19
- Romans 1:24-32
- I Timothy 1:8-11
- Jude 6:7
- I Corinthians 6:9-11

* **All Scriptures refer to someone's behavior and not the person him/herself.**

We believe...

1. There is no compelling evidence that anyone is determined from birth to experience SSA.

There is no conclusive scientific data that proves there is a simple genetic, hormonal, or biological cause for homosexuality. Scientific research indicates that although biological and genetic factors may play a part, homosexual desires stem from a complex interaction of psychological, environmental, and temperamental influences.

2. No one simply chooses to experience SSA.

These desires are very often the result of unresolved childhood wounds and unmet love needs. Choice is clearly involved in the decision of whether or not to act upon the desires.

3. People can be hopeful in their choice to change from a homosexual to a heterosexual orientation.

Research demonstrates that changing from SSA to OSA (Opposite-Sex Attraction) is possible. With strong motivation, effective treatment, and proper support, some people can and do change their orientation and sexual desires. The path to healing is fourfold: (1) understand the root causes of SSA, (2) gain support from others, (3) heal the wounds that created the desires in the first place, and (4) fulfill unmet love needs in healthy, healing, nonsexual relationships with those of the same gender.

DAY ONE

Biological and Genetic Studies of Homosexuality

There are two prevailing views about homosexuality:
Essentialist—those who believe that SSA is predetermined or innate.
Constructionist—those who believe that SSA is an acquired condition.

1. Simon LeVay

"A Difference in Hypothalamic Structure Between Heterosexual and Homosexual Men," *Science*, August 30, 1991, Vol. 253, pp. 1034-1037.

"It's important to stress what I didn't find. I did not prove that homosexuality is genetic, or find a genetic cause for being gay. I didn't show that gay men are born that way, the most common mistake people make in interpreting my work," Simon LeVay.

"Sex and the Brain," *Discover*, Vol. 15, no. 3 (March 1994), pp. 64-71

2. Michael Bailey, Ph.D.
Richard C. Pillard, M.D.

"A Genetic Study of Male Sexual Orientation," *Archives of General Psychiatry*, Vol. 48, December 1991.

"There must be something in the environment to yield discordant twins," J. Michael Bailey.

Newsweek, February 24, 1992, p. 46

3. Dean Hamer et al.

"A Linkage between DNA Markers on the X Chromosome and Male Sexual Orientation," *Science*, July 16, 1993, Vol. 261, pp. 3212-3217.

"These genes do not cause people to become homosexuals…ultimately it is the environment that determines how these genes will express themselves," Dean Hamer.

Time, April 27, 1998, pp. 60-61

200 Participants Reporting a Change from Homosexual to Heterosexual Orientation*

In October 2003, Dr. Robert Spitzer, former professor of psychiatry at Columbia University, published a study in the *Archives of Sexual Behavior*. He found that some men and women actually changed their sexual orientation.

> "Like most psychiatrists, I thought that homosexual behavior could only be resisted and that no one could really change their sexual orientation. I now believe that to be false. *Some people can and do change.*"
>
> Robert L. Spitzer, M.D., Columbia University
> (*Archives of Sexual Behavior*, October 2003, Vol. 32, No. 5, pp. 403-417)

- 200 Subjects: 143 Men, 57 Women

- 43% through Ex-Homosexual Ministries;
  57% through Therapists

- "Yearning for romantic involvement with same sex"
  BEFORE treatment:
    78% men and 81% women
  AFTER treatment:
    8% men and 4% women

- Achieved "their goal of good heterosexual functioning"
  66% men and 44% women

- Depression:
  BEFORE treatment:
    43% men and 47% women
  AFTER treatment:
    1% men and 4% women

- 87% reported that their change effort was "very helpful" in "feeling more masculine/feminine"

- 93% said it was "very helpful" in "developing nonsexual relations" with members of the same sex

* In May 2012, Dr. Spitzer apologized to the homosexual community for any harm his study may have caused them. However, this does not invalidate the findings. Many of my former clients and myself participated in his study and we are all living healthy, happy heterosexual lives. The same holds true for the vast majority of subjects who participated in this study.

DAY ONE

People Are Not Essentially Born with SSA

American Psychological Association

"Although much research has examined the possible genetic, hormonal, developmental, social, and cultural influences on sexual orientation, no findings have emerged that permit scientists to conclude that sexual orientation is determined by any particular factor or factors."

American Psychological Association © 2008
http://www.apa.org/topics/sorientation.html

What You Should Know about Sexual Orientation of Youth

American College of Pediatricians
www.FactsAboutYouth.com

- Homosexuality is not a genetically determined, unchangeable trait.
- Homosexual attraction is determined by a combination of familial, environmental, social and biological influences. Inheritance predisposing personality traits may play a role for some. Consequently, homosexual attraction is changeable.
- The homosexual lifestyle, especially for males, carries grave health risks.
- Sexual reorientation therapy has proven effective for those with unwanted homosexual attractions.

The Language of God: A Scientist Presents Evidence for Belief

Francis Collins, M.D., Ph.D., New York: Free Press, 2006, p. 260.

"An area of particularly strong public interest is the genetic basis of homosexuality. Evidence from twin studies does in fact support the conclusion that heritable factors play a role in male homosexuality. However, the likelihood that the identical twin of a homosexual male will also be gay is about 20% (compared with 2-4 percent of males in the general population), indicating that sexual orientation is genetically influenced but not hardwired by DNA, and that whatever genes are involved represent predispositions, not predeterminations."

My Genes Made Me Do It: A Scientific Look at Sexual Orientation

Dr. Neil & Briar Whitehead / http://mygenes.co.nz/download.htm

Review of the genetic, hormonal, and biological studies regarding SSA, debunking the innate, immutable theory.

There is (Still) No Gay Gene, 2019

A study was reported in the journal *Science* in 2019. The researchers were from Harvard and MIT. The subjects were 470,000 people who identified as gay. They gave permission for their DNA to be tested. This study was 100 times larger than any group previously studied. Their conclusion was that there is no way to look at someone's DNA and predict whether they are gay or straight.

- https://www.harvardmagazine.com/2019/08/there-s-still-no-gay-gene#:~:text=There%20is%20no%20one%20gene,complex%2C%20and%20anything%20but%20deterministic
- https://www.nature.com/articles/d41586-019-02585-6).

Sexuality and Gender
Findings from the Biological, Psychological, and Social Sciences

The New Atlantis, Lawrence S. Mayer, Ph.D, Paul McHugh, M.D., 2016
www.thenewatlantis.com

This report, conducted by world-renowned Johns Hopkins University scientists Dr. Lawrence S. Mayer and Dr. Paul R. McHugh, is a meta-analysis of data from over 200 peer-reviewed studies regarding "sexual orientation" and "gender identity." It is the most objective, exhaustive, and comprehensive study on the topic to date. Highlights of the study:

- "The understanding of sexual orientation as an innate, biologically fixed property of human beings—the idea that people are 'born that way'—is not supported by scientific evidence" (page 7 and Part One: Sexual Orientation).
- "Compared to heterosexuals, non-heterosexuals are about two to three times as likely to have experienced childhood sexual abuse" (page 7 and Part One).
- "Compared to the general population, non-heterosexual sub-populations are at an elevated risk for a variety of adverse health and mental health outcomes" (page 8 and Part Two: Sexuality, Mental Health Outcomes, and Social Stress).
- "The hypothesis that gender identity is an innate, fixed property of human beings that is independent of biological sex—that a person might be 'a man trapped in a woman's body' or 'a woman trapped in a man's body'—is not supported by scientific evidence" (page 8 and Part Three: Gender Identity).
- "Members of the transgender population are also at higher risk of a variety of mental health problems compared to members of the non-transgender population. Especially alarmingly, the rate of lifetime suicide attempts across all ages of transgender individuals is estimated at 41%, compared to under 5% in the overall U.S. population" (p 8/Part III).
- "Compared to the general population, adults who have undergone sex-reassignment surgery continue to have a higher risk of experiencing poor mental health outcomes. One study found that, compared to controls, sex-reassigned individuals were about five times more likely to attempt suicide and about 19 times more likely to die by suicide" (page 9 and Part Three).
- "Only a minority of children who experience cross-gender identification will continue to do so into adolescence or adulthood" page 9 and Part Three).

Meaning Behind Same-Sex Attraction (SSA)

Homosexuality is a symptom of:

- Unhealed wounds of the past (ten potential causes)

- Unmet needs for love

- Reparative drive to fulfill homo-emotional and/or homo-social love needs

Homosexuality is essentially an emotionally-based condition:

- Need for same-gender parent's/same-gender peers' love

- Need for gender indentification

- Fear of intimacy with members of the opposite sex

SSA represents a lack of gender indentity, caused by:

- Detachment from same-gender parent

- Detachment from same-gender peers

- Detachment from one's body

- Detachment from one's own gender

© Richard Cohen, M.A., 2023

Meaning Behind Same-Sex Attraction

As you will soon discover, there are many contributing factors that lead a boy or girl to develop homosexual feelings. Many professional therapists, myself included, have observed that most often SSA men and women are highly sensitive or hypersensitive individuals. Therefore, they experience events and relationships more deeply than other children. This temperament of hypersensitivity often leads these boys and girls to *perceive* rejection from their parents, peers, family members and/or friends. This perception becomes their reality: "I don't fit in. I'm different. I don't belong." These are often the core beliefs of children and adolescents who experience SSA.

If you are a parent of an SSA child, please do not blame yourself. This is not a blame game. My sole purpose in identifying what may have occurred is to achieve healing and reconciliation. Knowledge is power. Understanding the deeper meaning behind homosexual feelings is instrumental to bring about lasting change.

1. Homosexuality is a symptom of:

- Unhealed wounds of the past (see ten potential causes)
- Unmet needs for love
- Reparative drive to fulfill homo-emotional and/or homo-social love needs

Homosexual feelings, thoughts and desires are symptoms of underlying issues. They represent (1) a defensive response to conflicts in the present, a way to medicate pain, (2) unresolved childhood trauma, emotions and wounds that never healed, and (3) a *reparative drive* to fulfill homo-emotional love needs (bonding with same-gender parent, i.e., father-son, mother-daughter) and/or homo-social love needs (bonding with same-gender peers, i.e., guys with guys, girls with girls).

By "reparative drive" we mean that the individual who experiences SSA is seeking to obtain the love he or she did not experience in early childhood and adolescence, and is doing so by trying to connect with someone of the same gender. I need to stress that this reparative drive is most often completely unconscious. Dr. Elizabeth Moberly coined and Dr. Jospeh Nicolosi Sr. further developed the concept of a homo-emotional love need.

"It is here suggested that it is precisely this reparative urge that is involved in the homosexual impulse, that is, that this impulse is essentially motivated by the need to make good earlier deficits in the parent-child relationship. This persisting need for love from the same sex stems from, and is to be correlated with, the earlier unmet need for love from the parent of the same sex, or rather, the inability to receive such love, whether or not it was offered. This defensive detachment and its corresponding drive for renewed attachment imply that the homosexual condition is one of same-sex ambivalence" Elizabeth R. Moberly, *Homosexuality: A New Christian Ethic* (Cambridge, UK: Lutterworth Press, revised edition 2006), 6.

2. Homosexuality is essentially an emotionally based condition:

- Need for same-gender parent's / same-gender peers' love
- Need for gender identification
- Fear of intimacy with members of the opposite sex

We gain our sense of gender identity—masculinity for a man, and femininity for a woman—through successful bonding with our same-gender parent and then same-gender relatives and peers. Most case histories of those who experience SSA demonstrate that homosexual feelings originate in early childhood and preadolescence.

From the ages of one or one-and-a-half to three, the child begins to crawl, walk and then talk. This stage of development is known as a time of separation and individuation. The child begins to realize that he/she is different from mom, that he/she is an individual, separate and unique from mother. This time is also known as either the terrible or terrific twos, and the operative word is, "No." "No" essentially means that "I am not you, I am me, and I'm different from you." *However, the boy has an extra developmental task here.* He comes to realize that his genitals are different from his mother's. Who does he look like, who does he resemble?

The boy must then gender identify with his father, his role model of masculinity. If the father is absent, abusive or distant, another male mentor may help stand in the gap for the son. If there is no strong male presence in the toddler's life, he may continue to gender identify with his mother, internalizing her sense of femininity. This is one reason why many men who experience SSA may say, "From the time I was a child, I experienced homosexual feelings." They never successfully individuated from their mothers and gender identified with their fathers. On the other hand, the daughter, even though she is separating and individuating from her mother, will continue to gender identify with mom as her primary role model of femininity. She individuates while continuing to emulate her mother's behaviors. In the case of a potential SSA daughter, she may have been fearful of or detested her mother, and therefore didn't successfully internalize her own sense of femaleness (see other causes listed below).

"Just when he was developing his sense of masculinity and was especially receptive to the father's influence, the prehomosexual boy experienced a hurt or disappointment in his relationship with his father. To protect himself against future hurt, the boy developed a defensive posture characterized by emotional distancing. Not only does he fail to identify with father, but because of this hurt, he rejects father and the masculinity he represents" Joseph Nicolosi Sr., *Reparative Therapy of Male Homosexuality: A New Clinical Approach* (Northvale, NJ: Jason Aronson, Inc., 1991, Liberal Mind Publishers, updated edition, 2020), 105.

Same-sex attraction often represents a search for healthy parenting—a man seeking paternal love in the arms of another man, and a woman seeking maternal love in the arms of another woman (of course, this drive is most often unconscious). It may also represent a need for bonding with same-gender peers because these men and women never experienced successful bonding with those of the same gender in their preadolescent and/or adolescent years of development. Then, during puberty, those normal needs for bonding, with the same-gender parent and/or same-gender peers, became sexualized and/or eroticized. At this point the world tends to say to such a person, "You're born gay," or "You're born lesbian." This is a false label.

Labeling people with words like gay, lesbian, bisexual, or transgender is not only false, it also is done without a proper understanding of the situation. We are born as a man or a woman, as a son or a daughter. Those who experience SSA are merely stuck in early stages of psychosexual development. When they resolve past issues and fulfill unmet love needs in healthy, nonsexual, same-gender relationships, they will naturally develop opposite-sex desires. We are all heterosexually designed (men and women fit together beautifully and perfectly, biologically two men or two women simply do not).

If a man seeks to join sexually with another man, it means there is something lacking within him. He does not experience the fullness of his own masculinity. By joining with a man, he hopes to complete this lost part of himself. The same holds true for the woman seeking to join sexually with another woman. These yearnings represent the deep need of a child within—a need to experience love and secure bonding with someone of the same gender, to restore this lack of love. However, sexual relations will never satiate that need for love because this need is that of a child, and children do not want or need sex.

In many cases men who experience SSA have been over-attached to their mothers and detached from their fathers and the masculinity they represented. As a result of closeness to his mom and detachment from his dad, the son becomes internally more feminine in nature (research shows that about 85% of adult men who experience SSA had a close-binding intimate relationship with their mothers). In adulthood, this may block his ability to have a successful heterosexual relationship with another woman, because of this over-attachment and identification with the feminine (remember, opposites attract). The same may hold true for the daughter who is over-attached to her father and disconnected and dis-identified with her mother. She internalizes her dad's masculinity and rejects her mother's femininity. She may spend the rest of her life looking for that lost love and sense of connection with the feminine in the arms of other women.

"In one popular scenario of the homosexual male, he is the son of an unhappily married woman whose unhealthy, engulfing relationship with him may border on the incestuous. Though he becomes symbolically 'mother's little love,' she may stifle the boy's embryonic masculinity lest the relationship become overtly incestuous. However far it goes, he has feelings of guilt. Later, as an adult, he associates this guilt with all women because they remind him of the 'forbidden mother,' and therefore must not be touched. Many male homosexuals confess to strong attachments to their mothers, beginning from earliest childhood when their fathers were either absent, weak, withdrawn, or extremely harsh. Through this attachment, they 'identify' with women and seek the same sexual outlets as women" Robert Kronemeyer, *Overcoming Homosexuality* (New York City: NY, Macmillan Publishing Co., Inc., 1980), 60-61.

Many women who experience SSA might have also been sexually, physically, emotionally and/or mentally abused by men, and/or are hypersensitive. Not wanting to re-experience abuse with men, many turn to other women for affection, comfort and love. It is interesting to note that there is a higher percentage of domestic violence among lesbian couples than there is in the heterosexual population. Why? Underneath the exterior of these women are hurt little girls who were violated, and who take out their aggression and unresolved pain on each other.

3. SSA represents a lack of gender identity, caused by:

- Detachment from same-gender parent
- Detachment from same-gender peers
- Detachment from one's body
- Detachment from one's own gender

SSA often represents detachment between the individual and his or her same-gender parent and/or same-gender peers. Because a boy did not successfully or sufficiently bond with his dad and/or other male relatives and peers, he then rejects his own gender identity, not wanting to act or be like his father and/or other boys. After this occurs and puberty sets in, his emotional needs for bonding become sexualized. This is the construction of SSA and perhaps a gay identity—little boys and girls in adolescent or adult bodies looking for bonding through sexual relationships. Sexual behavior cannot and will not resolve their deeper needs.

Potential Variables Creating Same-Sex Attraction

Heredity	Temperament	Hetero-Emotional Wounds	Homo-Emotional Wounds	Sibling Wounds/ Family Dynamics	Body Image Wounds	Sexual Abuse	Social or Peer Wounds	Cultural Wounds	Others Factors
Generational Blessings and curses	Hypersensitive	Over-attachment to opposite-sex parent	Lack of attachment to same-sex parent	Abuse: mental, emotional, physical, and/or sexual	Late bloomer	Premature sexualization	Name-calling	Internet porn	Divorce
Unresolved family issues	High Maintenance	Abuse: mental, emotional, physical, and/or sexual	Abuse: mental, emotional, physical, and/ or sexual	Don't fit in	Physical disabilities	Homosexual imprinting	Put-downs	Media/ Entertainment Industry promoting sex	Death
Men resenting women, women resenting men	Artistic Nature	Parentified child: role reversal between parent and child	Parentified child: role reversal between parent and child	Don't belong	Shorter / Taller	Learned/ reinforced behavior	Teacher's pet	Sexualizing legitimate needs for love	Suicide
Addictions: substances, sex, gambling	Gender non-conforming behaviors:	Born the wrong sex	Born the wrong sex	Different from others	Heavier / Thinner	Sex used as a substitute for love	Goody-goody		Addictions: alcohol, drugs, sex, gambling, etc.
Medical/Mental health issues	Male more feminine	Imitation of behavior		Bullying/ verbal abuse	Skin color issues		Nerd		Intra-uterine experience: insecure attachment
Financial problems	Female more masculine				Lack of eye-hand coordination		Non-athletic		Adoption
Predilection for rejection							Lack of gender identification and/or gender non-conforming behaviors		War/genocide
Racial, religious, ethnic prejudice									Religion: toxic beliefs

The severity of wounding in each category will have a direct impact on the amount of time and effort it will take to heal.

Richard Cohen, M.A. © 2023

DAY ONE

Ten Potential Causes of SSA

The following is a list of ten potential causes that may lead an individual to experience SSA (see the chart). A combination of experiences and characteristics lead to SSA—never a single factor alone. Parents do not instill SSA in their children. It is the child's perception of their parenting combined with his/her innate temperament, e.g. hypersensitivity, which makes the difference.

1. Heredity

- Unresolved family issues
- Misperceptions
- Tendency to feel rejected

"It is assumed [by intergenerational and transgenerational family systems theory] that relational patterns are learned and passed down across the generations and that current individual and family behavior is a result of these patterns" ("Assessment of Intergenerational Family Relationships," *Family of Origin Therapy*, James Bray and Donald Williamson, Rockville, MD, Aspen Publishers, 1987, p. 31).

In family systems therapy, it is well known and accepted that unresolved issues and dysfunctional behaviors of preceding generations are passed down to subsequent family members. At the core of an individual who experiences SSA is a sense of not belonging, not fitting in, and feeling different from others. These thoughts and feelings may be inherited from family members depending upon their circumstances in life, culture, religion, race, and/or ethnicity.

What I and other sexual orientation therapists have observed is that men and women who experience SSA are highly susceptible to rejection, or perceived rejection, existing for any number of reasons which may stem from unresolved generational issues. Of course, this does not cause same-sex attraction in boys or girls; it is just one contributing factor among many.

2. Temperament

- Hypersensitive
- Artistic nature
- Gender nonconforming behaviors:
  Male more feminine; female more masculine

As I have mentioned, many or most SSA men and women as children were highly sensitive, or hypersensitive, which led them to react more deeply to the behaviors of their parents, relatives and peers. Often attuned to the emotions of their parents, these children will frequently modify their behaviors to avoid conflict. Other times, they will become pleasers or caretakers. Because of their hypersensitive nature, they may act more passively and therefore be unable to assert themselves in interpersonal relationships. Of course, not all sensitive children will develop SSA.

If the hypersensitive child has an artistic nature, and the parents, relatives or peers are non-supportive of this gift, she or he may experience further rejection. The sensitive and gifted child, in an insensitive and non-support environment, experiences undue stress and anxiety.

A further group of young children, who exhibit what we call "gender non-conforming behaviors," that is, the little boy who acts more effeminate and the little girl who acts more masculine, are particularly at risk for being either ostracized by family members and peers, or these days, encouraged to act upon those tendencies (the new transgender phenomenon). However, these character traits—(or behavioral phenotypes), the more effeminate boy and more masculine girl—in certain environments are expressed with the purpose of invoking a reparative or healing drive. By that I mean that a child is seeking to successfully bond with his or her same-sex parent, and thus not trying to summon a gay identity. When this drive for bonding is achieved, the child will have a healthy attachment with his or her same-sex parent and secure gender identity will ensue.

Therefore, with this understanding, instead of thinking, "Oh, he was born gay," or "She was meant to be a boy," and with deeper insight into the dynamics of the family system, we see an attempt by the birth of this child to heal generational wounds of detachment between either fathers and sons or mothers and daughters. If the father would take the time to join with this effeminate boy, see life through his eyes and experiences, eventually the boy will bond with his dad and internalize his father's sense of masculine identity. The same would hold true for the mother and her more masculine daughter.

Dr. Francis S. Collins, director of the National Institutes for Health and former director of the Human Genome Project, declares that homosexuality is "genetically influenced but not hardwired by DNA, and that whatever genes are involved represent predispositions, not predeterminations" (*The Language of God*, New York, 2006, Free Press, p. 260). With healthy intervention and parenting/mentoring, the child will experience a sense of his or her own gender identity and opposite-sex desires with ensue.

3. Opposite-Gender (Hetero-Emotional) Parental Wounds

- Over attachment to opposite-sex parent (enmeshment)
- Imitation of opposite-sex behaviors
- Abuse: emotional, mental, verbal, physical, and/or sexual

There has been much literature written about boys over-attached to their mothers and girls over-attached to their fathers. Again, this is not a blame game, but naming what took place for the purpose of healing. Drs. Irving Bieber, Charles Socarides, Joseph Nicolosi, Gerard van den Aardweg, Sigmund Freud, Robert Kronemeyer and many other psychologists and psychiatrists have observed that men who experience SSA have had an abnormally close mother-son attachment. They are inclined to internalize their mother's sense of femininity and become distant and detached from the masculinity represented by their fathers. On the other hand, the daughter may be closer to her father and estranged from her mother, thereby internalizing her father's masculinity and rejecting her mother's femininity. In other cases, the daughter views the mother as weak and/or ineffective, and models her behavior after the more dominant and powerful parent, her father.

Another phenomenon might be the child perceiving that his or her parents wanted a child of the opposite sex. The son therefore acts like a girl, and the daughter acts like a boy in order to please their parents and win their approval and affection.

As mentioned, many women who experience SSA have been abused by men, and not wanting to repeat these unhealthy bonding patterns, they seek their affectional needs from women.

4. Same-Gender (Homo-Emotional) Parental Wound

- Detachment from same-sex parent
- Neglect: lack of intimacy
- Abuse: emotional, mental, verbal, physical, and/or sexual

Lack of sufficient bonding between the son and his father and daughter and her mother is often at the core of anyone who experiences SSA (homo-emotional wound). Some of the experiences of detachment/neglect may be an angry, violent or scary parent, a physically or emotionally unavailable parent, etc., Additionally, because of the hypersensitive temperament, it may be the perception of the child who feels rejected and detached. For whatever reason(s), many children who experience SSA did not securely connect with the same-sex parent. The mismatch in character and temperament between father and son or mother and daughter often creates the sense of hurt in the heart of a pre-SSA child. Without the parent perceiving these cues, the daughter or son becomes susceptible to further rejection by same-sex peers. The stage is then set for the potential development of same-sex attraction and same-sex erotic feelings during or after puberty. Those desires represent a means to achieve bonding that never took place in the earliest years of child development.

5. Sibling Wounds / Family Dynamics

- Name calling
- Same-sex siblings/relative's rejection
- Abuse: emotional, mental, verbal, sexual, and/or physical

Yet another variable that may contribute to the development of SSA is insufficient bonding with siblings and/or relatives of the same sex, e.g., boys with brothers and male relatives, or girls with sisters and female relatives. These sensitive children are often people-pleasers, trying to keep everyone happy at the expense of their own needs. Over the past 35 years as a psychotherapist, I have heard so many parents say, "My son was the perfect little boy." Well, boys generally by nature are more assertive and mischievous, and not so sweet. Be careful of the "good little boys," encourage them to be themselves and not to please everyone else.

Some women who experience SSA had poor relationships with their sisters, and/ or were mocked and teased by men in their family. This leaves a deep wound in their hearts, not fitting in with their same-sex peers and relatives, and feeling hurt by men. Some boys who experience SSA grew up in families of all girls and women, and some SSA girls grew up in families of all men. These factors may also contribute to gender confusion.

6. Body Image Wounds

- Late bloomer
- Shorter/taller – thinner/larger
- Physical disability

Late bloomer, early maturation, physical disabilities, shorter, taller, thinner, or larger—these are some characteristics that may result in body-image wounds for the pre-SSA boy or girl. A hypersensitive boy who experienced insufficient bonding with his father and over-attachment with his mother, now incurs more self-esteem issues by being different from other guys, e.g., too tall, too thin, too short, too large, not athletically inclined. The result is a profound sense of gender inadequacy, feeling on the outside looking in. If they were late bloomers, they often felt different and alienated from their peers. And the pre-SSA girl may experience similar thoughts and feelings based upon her perception of her body image and the opinions of her parents, relatives and/or peers.

7. Sexual Abuse

- Homosexual imprinting
- Learned and reinforced behaviors
- Substitute for affection and love

Sexual abuse may be another contributing factor to the development of same-sex attraction, however, it is never the sole cause. The pre-SSA child is more susceptible to sexual abuse because of his or her lack of attachment to same-sex parent and/or same-sex peers. Sex then becomes a substitute or replacement for emotional and relational intimacy with others of the same sex. If the behavior is repeated over time, it may create a neurological basis for the further development of same-sex attraction in the male or female. Again, this is just another contributing factor and not a prerequisite to experience SSA. In my therapy practice, and the counseling practice of many colleagues, approximately 50% of our clients experienced some form of childhood sexual abuse.

There is usually a difference between SSA men and women when it comes to sexual abuse. Many boys who carry father and/or male peer wounds were easy targets for male sexual abuse, because they were longing for that connection with their dads and other guys. Many girls who develop SSA were sexually abused by men. They may seek female affection to soothe their wounds and protect themselves from further abuse by men.

8. Same-Sex (Homo-Social) Peer Wounds

- Name calling / put-downs
- Teacher's pet
- Non-athletic boy / more athletic girl

Both men and women who experience SSA often felt a tremendous sense of emotional wounding because of same-sex peer rejection—guys didn't fit in with other guys, and girls didn't fit in with other girls. Often they were called names such as "sissy," "faggot," "queer," "pansy," "dyke," "tomboy." Many boys who experience SSA hung out with the girls, and girls who experience SSA hung out with the guys. While boys who experience SSA were not athletically inclined and received teasing and taunting from their male peers, some girls who experience SSA were more athletic, and if detached from their female peers, may have been ostracized as well. Then, during or after adolescence, those normal needs for same-sex peer bonding became sexualized.

Another source of wounding for the pre-SSA child is boys mocking girls ("You're so butch," "You're a dyke") and girls mocking boys ("You're such a faggot," "You're so sweet and girlie"). Not only do they receive put-downs from their same-sex peers, but opposite sex peers as well.

9. Cultural Wounds

- Promotion of the homosexual myth—born that way and cannot change
- Cultural Abuse: media, Internet, educational system, and politics affirm and promote homosexuality
- Pornography

After a boy or girl experiences wounding or lack of attachment with their same-sex parent and/or peers, or incurs any of the other factors previously mentioned, then same-sex attractions develop during or after adolescence leading to homo-erotic feelings and desires. The world then mistakenly says, "You're gay," or "You're lesbian." As we have learned, this is a false paradigm leading hurt children down the road to homosexuality under false pretenses. Also, with behaviors from performers in the music and entertainment industries, it is becoming trendy to experiment sexually and identify as LGBTQ+, non-binary, etc.

Many kids are being raised in single-parent families, often lacking the attention and affection of the same-sex parent. This leaves him or her vulnerable to being enrolled into the false gay paradigm, whereby their normal needs for bonding will become eroticized by members of the same sex. The media, educational system and the entertainment industry, driven by the homosexual myth, have created false identities: LGBTQ+. But there is no such thing as a "gay." There are only hurt children looking for love in ways that will not fulfill their deepest desires for real love.

Again we go back to the Homosexual Manifesto and the false indoctrination of our youth and our culture into the innate, immutable paradigm. If boys or girls experience SSA in adolescence, we immediately label them as gay, rather than understand there are specific causes that led him or her to experience SSA. No one is born this way. There are always reasons why anyone develops homosexual feelings. (Remember, some kids experiment with same-sex friends at the onset of adolescence, but this does not make them gay or SSA.)

10. Other Factors

- Divorce
- Death
- Adoption
- Religion
- Spiritual factors

There are any number of other life experiences that may contribute towards the development of SSA and low self-worth in a sensitive boy or girl. If the parents divorce, the people-pleasing child may blame himself or herself. If a parent dies, the child may perceive it as personal rejection and abandonment. When a struggling child hears "hell and damnation" or homosexuality is an "abomination" from the pulpit of his or her place of worship, further feelings of guilt and shame burden this sensitive child (read the story of Kevin Jennings in the next chapter).

If the child was adopted, she or he may feel rejected by their birth parents and never securely attach to their adopted parents (read Greg Louganis's story in the next chapter). This sense of rejection may reside deep in the unconscious, creating a pattern of insecurity.

Note: Many people with a strong faith background believe there might be spiritual influences that drive homosexual feelings in boys or girls and men or women. Even if there is validity to this, it is imperative to realize that when the other ten potential factors are addressed, healing occurs and change will ensue. By strictly viewing SSA as a "spiritual problem," one will not fully heal and fulfill their innate heterosexual potential. As psychotherapist Jan Frank stated, "You cannot heal a spirit, or deliver a wound."

"For a homosexual adaptation to occur, in our time and culture, these factors must combine to (1) create an impaired gender-identity [feeling of masculinity or femininity], (2) create a fear of intimate contact with members of the opposite sex, and (3) provide opportunities for sexual release with members of the same sex" (Dr. Judd Marmor, as quoted in *Growing Up Straight*, Peter and Barbara Wyden, New York: Stein and Day, 1968, p. 18).

A combination of any of these ten factors may lead an individual to experience SSA: (1) Heredity, (2) Temperament, (3) Hetero-emotional wounds, (4) Homo-emotional wounds, (5) Sibling wounds and family dynamics, (6) Body-image wounds, (7) Sexual abuse, (8) Social and peer wounds, (9) Cultural wounds, and (10) Other factors. *The severity of wounding in each category will have a direct impact upon the amount of time and effort it will take to heal.*

Please read my book *Being Gay: Nature, Nurture or Both?* for a greater explanation about the potential causes of SSA, and a four-stage model of healing, plus remarkable stories of change.

- *No one is essentially born with SSA.*
- *No one chooses to have SSA.*
- *The only choice is to live a homosexual life or resolve unwanted SSA.*

Let me make it perfectly clear: I am not saying that people who decide to live a homosexual life are wrong. I respect all members of the LGBTQ+ community and the path that they have chosen. For me, I chose a different path, the road less traveled, and, as Robert Frost has written, that has made all the difference. What I wish to convey is that people are not essentially born with SSA, and that change is possible for those who pursue this option. The fact that there are underlying causes of homosexual feelings and there exists the potential for change is *not* widely publicized. There has existed for decades a heavily financed media mechanism, which would have us believe the opposite.

Causes of SSA

Heredity: Unresolved family issues   +
Temperament: Hypersensitivity and/or Gender Non-Conforming Behaviors

>   May create → Predisposition or predilection for SSA
>   But not predetermination for SSA

Eight other influential factors:

1) Opposite-sex parent wound
2) Same-sex parent wound
3) Sibling wounds
4) Body image wounds
5) Sexual abuse
6) Peer wounds
7) Cultural wounds
8) Other factors: Divorce/death/adoption/religion

Two invisible causes: Heredity and temperament
Eight visible causes: Parents, peers, and environment
The child's wounds are a mirror of the parents' and family's unresolved issues.
SSA is no one's fault, and we do have solutions.

COUNSELOR TRAINING PROGRAM MANUAL

The Heart of Female Same-Sex Attraction

Janelle Hallman, InterVarsity Press, © 2008

Profile 1: Empty, Depressed, Withdrawn and Isolated

- Developmental deficits arising out of perceived and actual *emotional* absence or neglect
- Internalized that her existence was an inconvenience and a nuisance
- Uncomfortable in her own skin
- Doesn't feel "normal" at least in social settings

Profile 2: Tough, Angry, Sarcastic, and Barricaded

- History of trauma and abuse, frequently involving severe physical or emotional abandonment
- Negatively affected by the underlying relational dysfunctions within the family system
- Carry a deep belief that the world is not safe
- Relies on toughness to protect her tender heart
- Method of survival starves them of intimacy
- Can feel their inner agony and therefore aggressively cuts off all vulnerabilities
- Works hard and is demanding; she is impatient but also deeply committed
- If she decides she is safe, she will do anything in the world for you
- Endless ability to take care of others, all the while denying her own needs

Profile 3: Energetic, Caretaking, Drama-Oriented, and Never "Home"

- Even though she is less likely to have typical trauma or neglect in her background as compared to women associated with profiles 1 and 2, she still suffers from severe, subtle and negative relational dynamics such as familial enmeshment or rigid gender roles within the family of origin
- Due to her attuned sensitivities and perhaps her deeper relational needs, she felt that she was neither acknowledged nor affirmed as special, particularly as a girl
- Although she felt close and loved, she also felt obligated to support or take care of other family members, including Mom and Dad
- Nevertheless, her basic needs were usually met, and she experienced the greatest level of stability among the four profiles. She is active, often athletic and typically overachieving

Profile 4: Pragmatic, Perfectionistic, Distant, and Smugly Self-Assured

- Various backgrounds but typically compensate for her losses and defend against her pain by avoiding all vulnerability and identifying with her ability to pursue excellence and success
- Often the movers and shakers within her field of expertise and finds value through achievement
- Very intelligent/extremely gifted; often so accomplished, she is also arrogant and contemptuous of others (especially men)
- She may unconsciously use others to serve her own purpose or meet her own needs

DAY ONE

Process of Healing Unwanted SSA*

- Key: Discover the root causes of SSA.

- There is a message in the desires.

- Motivation is paramount for change.

- Marriage is never the solution for SSA.

- Path of healing:
  1) Personal motivation
  2) Effective treatment
  3) Support from others
  4) Love of God

- You must feel in order to heal.

*Throughout the series/manual, I often use the masculine pronoun; however, this process applies to both men and women.

Four Stages of Resolving Unwanted Same-Sex Attraction (SSA)

Stage One: Transitioning (Behavioral Therapy)

- Cutting off from sexual behaviors: playgrounds, playmates, playthings
- Developing a Support Network
- Building self-worth and experiencing value in relationship with God

Stage Two: Grounding (Cognitive Therapy)

- Continuing with the Support Network
- Continuing to build self-worth and experience value in relationship with God
- Building skills: assertiveness training, communication skills, problem-solving techniques
- Beginning inner-child healing: identifying thoughts, feelings, and needs

Stage Three: Healing Homo-Emotional/Homo-Social Wounds (Psychodynamic Therapy)

- Continuing all tasks of Stage One and Two
- Discovering the root causes of homo-emotional/social wounds
- Beginning the process of grieving, forgiving and taking responsibility
- Developing healthy, healing same-gender relationships

Stage Four: Healing Hetero-Emotional/Hetero-Social Wounds (Psychodynamic Therapy)

- Continuing all tasks of Stage One, Stage Two and Stage Three
- Discovering the root causes of hetero-emotional/social wounds
- Continuing the process of grieving, forgiving and taking responsibility
- Developing healthy, healing opposite-sex relationships and learning about the opposite sex through the perspective of one's own gender

© Richard Cohen, M.A., 2023

DAY ONE

How to Assist Those Who Experience Unwanted SSA

Through my own journey of healing, and through my clinical practice since 1989, I have developed a four-stage model of recovery. It has proved successful for those who experience unwanted same-sex attraction, whether they have been sexually active or not. The same protocol applies to both populations. Additionally, heterosexual marriage is never the solution for anyone who experiences SSA, because a woman can never meet the homo-emotional/homo-social needs of a man, and a man can never meet the homo-emotional/homo-social needs of a woman. In the process of recovery, first a man must heal with other men, and a woman must heal with other women.

> "Attempted heterosexual relationships, or social contact, with the opposite sex, are not the solution to homosexuality, since increased opposite-sex contact can do nothing to fulfill same-sex deficits" Elizabeth R. Moberly, *Homosexuality: A New Christian Ethic* (Cambridge, UK: Lutterworth Press, revised edition 2006), 18.

Over the years, I basically had four types of clients:

1) Young people confused about their sexuality and/or gender identity.
2) Married men or women (in heterosexual marriages) who wish to resolve their unwanted SSA.
3) Those who lived a gay/lesbian life, never found the right person(s), and wish to explore the possibility of change.
4) Religiously motivated men and women who sought to resolve their unwanted SSA.

Of course, the first three types may also be motivated to resolve unwanted SSA because of their spiritual beliefs.

Before I sought help, some of my well-intentioned friends told me, "Richard, just find the right woman and she'll straighten you out," or "Just pray hard enough, and God will take those desires away. If not, then you're doing something wrong." Well, I wish it would have been that simple, but it was not. I prayed and prayed for God to take away my SSA, but He did not. I married, hoping it would straighten me out, but my same-sex desires only intensified. I came to understand that I had been praying the wrong prayer for over twenty years. What I needed to pray was: "God, please reveal to me the meaning behind my same-sex desires." Later, I understood that God could have but would not take away my SSA, because it was connected to the hurts in my heart that required healing, and legitimate needs for love that required fulfillment in healthy non-sexual relationships with heterosexual mentors and friends.

A Brief Summary of the Four Stages of Recovery

Stage One: The individual needs to cut ties with gay porn, stop homosexual behavior, terminate homosexual relationships and build a strong Support Network of healthy love. He/she needs to develop a sense of self-worth through experiencing a personal relationship with God/Higher Power. This is behavioral therapy, modifying unhealthy behaviors and replacing them with positive, healthy sources of love.

Stage Two: The individual needs to develop skills to create happiness in his/her present-day relationships. This is cognitive therapy, teaching communication and problem-solving skills, assertiveness training and correcting faulty thinking. Then he/she begins inner-child work, learning about feelings and needs, and fostering self-love and compassion. If an individual bypasses this stage, chances are that he/she will terminate treatment, give up and/or revert to homosexual behavior.

Stage Three: The individual needs to identify homo-emotional/homo-social wounds, heal them, and then fulfill them in healthy, nonsexual same-gender relationships. This is the psychodynamic work of recovery, exposing the wounds, grieving the pains and losses of the past, learning to forgive, and finally moving on. The result is a renewed and empowered sense of one's true gender identity.

Stage Four: The individual needs to identify hetero-emotional/hetero-social wounds, heal them, and then fulfill them in healthy opposite-sex relationships. He needs to learn about women from a male perspective, and she needs to learn about men from a female perspective.

People always ask me how long it will take to complete the four stages of healing. It all depends on the severity of the wounds and the amount of time and energy the individual is willing to invest in his healing. One-and-a-half to three years is the average time of treatment. Our job as therapists is to equip our clients with the proper tools and skills to take care of themselves throughout their lives.

Please read Chapters Four and Six in *Being Gay* for a much more detailed explanation of the Four Stages of Healing.

The Initial Session

When someone comes for help and shares about the nature of his situation and current conflicts, the first thing I ask is, "What are your goals for our work together?" Quite often, many who seek counseling are not clear about their goals. However, they must address and answer this question. It makes them think about what they want and need, and it gives the client and the helper a clear direction for their work.

When we decide to work together, I begin by taking a thorough history. Generally, this takes from two to three hours, sometimes more. During this time, the client has an opportunity to share much about his/her life, many things that he/she has never shared with anyone before. It gives the therapist/coach a bird's-eye view of the multi-generational family system and many other contributing factors that the client will need to address along the road of recovery.

Instead of going over the history in two or three sessions, the therapist may email the client the Family History Questionnaire. Ask him/her to respond to each question succinctly, with a maximum of 8 pages. Additionally, I ask him/her to draw a genogram of three generations (examples of genograms are readily available online). I show the client an example of a genogram: beginning with paternal and maternal grandparents, the client's parents, siblings, and the families of the client and siblings (if they exist). It is very interesting to see how much the individual does or does not know about his/her parents and grandparents. This in itself may be very revealing about family relationships, or lack thereof.

DAY ONE

Family History Questionnaire

Section One:

1. Name your father's parents (your paternal grandfather and grandmother) and name your father's siblings in birth order from oldest to youngest, including your father. Include the year that each person was born (grandparents and siblings). Identify who is/was married to whom, and who might have passed away. Also include if there were any miscarriages, stillbirths, abortions, or if a child died.

2. Name your mother's parents (your maternal grandfather and grandmother) and name your mother's siblings in birth order from oldest to youngest, including your mother. Include the year that each person was born (grandparents and siblings). Identify who is/was married to whom, and who might have passed away. Also include if there were any miscarriages, stillbirths, abortions, or if a child died.

3. Names, birth years, and children that your parents had (your siblings and you). List if your siblings are married, and their spouses' name(s), and number of children.

4. Include the age, name, and gender of each of your children (if you are married). If there was a miscarriage, stillbirth, abortion, or a child died, please include each of them as well. List their birth order, the year they were born, and if applicable, when they passed away.

Section Two:

1. Describe the relationship between your father and his father, your father and his mother, your father and his siblings (if he had any), and your father and any other significant people in his life while he was growing up. Include the names and birth order of all your father's siblings.

2. Describe the relationship between your father's parents—past to present.

3. Where did your father's family live? Where did he grow up?

4. What was their ethnic background? What was their religious background?

5. Describe the relationship between your mother and her father, your mother and her mother, your mother and her siblings, and any other significant people in her life growing up. Include the names and birth order of all your mother's siblings.

6. Describe the relationship between your mother's parents—past to present.

7. Where did your mother's family live? Where did she grow up?

8. What was their ethnic background? Religious background?

9. Be sure to describe any major issues or events on both the paternal and maternal sides of the family, such as war experiences, immigration, sexual abuse, physical abuse, emotional-mental abuse, drug/alcohol/sexual addictions, gambling addictions, eating disorders, sexual problems, major depressions, divorce, suicide, rape, murder, theft, autism, abortions, homosexuality, adoption, moving, etc.

Section Three:

1. Describe your relationship with your father—past (from your earliest memories) to the present (current-day relationship).

2. Describe your father's personality—past to present.

3. Describe your father's education, employment history, and religious history.

4. Describe your relationship with your mother—past to present.

5. Describe your mother's personality—past to present.

6. Describe your mother's education, employment history, and religious history.

7. Describe the relationship between your father and mother—past to present.

8. Describe your relationship with your siblings (if you have any)—past to present.

9. Describe your siblings' personalities.

10. Describe your relationship with any other significant people in or out of your family system (e.g., grandmother, grandfather, uncle, cousin, neighbor, stepparent).

11. What was your role in the family system (e.g., hero, pleaser, clown, rebel, substitute spouse, golden child, caretaker, loner, scapegoat, peacemaker)?

12. Describe your school history—academically and socially, past to present.

13. Describe your sexual history—from your earliest memories to the present. Include all references to sex and sexuality, in or outside of the family. When did your homosexual feelings and desires begin?

14. Describe your history of masturbation—when it began, how it progressed, and how frequently you masturbate today. Are there any special rituals you perform while masturbating? Is masturbating accompanied by fantasies and pornography? If so, please describe what images you like to view?

15. Describe your sexual fantasies—from past to present, as they may have progressed over time. What kind of person/people are you attracted to? What are his or her characteristics (physical attributes and personality traits)? What activities are performed in your fantasies and in what environment? Do you have any particular fetishes? If so, please describe them, when they started, and how they manifest in your life today.

16. Describe your religious history—past to present.

17. Describe yourself—how you see yourself today.

18. List any other significant issues about your life or your family that were not covered in these questions, such as health issues, marriage issues, extramarital affairs, career issues, money issues, and previous treatment or therapy.

19. How do you feel about your body? Are you pleased with how you look? Has this changed over time?

20. List your current and past employment history, and your age.
21. Please list your goals for the therapy.

Example of a genogram from *Being Gay,* Richard Cohen, PATH Press, 2020.

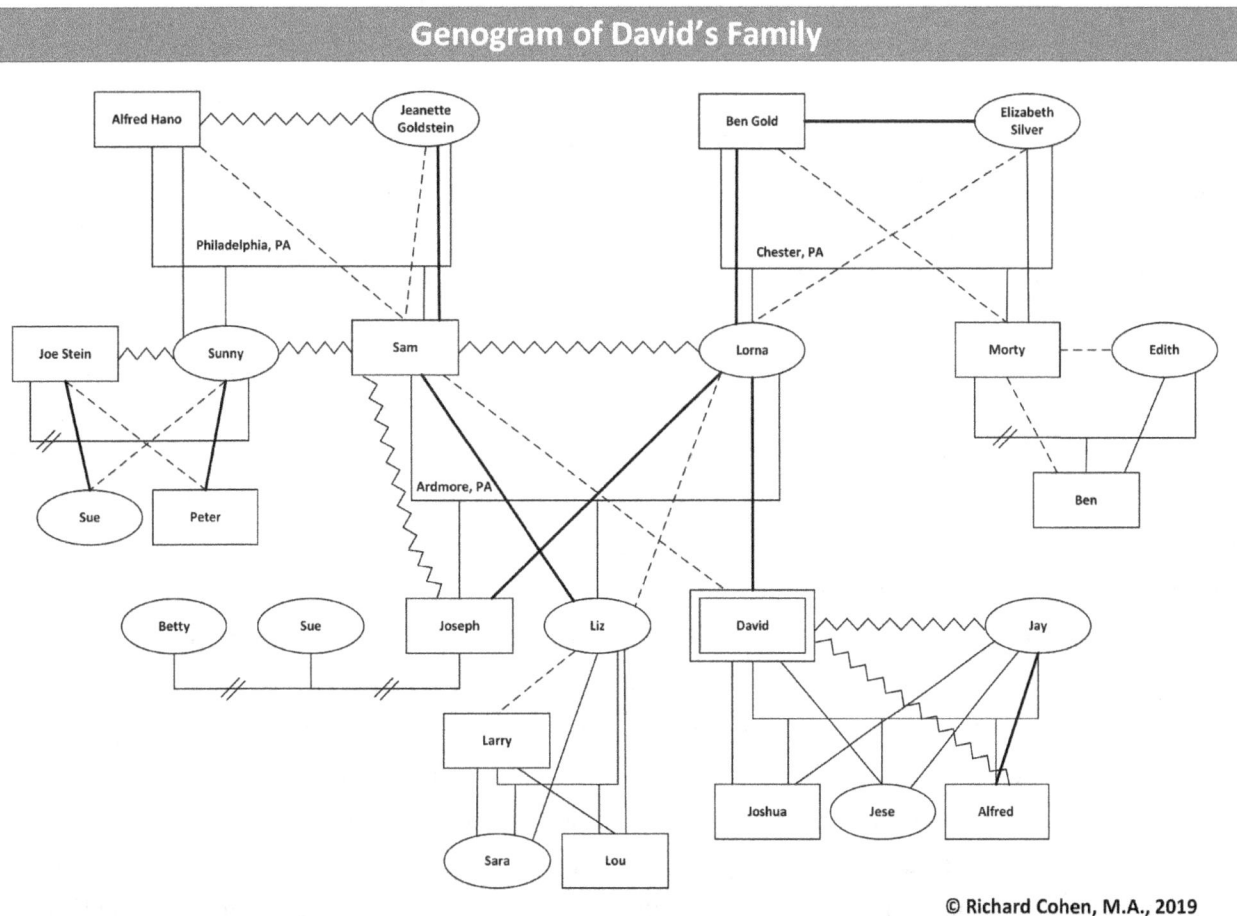

One thing that becomes apparent while reviewing the client's family history is the generational detachment between same-gender parents and their same-gender children, e.g., the distance between fathers and sons, and mothers and daughters. I have observed in many of my male clients' weaker paternal figures and much stronger maternal figures. This leads a male to identify more easily with the feminine, the stronger of the sexes in the family system.

While sharing about his family history, one client stated, "I wanted to be a girl because my father liked my sister more than me. He was always working and while at home he was angry. My mother was more fun, could speak her mind and was more loving."

It is important to have him/her share about his/her earliest childhood memories because it is the fertile soil that cultivates future SSA. Pay close attention to memory lapses—there is much useful information locked in the unconscious. *The conscious mind cannot hold that which was too painful to remember.* These places will be important to revisit when working through stages three and four of recovery.

When reviewing the individual's social life during school years, I most often hear "I'm different," "I don't belong," and "I don't fit in." Inquiring about sexual fantasies or fetishes is important. There is much useful information here since the homo-emotional/homo-social wounds hide beneath the fantasies/fetishes. There is generally a progression of fantasies as well. Sometimes it starts by just observing naked men or women, and then progresses to sexual activity. This will be unique to each individual, depending upon the specific needs and intensity of detachment from self and others.

Some feel attracted to older men, displaying a need to be taken care of or fathered. Some adolescents and adult males feel attracted to peers, seeking in other men what they feel lacking within themselves. Most men feel drawn to muscular, strong and confident men—all the qualities they wish to possess. Some want to feel dominated, held, cared for or mentored by the men they admire. Others have an attraction to younger boys or teens. This may represent several things: 1) unresolved trauma at that particular age; 2) unmet needs in that stage of development; and/or 3) a connection to some form of abuse at that age (oftentimes a repressed or suppressed memory of sexual abuse).

It is important to realize that sexual fantasies are a mask for unmet homo-emotional/homo-social love needs or fear of intimacy with someone of the opposite sex. I have also found that these fantasies may hide repressed anger toward one or both parents, anger that the child felt unable to express and is now being manifest as sexual desires. Still others, disconnected from their own sense of gender identity, want to watch heterosexual men having sexual relations with women. In this way, they find their lost identities in the men they wish to be. There are many variations of sexual fantasies. It is important to find out as much detail as possible in order to understand the deeper meanings behind their SSA.

It is important to see what part religion has played in the client's life and what role it now plays. Many experienced judgement and/or persecution within their particular faith. I have heard horror stories of how they sought help from their clergy and were then asked to leave the congregation. Others feared to reveal their struggle because of the strong judgmental attitudes of those in their faith. In other cases, if they have strongly detached from their parents, then they may easily detach from their parents' religious beliefs. **Oppositional behavior is an integral part of SSA.** One young client shared with me, "I consciously chose to be different from my father. If he liked country music, I chose rock. If he liked white, I chose black. This was my way of telling him that I didn't like him at all."

After reading the client's responses, I write an evaluation or content analysis, offering my observations and hypotheses why I believe he/she experiences SSA, based on the ten potential causes. When I present this evaluation/content analysis to the clients, I invite them to first listen. If I have made a mistake or misperceived something, I ask him/her to correct me. This is generally a positive and deeply moving experience for the client. Finally, someone truly understands him/her from the inside out. There are often many tears during this session. "No one has ever understood me so deeply before."

After completing the evaluation, I also give him/her a personalized treatment plan based on the four stages of healing (see an example of a treatment plan later in this Manual). Then we begin therapy. If a client is in extreme pain at the initial session or sessions, please give him/her time to express his/her feelings and thoughts before doing a thorough history. This may be the first time for him/her to have found a safe space to let go and release his/her pain and frustration. The therapist, counselor or coach must create a sacred setting that is confidential, safe and nonjudgmental.

Resources for Resolving Unwanted SSA*

Therapeutic / Healing Organizations
- Alliance for Therapeutic Choice and Scientific Integrity (Professional Therapists)
  www.therapeuticchoice.com
- Brothers Road (Online support groups for men / JIM weekend experience)
  https://www.brothersroad.org
- Institute for Healthy Families
- https://instituteforhealthyfamilies.org
- Joel 225: Online Support Groups in many languages
  www.joel225.org
- Positive Approaches To Healthy Sexuality (PATH)
  www.pathinfo.org

Faith Ministries
- Courage / Encourage (Catholic)
  www.couragerc.net
- North Star (Mormon)
  www.northstarlds.org
- Restored Hope Network (Christian)
  www.restoredhopenetwork.com
- One by One (Presbyterian)
  www.oneby1.org
- Strong Support (Muslim)
  https://www.strongsupport.co.uk
- Transforming Congregation (Methodist)
  www.transformingcong.org
- Wife's support groups
  http://www.brothersroad.org/whj/helpforwives/

Parents & Children's Organizations
- PFOX: Parents and Friends of Ex-Gays and Gays (Christian)
  www.pfox.org
- Support for Children of LGBTQ+ Parents
  www.dawnstefanowicz.org

Testimonies of Change
- Videos, audios, and written stories of transformation
  www.voicesofchange.net

* For a more comprehensive list of organizations, please visit our website: https://www.pathinfo.org/organizations

Bibliography

Male Homosexuality

1. *Being Gay: Nature, Nurture, or Both?* Richard Cohen, M.A., PATH Press, Bowie, MD, 2020.
2. *Reparative Therapy of Male Homosexuality,* Joseph Nicolosi, Ph.D., 1991
3. *Shame and Attachment Loss: The Practical Work of Reparative Therapy,* Joseph Nicolosi, Ph.D., 2016.
4. *Growth into Manhood,* Alan Medinger, WaterBrook Press (Shaw), Colorado Springs, CO, 2000.
5. *Practical Exercises for Men in Recovery,* James Phelan, Psy.D, Morris Publishing, Kearney, NE, 2006.

Female Homosexuality

6. *The Heart of Female Same-Sex Attraction: A Comprehensive Counseling Resource,* Janelle Hallman, InterVarsity Press, Downers Grove, IL, 2008.
7. *Restoring Sexual Identity: Hope for Women Who Struggle with Same-Sex Attraction,* Anne Paulk, Harvest House, Eugene, OR, 2003.
8. *Female Homosexuality: Choice without Volition,* Elaine V. Siegel, Ph.D., Analytic Press, Hillsdale, NJ, 1988.
9. *Practical Exercises for Women in Recovery,* James Phelan, Debora Barr, Phelan Consultants, 2011.

Family / Friends

10. *Gay Children, Straight Parents: A Plan for Family Healing,* Richard Cohen, M.A., PATH Press, Bowie, MD, 2016.
11. *A Parent's Guide to Preventing Homosexuality,* Joseph Nicolosi, Ph.D., Liberal Mind Pub., 2017

General Books on Homosexuality

12. *Understanding Our LGBTQ+ Loved Ones,* Richard Cohen, M.A., PATH Press, Bowie, MD, 2022.
13. *My Genes Made Me Do It: A Scientific Look at Sexual Orientation,* Neil and Briar Whitehead, Huntington House Publishers, Lafayette, LA, 1999.
14. *You Don't Have to Be Gay: Hope and Freedom for Males Struggling with Homosexuality,* Jeff Conrad, Pacific Publishing House, Newport Beach, CA, 2001.
15. *Desires in Conflict: Answering the Struggle for Sexual Identity,* Joe Dallas, Harvest House, Eugene, OR, 1991.

Political Influence of Homosexuality in the American Psychiatric Association

16. *Homosexuality and American Psychiatry,* Ronald Bayer, Princeton University Press, Princeton, NJ, 1981.

Initial Client Intake

Five phases of the initial consultation/evaluation session:

1. Review their history:
- Based upon their answers to the Family History Questionnaire / Genogram

2. Content analysis:
- Using the ten variables from Chapter Two of *Being Gay* as a guideline, define why you believe they experience SSA

3. Treatment plan*:
- Create a treatment plan based on the Four Stages of Healing (refer to Chapters Four and Six of *Being Gay*)
- Strategic approach to the healing of unwanted SSA and fulfillment of their goals

4. Teach about the true meaning of Same-Sex Attractions (SSA)
- Not about sex—emotionally based condition
- Not an identity—you are either a son or daughter of God (Higher Power)
- Homosexuality is only a description of one's thoughts/feelings/desires
- Basis of all SSA is:
    1) Wounds that have not healed
    2) Legitimate needs for love that have not been met

5. Liability clause
- Protect your practice or ministry

---

* If the client has an addiction (drugs, alcohol, sex, etc.) as well as SSA, you must help him/her stabilize before addressing the underlying causes of SSA.

Example of an Evaluation/Content Analysis and Treatment Plan for a Male Client

CAUSES OF UNWANTED SSA

1. Father's family: It appears that your grandfather was not involved in raising your father, and there was no emotional intimacy between the two of them. You mentioned that your father treated you in the same manner while you were growing up. Additionally, your father was not close to his brothers or sisters. As stated, your paternal grandmother was quite strict and abusive to your father—both verbally and physically. Their family was very poor, and lived in the country.
2. Mother's family: Your maternal grandfather was a tailor who died when your mother was ten years old. As stated, he was verbally abusive, shouted, and drank a lot. Your mother reported that your maternal grandmother was a very good provider for the family after her husband died, and that she had a very strong faith in God.

Your parents married when your mother was eighteen years old. Your maternal grandmother lived with you and your family. You mentioned that your dad and she did not get along. They quarreled often and had poor or little communication. You stated that their relationship was hard on your mother.

Your grandmother helped to raise you, along with your mother. It appears that your father was not involved much at all. Furthermore, your mother and father did not teach you how to express your emotions, as they didn't express theirs.

Also, your mother stated that both of her brothers dealt with alcoholism.

3. Relationship with father: It appears that there was no emotional relationship between you and your father while growing up. You lived together, but he was like a stranger to you. He worked hard, and you stated that was the only positive quality you admired about him. You said that you felt "nothing" for him—"no love, no hate." There was no deep communication, only "superficial conversations," and "no emotional connection." He is "malcontent, shouts, and works hard." He doesn't "expect much from life." "He thinks he's a loser." Your mother earns more money than he does, and you stated that "she is the head of the family."

FATHER WOUND: Your father did not experience a salient, loving, supportive father. As well, you did not experience a salient, loving and supportive father. There was no emotional attachment and connection between your dad and yourself while you were growing up. This leaves a hole in the soul, a deep need for *bonding with men* (homo-emotional wound). He didn't play with you, which developmentally impeded your ability to play and socialize with other boys. This created a *male peer wound* (homo-social wound).

4. Relationship with mother: As you mentioned, your mother was both father and mother to you because your dad did not participate in raising you. You mother loved and loves you very much. You two shared a very close relationship, and you were her "special boy." You did very well in school, you were a "good child," and made no trouble for your mother. She has no idea about your relationship with men or your SSA.

As you stated, she is "open, smiling, cheerful, social, smart, active, and successful in her work." She graduated university in accounting, and is a Christian.

MOTHER WOUND: As you stated, you were more connected and attached to your mother than your father. She was the source of love in your family. At times, in such a situation, the child appears to model his character and way of life after his mother, the more dominant and successful person, the "head of the family." Then he becomes internally more like her, more feminine, rather than more masculine, like his dad.

Being too close to one's mother is potentially emasculating for a boy without the active participation of his father. He may align himself with her feminine viewpoint, and then perceive his father as weak, and his mother as strong. This damages his sense of gender identity and masculinity. Seeing the male role model as weak and ineffective, he ends up rejecting his own masculinity, and then looks for that lost connection and part of himself in other men.

Perhaps you fell into the "good boy" syndrome. Many SSA boys were pleasers, good little boys trying to please everyone. The problem is, they end up losing themselves, being out of touch with their own thoughts, feelings, and needs. And most boys are not naturally so "sweet." They often make trouble, are gregarious in nature, and mess around with other guys. You, however, did not experience this important stage of male homo-social bonding with other boys while growing up.

5. Parents' relationship: "Superficial." "They didn't express affection or display emotional intimacy." You mentioned that your mother often complained about your dad.

PARENTS WOUND: Most likely, it was hurtful not to see a warm, supportive, and loving husband-wife relationship. Parents are to model healthy masculinity and femininity to their children. As you mentioned, you did not experience healthy male bonding with your father. Furthermore, you didn't see him taking good care of your mother. When your mother complained about your father to you, this further distanced you from him and your own sense of masculinity. Your mother was the primary source of love in the family. Therefore, if you were like your dad, meaning masculine, then perhaps your child's mind thought that she wouldn't love you. This further detaches you from a healthy sense of gender identity.

6. Relationship with maternal grandmother: As you stated, she was a strong influential figure in your emotional development. **Again, here is another strong female figure to model yourself after. This may have served to further distance you from your masculinity and a healthy sense**

of your gender identity as a male. There were no healthy grandfathers to counterbalance the strong female presence in your life while growing up.

7. Your family role: "Golden child, pleaser, sweet boy"—good grades, female friends, no male friends, mocked by male peers at school, name calling.

TEMPERAMENT: Sensitive or hypersensitive. This characteristic, when combined with a lack of father-son and male peer bonding, leads to confusion in any boy about his own secure sense of masculinity and gender identity. He finds it easier to fit into the world of women, the feminine. He then becomes a "good boy, a nice guy," and a "pleaser."

8. Social and school history: The boys laughed at you during gym class and at lunch. As mentioned, you experienced being called names and criticized by the other boys in your class. Consequently, you had more girl than boy friends. You mentioned that you were helpful and always the good kid, at the top of your class. You did very well in college, and are very successful in your profession.

PEER WOUNDS: Being the "good, smiling" boy is typical of many SSA guys. They are very sensitive and caring, living from the more feminine side of their character. The relationship with your (gay) boyfriend is one of the most genuine parts of your life. On one level, it may represent your rebelliousness, as if to say "Screw you" to everyone else because you never got to be the strong male in real life. Of course, this relationship is also a means whereby you fulfill a legitimate need for male love and affection. However, the origin of this need is that of a child—seeking bonding with dad and other boys. And children do not want or need sex. Sex prevents one from experiencing the very thing he is looking for—to be loved for who he is, not for what he does or how he looks.

9. Sexual history: From eight years old, your seventeen-year-old neighbor introduced you to sex. This was sexual abuse—where an older male used you for his sexual pleasure. He awakened your sense of sexuality prematurely. This is abusive to a child.

SEXUAL ABUSE: With your father and male peer wounds in place, it was natural that you wanted a strong male's attention and affection. This came in the form of sexual activity. To a hungry soul, it's a tradeoff—I will give you sex if you pay attention to me. This was the only form of acceptance you got from a male at that time of your life. This created a pattern that would later be emulated in your relationship with your boyfriends.

Even though your parents, and the neighbor's parents, knew about this, they never did anything to help you heal. It was kept a secret. This was detrimental to your emotional, mental, physical, and spiritual growth and development. They should have helped you express and share all your confused feelings. They should have helped you understand that it wasn't your fault. The most divisive thing about sexual abuse is this: It feels good physically, but it is confusing and splitting emotionally, mentally, and spiritually. Instinctively, you knew it was wrong, but physically, it felt good because

the penis has many nerve endings which were created for pleasure. The payoff was that a male was interested in and paid attention to you.

Basically, this neighbor used you for his pleasure. Several years later he left the community and it was over. You, however, internalized it because of your father hunger and male peer wounds. It became a way to get another man's attention and affection—by giving him your body and having sex. This pattern was established from the time you were eight years old.

These experiences awakened your sexuality, and masturbation to fantasies of men began. This was a natural consequence, equating sex with men. You fantasized about the men you saw in porn magazines and on-line, and the naked guys in the shower room at school. You hungered for male attention and affection, and the legitimate, primal need for paternal and fraternal bonding then became eroticized.

10. Compulsive masturbation (often daily): You thought about sex with strong, powerful, competent, masculine guys.

This activity was very punishing because you believed, as a devote Christian, that homosexual behavior was viewed as "sinful." You tried to stop but were unsuccessful because you had no positive alternatives or understanding of the dynamics of what was happening in your life. Compulsive masturbation is a way to avoid feelings and legitimate needs for love. It numbs one emotionally, mentally, and spiritually.

11. Sexual fantasies: You fantasized about your former boyfriend—muscular, strong arms, well endowed, confident—and about oral and anal sex you had with him.

HOMO-EMOTIONAL AND HOMO-SOCIAL WOUNDS: The need for healthy male affection and attention became sexualized and eroticized from the time you were eight years old. After the homo-emotional (father hunger) and homo-social (peer bonding) needs become eroticized, the craving for male affection grows more intense. Many SSA men seek to join with the "strong, muscular, confident" male. This may have a double meaning: (1) longing to be loved by a strong man, and (2) longing to be that person himself. This reflects a deficit in one's gender identity, so he seeks in the other what he lacks within himself.

12. Strong faith in Christ: Presently you are deepening your relationship with God, and wanting to study the Word more, to change your life and not be identified as gay.
13. You want to become a "real man, both mentally and physically," and not be so soft—to be a "healthy man."

CONCLUSION:

1. Lack of connection, attachment, and bonding with father.
2. Over-attachment and connection with mother and grandmother.
3. Internalized feminine character/nature, and dis-identified with masculinity.
4. Hypersensitive temperament—reacting quite deeply to others. Became a pleaser, the nice guy, fulfilling other people's needs while ignoring your own; lacking in masculine strength and power.
5. Sexual abuse by neighbor at eight years old set up a pattern of sexualizing/eroticizing the need for male bonding (both paternal and fraternal).
6. Lack of peer bonding. Fit in with the girls but not with the boys.

The term "gay" is a socio-political term. Having same-sex attractions (SSA) is the result of many different factors. We are all designed heterosexually. You simply got stuck in various stages of early psychosocial and psychosexual development. When you resolve those past issues, and fulfill your legitimate needs for male bonding in healthy same-gender relationships, your same-sex attractions (SSA) will naturally wane and heterosexual desires will ensue.

Because you were sexually abused as a young boy, and have engaged in homosexual activity, those desires may linger later on. However, they will never have power or control over you. SSA is your friend, not foe. It lets you know when your life is out of balance and you need to take better care of yourself. SSA is a message from your soul, trying to get your attention so that you may become the true man that God created you to be.

CLIENT'S STATED GOALS FOR THERAPY

1. Stop being "gay" and become a healthy man.
2. Terminate the relationship with your boyfriend.
3. Learn how to develop healthy relationships with men.
4. Date women and eventually marry and have children.

Example of a Treatment Plan

Stage One: Transitioning (Behavioral Therapy)

1. Cut off from sexual behavior (playgrounds, playmates, playthings).

    a. Begin journaling to identify the triggers that lead you to masturbate and/or act out sexually. Journal before or after you masturbate or have sex.

    b. Use the HALT diagnostic tool:
    (1) **H**ungry: emotional hunger for a man, often when feeling rejected
    (2) **A**ngry: unexpressed emotions turned inward
    (3) **L**onely: legitimate need for love and connection with a man
    (4) **T**ired: stressed, overworked, life out of balance

    c. Work on those issue, resolve conflicts, and get your needs met in healthy way and in healthy relationships.

    d. Do not focus on the problem (masturbation, sex, or porn). Focus on the real issue(s), and create positive solutions:
    (1) Call someone, using the HALT diagnostic tool
    (2) Pray/meditate to identify causes and real needs
    (3) Work out your issues with the person you have unresolved feelings about
    (4) Get your needs met in healthy, same-gender, non-sexual relationships
    (5) Create a more balanced schedule
    (6) Exercise
    (7) Direct your energy outward, for others

    e. Use exercises in *Practical Exercises for Men in Recovery of SSA* by Dr. James Phelan, 2006, Morris Publishing, Kearney, NE.

    f. Share with accountability partners.

2. **Develop a support network.**

    a. Find and develop healthy relationships with men and male mentors—emotionally healthy men who can give and share with you positive love, attention, and affection. Be proactive: call them and suggest activities. If someone can't do the activity you suggest, call another person. Make a list with phone numbers of:
    (1) SSA strugglers on the path of healing

(2) Heterosexual men who don't know about your struggle and support you

(3) Heterosexual men who do know about your struggle and support you

(4) Heterosexual mentors, elders to bless you in different aspects of your life: spiritual, sports, financial/career, holding/healthy touch, etc.

Have your mentors read:

Gay Children, Straight Parents: A Plan for Family Healing.

b. Participate in groups with other men (e.g., church groups, social activities, etc). The more healthy, authentic male relationships you develop, the better. Learn how to be authentic, honest, and genuine in the presence of other men. You must be real and feel in order to heal. Everyone has issues. You are not alone. Participate in social activities (e.g., men's book club, MeetUp groups, card group, "guy's night out" group, movie group, sports night, etc).

c. Join local support groups for men with unwanted SSA:

(1) JIM (Journey Into Manhood) group

(2) On-line groups: www.joel225.com

(3) Ministry groups: Restored Hope Network, Courage, Strong Support, etc.

(4) SA (Sexaholics Anonymous) 12-step group / Celebrate Recovery

d. Begin a program of regular exercise. Ideally, find another man to work out with. You may hire a personal trainer to coach you. Have men teach you how to play sports (attend Courage Sports Camp in the summer time).

e. Read books about healing unwanted same-sex attraction (SSA):

  - *Being Gay* by Richard Cohen

  - *Growth Into Manhood* by Alan Medinger

  - *Reparative Therapy of Male Homosexuality* by Joseph Nicolosi

  - *Desires in Conflict* by Joe Dallas

  - *Homosexuality: A New Christian Ethic* by Elizabeth Moberly

  - *You Don't Have to Be Gay* by Jeff Konrad

f. Eat a healthy diet. Cut down on sugars and caffeinated drinks.

3. Build self-worth and experience value in relationship to God.

a. Spend time in prayer and meditation with God. Experience being loved for who you are, SSA and all. Develop a personal love relationship with God.

b. "Gay," "homosexual," or "bisexual" are man-made terms. You are inherently a man. You are a son of God. That is your true identity. Begin to let go of identification with "gay" terminology and concepts. Recognize that SSA is the result of many contributing factors. You are a latent heterosexual male in the process of healing your gender identity. If same-sex attractions emerge, learn to listen to them, and discover what they are trying to teach you about yourself. Make SSA your best friend.

    c. Affirmation MP3

    (1) Read *Words That Heal: Affirmations and Mediations for Daily Living* by Douglas Block (New York: Bantam Books, 1988).

    (2) Make a list of things you wish your father had said and done with you while you were growing up. Make a list of things you wish male peers had said and done with you while growing up.

    (3) Create an MP3 from this list: Have a few men you trust make the recording. Put equal space between each line so you may repeat the affirmation in your mind. Put beautiful music in the background.

    (4) Use this on a daily basis, ideally morning and night. Process your feelings as they come up by stopping the recording as necessary. If daily use is too much at first, listen a few times per week. Be consistent, and then slowly increase the dosage until you are listening to it twice daily. *Succeed small rather than fail big.*

Stage Two: Grounding (Cognitive Therapy)

1. Continue with the support network.

2. Continue to build self-worth and experience value in relationship to God.

3. Build skills: assertiveness training, communication skills, problem-solving techniques.
   a. Read and do the exercises in *Ten Days to Self-Esteem* or *Mind Over Mood*—one lesson every one to two weeks. Make a time commitment. Review with your therapist/coach/mentor.

   b. Learn and utilize good communication skills:
   - How to share yourself responsibly
   - How to listen effectively

   d. Begin inner-child healing: Identify thoughts, feelings, and needs. Read *Recovery of Your Inner Child* by Lucia Capacchione (New York: Simon and Schuster Fireside Book, 1991). Purchase a sketchpad and crayons or colored pencils. Do one chapter every two weeks, or more as you are motivated. You need to become a good parent to your own soul. Hold a pillow or doll, and imagine that you are sharing with the little boy that you used to be.

   e. Listen to the *Inner Child* and *Memory Healing* MP3 several times per week (www.pathinfo.org / Digital Download page).

Stage Three: Healing Homo-Emotional and Homo-Social Wounds (Psychodynamic Therapy)

1. Continue all tasks of Stages One and Two.

2. Discover and heal the root causes of homo-emotional/social wounds.

    a. Attend healing seminars (in order is suggested):
    - *Journey Into Manhood (JIM)*: www.brothersroad.org
    - *New Warrior Weekend*: www.mkp.org
    - *Adventure In Manhood (AIM)*: https://familystrategies.org/adventure-in-manhood

    b. Identify homo-emotional and homo-social wounds.
    - Refer to evaluation: father wound, male peer wounding, sexual abuse.

3. Begin the process of grieving, forgiving, and taking responsibility.

    a. Find male mentors who are able to "be" with you while grieving the many losses of your past. You need to be blessed by healthy mentors (those who experience the fullness of their gender identity and have healthy love to give and share with you).

    b. Work through sexual abuse issues: anger, grief, and forgiveness.
    - Read: *A Door of Hope* by Jan Frank (Thomas Nelson Publishers, 1995).

    c. Focusing:
    - Read *Focusing* by Eugene Gendlin.
    - Practice the six-step method to identify feelings and resolve present-day conflicts.

    d. Voice Dialogue:
    - Read *Embracing OurSelves* by Hal and Sidra Stone.
    - Practice voice dialogue method.
    - Learn to know yourself better by identifying the different parts of your inner personality.

    e. Healthy Touch: Work on energy blocks and grounding techniques to melt the protective armor that has developed around your body.
    - Begin Bioenergetic work. Read *Bioenergetics* by Alexander Lowen (New York: Penguin, 1975).
    - Healthy massage—by a licensed heterosexual massage therapist.

4. Develop healthy, healing same-sex relationships with men.
    a. SSA men on the path of healing.
    b. Heterosexual friends who know about your struggle and support you.
    c. Heterosexual friends who don't know about your struggle and support you.
    d. Heterosexual mentors.
    e. Mentor other men (SSA strugglers and other heterosexual guys).

Stage Four: Healing Hetero-Emotional and Hetero-Social Wounds (Psychodynamic Therapy)

1. Continue all tasks of Stages One, Two, and Three.

2. Discover and heal the root causes of hetero-emotional/social wounds.
   a. Refer to evaluation: mother wound, too close to girls.

3. Continue the process of grieving, forgiving, and taking responsibility.
   a. Read *Emotional Incest Syndrome* by Patricia Love, with Jo Robinson (New York: Bantam Books, 1990).
   b. Explore the unhealthy ties related to your relationship with your mother.
   c. Grieve the losses of your past, and the unhealthy attachment with mother.
   d. Process and appropriately release any stored emotions related to your mother that will allow you to grieve, forgive, and take responsibility.
   e. Separate and individuate from her in the present day.
   f. Establish healthy boundaries in the relationship with your mother.

4. Develop healthy, healing opposite-sex relationships and learn about the opposite sex through the eyes of your own gender.
   a. Study about marriage and women:
   Learn about the hidden meaning behind relationships before you wish to be intimate with a woman. You will need to learn about women from a male perspective. You experienced inappropriate closeness with your mother and girls. You will need men to teach you about women from a masculine perspective.

   b. Read:
   - *Getting the Love You Want: A Guide for Couples* by Harville Hendrix
   - *How to Get a Date Worth Keeping* by Henry Cloud
   - *Conscious Dating* by David Steele
   - *You Just Don't Understand* by Deborah Tannen
   - *Real Love in Marriage* by Greg Baer

   c. Find female mentors to teach you about women.
   - Have female mentors coach you about dating women.
   - Discover what women want and need in a relationship.

   d. Before dating, define who you are, and what kind of person you wish to be with. Explore the differences between men and women from a male point of view with the help of male mentors.

   e. Create a Relationship Vision, and utilize imagery with the end result in mind.
   (1) List your positive traits.
   (2) List the positive traits you want in a woman.

(3) List your non-negotiable needs for the relationship (things that you need for a lifetime of love and fulfillment).

(4) See yourself with that person doing activities that you enjoy.

(5) Visualize this image (do this at least three times per week).

Additional books:

1. *Healing Homosexuality: Case Studies* by Joseph Nicolosi
2. *My Genes Made Me Do It!* by Neil and Briar Whitehead
3. *The Truth about Homosexuality: Cry of the Faithful* by Father John Harvey
4. *Gay Children, Straight Parents: A Plan for Family Healing* by Richard Cohen
5. *Healing Humanity: Time, Touch and Talk*, by Richard Cohen

Submitted by:

Richard Cohen, M.A.
Positive Approaches To Healthy Sexuality, www.pathinfo.org

Books for Healing

Family of Origin

Family Ties That Bind by Ronald Richardson

Cognitive Therapy/Dealing with Negative Thought Processes

Ten Days to Self-Esteem by David Burns
Feeling Good Handbook by David Burns
The Four Agreements by Don Miguel Ruiz
Mind Over Mood, Dennis Greenberger, Christine Padesky

Anger Work

The Anger Workbook by Les Carter and Frank Minirith
Rage: A Step-by-Step Guide to Overcoming Explosive Anger by Ronald Potter-Efron

Assertiveness Training

Your Perfect Right by Robert Alberti and Michael Emmons

Obsessive-Compulsive Behavior

Brain Lock by Jeffrey Schwartz

Sexual Addiction

Out of the Shadows by Patrick Carnes
Faithful & True: Sexual Integrity in a Fallen World by Mark Laasser
False Intimacy: Understanding the Struggle of Sexual Addiction by Harry Schaumburg

Sexual Abuse

A Door of Hope, by Jan Frank
The Wounded Heart: Hope for Adult Victims of Childhood Sexual Abuse by Dan Allender
Counseling Survivors of Sexual Abuse by Diane Mandt Langberg

Inner Child Healing

Recovery of Your Inner Child by Lucia Capacchione
Self-Parenting, by John Pollard
Where Were You When I Needed You, Dad? by Jane Meyers Drew

Psychodynamic Therapy (Getting in touch with thoughts, feelings, needs)

Focusing by Eugene Gendlin
Voice Dialogue by Hal and Sidra Stone
Bioenergetics by Alexander Lowen

Family Healing Sessions

Holding Time by Martha Welch

Understanding Male/Female Relationships

Getting the Love You Want by Harville Hendrix
How to Get a Date Worth Keeping by Henry Cloud
Real Love / Real Love in Marriage by Greg Baer
Conscious Dating by David Steel

DAY ONE

Example of a Liability and Release Form

INFORMED CONSENT AND LIABILITY WAIVER AND RELEASE FORM

To participate in therapy sessions with ____, please read and sign this Informed Consent. Your signature constitutes an understanding and acceptance of all terms mentioned.

1. I am responsible for arriving at my scheduled therapy session on time. If I am late, I understand that (your organization/practice) may need to re-schedule the session so that it does not impede on the time of the next person who has scheduled a therapy session. Out of courtesy, I will give at least 72 hours (3 days) prior notice before canceling an appointment, unless the cancellation is due to sudden illness or an emergency. If I do not provide timely notice, I agree to pay (your organization/practice) for its commitment of time. I understand that therapy sessions typically last 50-60 minutes. If I wish to commit a longer or shorter period of time, I will contact (therapist) in advance to discuss my preference and determine if that time is available.
2. I understand that I may not email, text, or call _____ in between sessions except to schedule appointments and address other administrative matters, unless otherwise stipulated.
3. Psychotherapist _____ will facilitate the therapy sessions. He is under supervision by ___.
4. By signing this Informed Consent, I hereby release, acquit, discharge, and indemnify, and hold harmless the (your organization), its officers, board members, employees, agents, representatives, and/or volunteers from any and all actions, claims, demands, damages, and expenses, including attorney's fees or other legal expenses, arising from and/or in connection with the therapeutic services provided by the (your organization).
5. I understand that (your organization) will make every reasonable effort to safeguard my communications with _____ and treat them as confidential and privileged information. I further understand that the (your organization) will comply with any applicable federal or state laws regarding maintenance and safekeeping of its records pertaining to my therapy sessions and my right to inspect and copy them. Notwithstanding the foregoing, I understand that ____ may need to share my confidential information with (your supervisor) for the sole purpose of assisting in my healing and personal growth, and with (your supervisor) and/or the appropriate authorities if:
   a. he suspects that a child, or other person, has been physically abused, neglected, and/or sexually abused;
   b. he suspects that I have a condition or am engaging in behavior that may require restraint and/or hospitalization to protect me and/or others;
   c. I have committed or am about to commit a crime or other violation of the law and he or the (your organization) is required or permitted to report it;
   d. a court of law issues a legitimate subpoena for your records; and/or if I provide written consent to release information about me and/or my family members.

    e. If the circumstances described above arise, I will not require the (your organization), and _____ and (supervisor), to obtain a release-of-information form from me designating each person to whom they will be communicating.
6. The use of touch in the therapeutic setting is strictly at the discretion of the client and for the sole purpose healing. We adhere to the Ethics Guidelines of The United States Association for Body Psychotherapy (https://usabp.org/USABP-Code-of-Ethics).
7. I understand that all clients experience healing in different ways and may have varying degrees of success, and that change is determined by each individual client.
8. I agree to pay the (your organization) a fee of $_____ per session. I understand that the (your organization) is able (or is not able) to accept insurance at this time.
9. This Informed Consent represents the entire agreement between us regarding the therapeutic sessions I will be receiving from the (your organization) and shall not be modified unless done so in writing signed by both the (your organization) and me for the duration of the services it provides me. There are no other promises, representations, or warranties of any kind not included in this Informed Consent. If any provision is declared void or unenforceable, it shall not affect the validity or enforceability of any other provisions.

My signature demonstrates my understanding of the foregoing points.

By signing below, I accept the terms of this agreement.

_____

Name   Date

DAY ONE

Therapeutic Relationship Between Therapist / Coach and Client

1. **Create a positive, healthy alliance with your client:** Empathy, joining, providing a safe place and safe container for him/her to share without judgment.

2. **Begin and end each session with either prayer or quiet meditation.** Ask the client which s/he would prefer. Then ask if s/he would like to pray, or if s/he would like me to pray. Always give the client/individual "control."

3. **Utilize good listening and communication skills** (paraphrase/mirroring, thought and feeling empathy).

4. **Ask questions.** Do not offer unsolicited advice without first asking permission: "Would you like some feedback?" "Would you like some suggestions?"

5. **After you have established a strong therapeutic alliance and trust has been established, you must be directive in your approach**, as opposed to Rogerian (humanistic existential: allowing them to share without any clear guidance or direction). Gently but firmly guide him toward his goals: Give homework assignments, hold him accountable for fulfilling his commitments. If he doesn't, discuss what is in the way of his commitment to doing his assignments. Process through this until he decides to do it for himself—not for you, not for anyone else. Be careful of the "good little boy" syndrome, as SSA often implies a "pleasing personality." Oftentimes, SSA clients lack the will to complete assignments. Discuss how to work through his lack of discipline or committment.*

---

* **Many who experience SSA are weak-willed.** One reason is because they did not successfully separate/individuate from their mothers in the second stage of child development—when a child usually develops will-power and self-determination, from 1½ to 3 years of age. Such individuals will need more community involvement and support.

Components of Session

1. **Prayer or quiet meditation** (centering and grounding).

2. **Two feeling words check-in.** Using The Feelings Wheel (many versions are available online), s/he shares how she/he is feeling, and what is behind her/his feelings.

3. **Goals for the session**: Go over what he wants to do/accomplish at the start of each session. It's important for him to identify the agenda/issues he wants to deal with, expressing his needs. Many times he won't be clear, but the more you place responsibility on him, the more clear he'll become about his wants and needs—instead of you directing the healing process.

4. **Homework**: Review what he's been working on (*Ten Days to Self-Esteem, Recovery of Your Inner Child*, affirmations, focusing, relationships with men, exercise program, meditations, support group, spiritual life, etc.).

5. **Psycho-educational training**: Responses to his homework and/or issues he brings up. Teach about the meaning behind his SSA and the healing process.

6. **Healing/process work (psychodynamic therapy)**: Use different skills/therapeutic modalities to address current or past issues (e.g., voice dialogue, focusing, role play, inner child work, bioenergetics, creative visualization, healing prayer, etc.).

7. **Review processing work**: What he went through, what he learned.

8. **New homework assignments**: Depending upon what stage of healing he is presently working through.

9. **Two feeling words and check-out**: Share how he feels at the end of the session. Then prayer or meditation (centering and grounding).

Day Two

Homework
1. Continue reading *Being Gay* Chapters Four and Six
2. Read *Ten Days to Self-Esteem* by David Burns
3. Read *Recovery of Your Inner Child* by Lucia Chapacchione

Class Syllabus:

Stage One: Transitioning (Behavioral)

1. Cut off from 3 Ps (Playgrounds, Playmates, and Playthings)

    a. Masturbation and Sexual Fantasies

2. Develop a Support Network

    a. Healthy Same-Gender Relationships
    b. How to Share with Heterosexual Friends and Mentors
    c. Mentoring Relationships

Break

3. Relationship with God

    a. Spend Time in Prayer and Meditation
    b. Not Gay, Bisexual, Lesbian, Transgender: Child of God (Son or Daughter)
    c. Affirmations

4. Group Process Protocol

Stage Two: Grounding (Cognitive/Affective)

1. Cognitive Therapy: *Ten Days to Self-Esteem* by David Burns

    Your Perfect Right by Alberti and Emmons

2. Communication Skills: Showing Up in Life

3. Journaling

4. Affective Therapy: *Recovery of Your Inner Child* by Lucia Capacchione

Stage One: Transitioning (Behavioral Therapy)
===

1. Cut off from playgrounds, playmates, playthings (stop having sex with self & others).
    a. Discuss where s/he's at with sex (self and others) and use of porn.
    b. Begin to journal using HALT diagnosis, learn to identify triggers.
    c. Work on those issues, resolve conflicts, and get needs met in healthy ways and in healthy relationships.
    d. Focus on the solution(s).

2. Develop a support network.
    a. Healthy same-sex relationships.
    b. How to share with opposite-sex attracted (OSA) friends and mentors.
    c. Mentoring relationships.
    d. Attend support groups/Join on-line support group(s):
        (1) JIM groups / Joel225.com groups
        (2) Ministry groups: Restored Hope Network, Courage, North Star etc.
        (3) New Warrior or Women Within groups
        (4) Church men's/women's groups/Synagogue groups/Mosque groups
        (5) Twelve-step groups (be careful because many are gay affirming)
    e. Exercise: work out, and find an exercise partner and/or trainer.
    f. Healthy diet: reduce sugar and caffeinated drinks.
    g. Read books and do homework assignments:
        - *Being Gay* by Richard Cohen
        - *Growth into Manhood* by Alan Medinger
        - *Reparative Therapy of Male Homosexuality* by Joseph Nicolosi
        - *Restoring Sexual Identity* by Anne Paulk
        - *The Heart of Female Same-Sex Attraction* by Janelle Hallman
        - *Desires in Conflict* by Joe Dallas (Christian)
        - *Homosexuality: A New Christian Ethic* by Elizabeth Moberly
        - *You Don't Have to Be Gay* by Jeff Konrad (Christian)
        - *The Battle for Normalcy* by Gerard van den Aardweg
        - *Practical Exercises for Men in Recovery of SSA,* James Phelan

3. Develop a personal relationship with God, use affirmations.
    a. Spend time in prayer and meditation, study God's Word.
    b. Feel loved for being a "Son/Daughter of God" (loved even with SSA).
       Change identification: not homosexual, not gay, not bisexual.
       Simply, a "Son of God" or "Daughter of God."

One doesn't have to "change" in order to be loved.

    c. Read *Words That Heal: Affirmations and Mediations for Daily Living* by Douglas Block (New York: Bantam Books, 1988).

    d. Make a list of things you wish your father had said and done with you while you were growing up. Make a list of things you wish male peers had said and done with you while growing up.

    e. Create a MP3 from this list: Have a few men/women you trust make the recording. Make a space in between each affirmation so you may repeat the lines in your mind. Put beautiful music in the background.

    f. Use this on a daily basis, ideally morning and night. Process your feelings as they come up by stopping the recording as necessary. If daily use is too much at first, listen a few times per week. Be consistent, and then slowly increase the dosage until you are listening to it twice daily. *Succeed small rather than fail big.*

4. Group process protocol.

Masturbation*

Your sexuality as a man or woman is good. Being aroused by seeing another person of the same sex is not morally wrong. It is a message from the soul. It is a message from the child within who didn't experience healthy male or female bonding with Dad/Mom and/or same-sex peers. When you get aroused by a man/woman, do not beat yourself up. Suspend judgment. Do away with guilt. Find the message in the desire, and you will heal your heart. Fulfill basic love needs for male/female bonding in healthy relationships with other men/women. Sex may give you what you want temporarily, but not what you need in the long run. Only healthy, non-sexual relationships will heal the wounds and fulfill basic needs for love.

Masturbation

1. Being a sexual male/female is good, healthy and a God-given gift. "I thank God for my sexuality."

2. Sex is a gift, and ideally, an act of marriage. It is an act of love and intimacy.

3. Many faiths have different teachings about masturbation.

4. Many experience guilt, shame, and anxiety about masturbating, which feeds an already wounded part of the psyche. It becomes an endless cycle or unmet needs, anxiety, masturbating/fantasizing, guilt/shame, and over and over again.

5. We need to stop the cycle and find out what drives us to WANT to masturbate in the first place. The CAUSE is more important and more powerful than the EFFECT.

6. <u>Some reasons why we masturbate</u>:
    a. To self-soothe: comfort from stress or conflict in present-day relationships.
    b. Inner child's way of getting your attention.
    c. Way to get back into your body. By being a pleaser, one gets disconnected from the true self. Touching yourself and masturbating then becomes a path of re-entry to the soul.
    d. Substitute for intimacy with others. Fantasy and masturbation are easier than creating and/or maintaining relationships.
    e. Reward yourself for hard work or a job well done.
    f. Numb physical or emotional pain.
    g. Habitual: physiology of addiction—enough is never enough.
    h. HALT: Hungry/Hurt, Angry, Lonely, Tired.

7. Masturbation becomes habitual from adolescence. It is a way to take care of myself when no one else is. It generally is accompanied by sexual fantasies.

8. Many who experience SSA were/are pleasers—so masturbation is a way of getting dirty, rebellious and real. By masturbating, *I* have control.

9. We need to stop the guilt/shame cycle. Identify causes and give ourselves grace. Because many of us were pleasers and perfectionists, we feel guilty and shameful about masturbating.

10. Marriage is not a solution for compulsive masturbation and sexual fantasies. Many men continue to do this throughout marriage. It is a habit for various reasons. Find the causes and create positive alternatives.

11. When you decrease/stop masturbating, you may have more nocturnal emissions—a natural release when you sleep. This is nature's way of taking care of sperm buildup.

12. Become the CEO of your body. The desire to masturbate is one part of you. Don't let your body be in control. Find the causes and create positive alternatives.

13. <u>How to resolve unwanted masturbation</u>:
    a. Breathe through it. Listen to the message from your soul. Embrace your desires! Listen and learn from your (inner child) soul.
    b. Forgive yourself if you already masturbated, and then…
    c. Pray or meditate to identify the cause(s) and/or genuine need(s).
    d. Journal: **Identify the triggers** that led/lead to masturbation and/or unwanted sexual behavior (use HALT diagnostic tool).
    e. Call an opposite-sex attracted (OSA) friend, OSA mentor, or SSA comrade and use the HALT diagnostic: Hungry or Hurt/Angry/Lonely/Tired.
    f. Deal effectively with the cause(s):
       (1) Resolve conflicts in relationships—make peace with the person you're upset with
       (2) Heal painful emotions—work through it yourself or seek help
       (3) Stop isolating yourself and get your needs met in healthy, same-gender, non-sexual relationships
       (4) Reduce stress—create a more balanced life.
    g. Create positive alternatives:
       (1) work out/exercise
       (2) give to others—direct your energy outward
       (3) receive healthy touch—massage, healthy hugs, holding by OSA mentors.
    h. Use inner child dialogue, drawing, and/or meditations.

12. Keep your focus balanced—inward and outward. There is a danger that during the healing process you may become too introspective. Create joy in your life. Give to others. Keep your energy flowing outward as well as inward. Make sure you exercise, give to others, engage in healthy relationships, experience joy, and play!

13. Ask God to help you:
    a. Identify the causes.
    b. Understand how to heal the wounds.
    c. Guide you to meet the unmet needs for love and connection in healthy relationships.

Homework:

1. Write down the causes/reasons why you masturbate—identify the triggers.
2. Write down your sexual fantasies—who you're attracted to, his/her characteristics, what takes place, and where it takes place.
3. Accountability partners—get support from other men. Call each other when you want to masturbate or have sex with another person other than your spouse (or after you did it), and use the HALT diagnostic tool.
4. Stop judging yourself. Pray. Identify the causes and resolve in healthy ways.
5. Keep a journal to identify the triggers that lead to masturbation or sexual behavior, and create positive alternatives.

*Some of the information about masturbation comes from ministry leader and psychotherapist Jerry Armelli. Used by permission from the author.

DAY TWO

Sexual Fantasies

1. We fantasize about and envy, idolize, or lust after:
   a. Those who carry our undeveloped, unconscious, or repressed parts: disowned parts (characteristics we had in the past but gave up because of rejection and criticism by others); and lost parts (characteristics we never experienced, such as being more assertive, masculine looking, confident, and/or muscular men).
   b. Those we wish to be loved by: older (need for parenting), same age (peer acceptance or self-acceptance), younger (generally represents the age when we were abused or developmentally stuck).
   c. Those who hurt us: homo-emotional (parent) and homo-social (peers). Identification with the perpetrator, as a means of self-protection.
   d. Someone to take care of: giving to others what I long for myself. Intimacy is too threatening, so it's safer to give rather than receive. Many therapists, clergy, and ministry leaders fit into this category.
   e. Those we want to be like: Envy what he can do, want to be like him.

2. Sexual fantasies essentially have nothing to do with sex. They represent:
   a. Wounds that have not healed, and
   b. Needs for love that have not been fulfilled.

3. Sexual fantasies are also progressive, changing over time. The chemistry of the brain adapts to a certain level of excitement over time, and therefore, it will need to be enhanced periodically. Therefore, enough will never be enough.

4. Sex between two men or two women is incomplete. A man gives his masculinity to a woman, and a woman gives her femininity to a man, during sexual union. It is an exchange, sharing, giving of masculine and feminine energies. This creates harmony between the two polarities. Opposites attract.

5. Self-sex and same-sex relations do not share, give, or exchange different energies—each partner seeks to gain from the other that which is lacking within him or herself. There are no dual polarities, so the exchange is not lasting or harmonizing. It is like getting an injection of masculinity or femininity from the other, rather than sharing male/female energies.

Men/women with homosexual desires are trying to restore homo-emotional wounds (need for paternal bonding) and/or homo-social wounds (peer bonding and acceptance). It represents a need to belong, to be loved, and to be accepted into the world of men/women.

Men with heterosexual addictions are often attempting to restore hetero-emotional wounds (need for maternal bonding) and/or hetero-social wounds (need for bonding with healthy women) = Opposite-Sex Attachment Disorder (OSAD). It represents a need to belong, to be loved, connected and accepted by healthy women. However, their normal need for bonding has become sexualized and then eroticized. The same may hold true for OSA women, seeking father's love through sexual relations or by flaunting their sexuality to attract men. Also, men may have experienced cultural/peer wounds, having learned that it's "masculine," "hip," "cool," "in," to gawk at and sexualize women. And in turn, some women then modify their behavior and appearance in order to appear "sexy" for men, in an attempt to gain their love, affection, and acceptance.

6. Another variable influencing sexual fantasies is one's personality—more assertive, a gentle-soul, etc. These personality traits may impact the one that he or she is attracted to.

7. Generally, people are caught up in a cycle of guilt and shame about their sexual fantasies and masturbation. They magnify their negative feelings about themselves (doing what they believe they shouldn't do), while minimizing what caused the act in the first place. The truth is that the cause(s) holds the key to freedom and love.

Therefore, until we understand what is behind our sexual fantasies and need to masturbate, our soul will continuously work to get our attention through these fantasies until we learn how to take care of ourselves in healthy, loving and responsible ways.

8. Attractions to different types of people:
    a. Older: homo-emotional wound (need for parental/maternal love).
    b. Same age: homo-social wound (need for peer love and acceptance), or need for gender identification—trying to claim manhood/womanhood through another man/woman, or need to obtain the lost or disowned parts of self by joining with someone of the same gender.
    c. Younger: trying to restore abuse issues or work through arrested developmental issues of a particular age.

9. Dominating: Tired of being controlled, tired of being the "nice guy" and "pleaser," he wants to take control, to be the powerful person of his fantasies ("The Secret Life of Walter Mitty"). In the fantasy, he can be powerful, aggressive, in control—the take-charge guy. It is too threatening to be assertive in real life, so he uses fantasies instead.

10. Dominated: Tired of being in control, tired of being in charge, he wants someone to take care of him. Also, love = home. Therefore, if while growing up he experienced love as being dominated, controlled or abused (emotionally, mentally, physically, and/or sexually), then this will become a core pattern of behavior. Yes, the human psyche is very strange indeed.

11. Fetish = Psychic Splitting. This is a survival skill, a built-in defensive mechanism. If the reality of the child was too painful, or he was unable to mentally process both the good and bad qualities of a loved one, he may have developed a fetish—underwear, feet, shoes, wrestling, boxing, genital size—as a source of comfort and relief. In this way, he was able to cope with the intolerable situation that he (believed he) could not change. Fetishes are not about the fetish. They mask feelings that were buried alive. Discover the hidden meaning behind the fetish. It is a coping mechanism and should not be removed until understood. Healing the cause(s) is the key. Grieving is necessary. Learning new coping skills is important for mental and emotional health.

12. Murder fantasies: Unexpressed anger toward parents or a perpetrator may manifest in murderous fantasies, a way to conquer the abuser that he is unable to confront in real life.

13. Penis size: Many men have an issue with the size of their penis, i.e., it doesn't hang long enough, it's too short, it hangs crooked, it's not long enough when erect, etc. SSA men generally are unaware of the fact that all men check out each other's penises. It seems the size of one's penis is more important to men than women! Most men hang short when flaccid, and most erections are similar in length. About ninety-eight percent of the time the penis is used for urinating. The other 2% of the time is used to pleasure one's wife. During intercourse, the size of the penis is not what's important. Stimulating her clitoris is (technique is more important than length or circumference of the penis).

14. Solving sexual fantasies: Focus on the solution, not the fantasy!

Create healthy solutions through the following approaches:

   a. Stop the cycle of guilt and shame. Stop berating oneself. Let go of toxic guilt. This obstructs healing and growth. Self-deprecation is ungodly and not useful in the healing process.

   b. Key is to understand what is behind the desire. Listen to your body and soul. Find your "truth." Identify your feelings and needs. Oftentimes, fantasies or sex are used to escape uncomfortable situations and/or feelings. Use Focusing, Voice Dialogue, or Inner Child drawing and/or non-dominant handwriting.

   c. Resolve present-day conflicts in a healthy manner. Be assertive in a positive way. Stand up and share your truth. Be authentic and real in the presence of others. Practice good communication skills, i.e. "I think…", "I feel…", "I need…"

   d. Create healthy relationships:
   (1) SSA/OSA mentors: Receive love ("Restore the years the locust have eaten).
   (2) SSA/OSA peers: Give and receive love from friends. A friend is someone who isn't impressed by you! Someone who will speak truth into your life, and be there for you when you need.
   (3) SSA/OSA mentees: Give love to those younger, your spiritual children.

5. Keep a masturbation/fantasy journal. Figure out the triggers that invokes the desire to masturbate and/or fantasize. Use the HALT technique.

Let me repeat: Embrace one's same-sex attractions and sexual fantasies. They help us to identify our wounds and unmet love needs. I am not implying to act upon those desires, not at all. However, they have a lot to teach us about ourselves. Our fantasies may be a pathway to the heart. Listen, learn, and love God, oneself and others in healthy ways.

Use the **Sexual Fantasy Exercise** to identify core wounds and unmet love needs. You may listen to the explanation of this exercise on the MP3 series. This may be used at different times and different stages in the healing process.

SUPPORT NETWORK

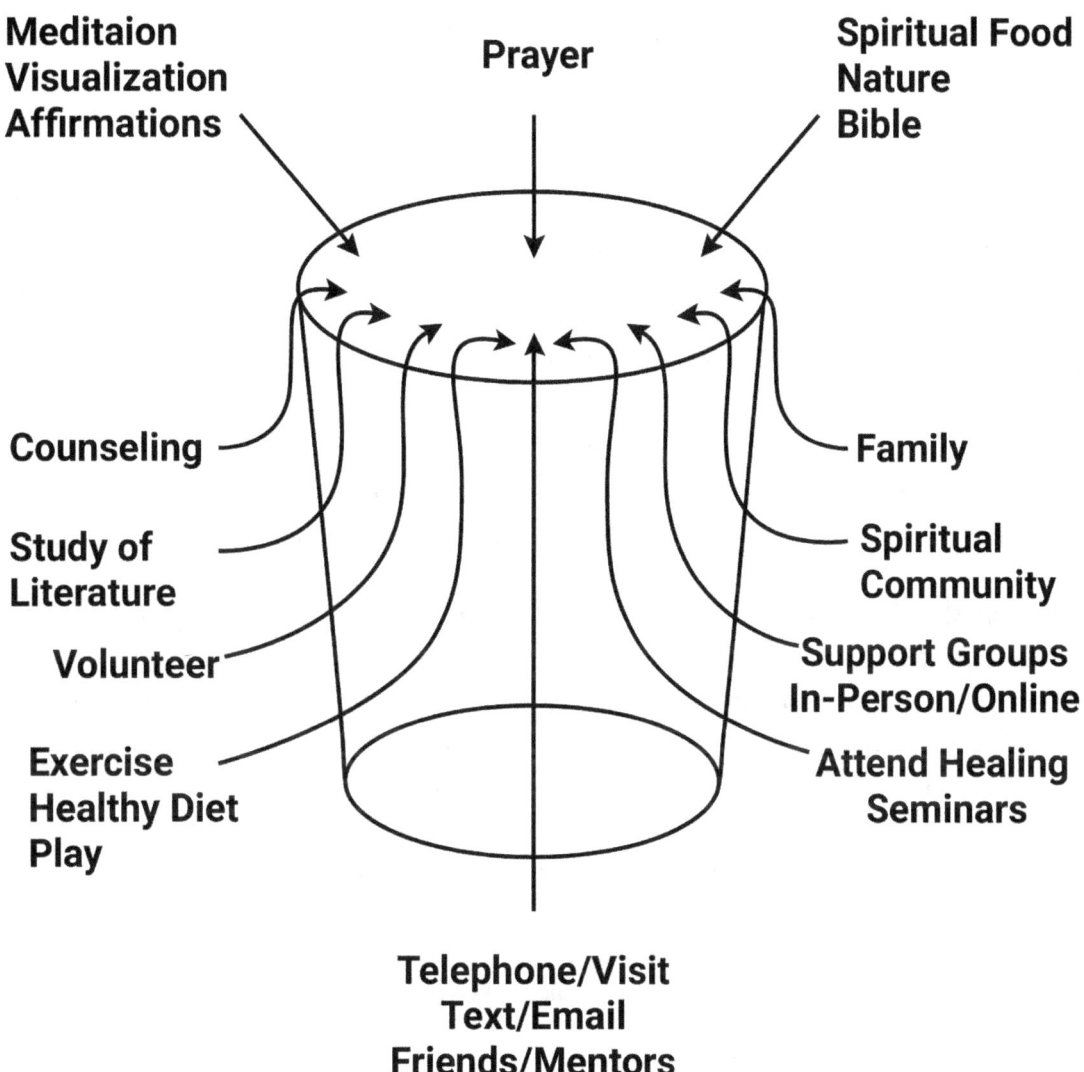

Richard Cohen, M.A. © 2023

Creating Healthy Same-Sex Relationships

Isolation = Death / Ideally Have 6-12 Relationships (elders, peers, mentees)
On a brick wall, each brick is surrounded by: 1) two bricks above, 2) two bricks on the sides, and 3) two bricks below = six bricks to stay on the wall! Encourage SSA strugglers to create healthy same-gender relationships. Affirm each step they take. Make small, measurable assignments for outreach.

Five Types of Healthy Same-Sex Relationships

1. Same-sex attracted (SSA) strugglers who are on the same journey of healing (from Joel225.org support groups, ministries, JIM weekends, JIM on-line groups, etc.).
Pray for each other. Encourage and lift each other up on the path of healing. When one is down, the other helps his/her friend out. Look for "sponsors," those who are further along in their recovery. Be careful not to create co-dependent and/or romantic relationships with other SSA strugglers. Remember, you are both looking for the same thing. Take responsibility for your own healing, and be sure to find opposite-sex attracted (OSA) friends and mentors to assist you on the journey.

2. Heterosexual (OSA) men/women who know about your struggle and are loving, supportive friends.
Make up for what you didn't experience while growing up during your pre-teen and teenage years. Hang out with the guys/women. Do guy things. Do women things. Share about yourself, your sexuality, ask questions. Be free and open. Learn about him/her. Love goes in two directions: Give and receive. Create mutuality.

3. Heterosexual (OSA) men/women who do not know about your struggle and are loving, supportive friends.
Same principles apply; you just don't need to share about your SSA. Meet men/women through common interests, e.g., church, synagogue, gym, clubs, sports. Learn to be a man among men, or a woman among women. Just because you experience SSA doesn't mean you are less than other men/women. All people deal with their own issues and insecurities, all people. Yours is not all that different. The more you get to know other men or women, and be genuine and real, you will be surprised how similar we all are. *Remember, be real and feel in order to heal.*

4. Mentors: OSA Elders who know about your struggle and offer healthy paternal/maternal love and affection.
Seek various mentors to fulfill different needs, e.g., financial, spiritual, athletic, professional occupation, demonstrative. Make up for past deficits by doing things you were unable to experience with your own dad/mom. Mentors are "second chance fathers/mothers." Don't expect that one mentor to meet all of your needs.

5. Mentees: Mentor younger men/women (emotionally/mentally/spiritually) in the process of healing.
Be an elder to younger men/women (equivalent to a "sponsor" in the 12-step programs).

DAY TWO

Create healthy same-sex relationships

We are all like bricks on the wall.

Each brick is surrounded by six other bricks:
    2 bricks above
    2 bricks on the side
    2 bricks below

If we don't have at least six relationships in our life, we will fall off the wall!

COUNSELOR TRAINING PROGRAM MANUAL

How to Tell a Straight Friend

By Joseph Nicolosi, Sr., Ph.D. / Used by permission from the author.

How can the client disclose his homosexual struggle to a straight friend, particularly a straight friend he looks up to? From my many years of experience, there seems to be a basic outline that works best for this procedure.

First, when telling a straight friend, it is advisable to avoid such words as "homosexual" or "gay." It is best, instead, to speak from personal experience. Unfortunately, many heterosexual men have been subliminally influenced by popular misinformation and tend to see their homosexually oriented friend as "gay"—that is, someone fundamentally distinct from "straight."

That's why it is wise to speak in terms of childhood deficits and the need for acceptance by men. Reference to homoeroticism is best presented not as an "identity" but as a *consequence and a symptom* of these earlier unmet male needs.

Disclosure to the straight friend should be done in four steps—either during one meeting or over a period of time:

1. *Family Background.* Offering information such as "This is the kind of father I had." "This is the kind of relationship I had with my mother, older brother, and younger sister"
   "These are my childhood experiences (sexual abuse, intimidation by peers, etc.)." The client can then describe the deficit that causes him not to feel confident about his masculine identification.
2. *Results of Family Background.* "I was left with feelings of insecurity, inferiority or inadequacy regarding my masculinity and my connection with other men. I didn't feel like one of the guys. I didn't know how to fulfill that deficit inside myself."
3. *Same-Sex Exploration.* "As a result of those feelings about myself, I found myself searching for masculine connectedness, and that search led me to sexual behaviors and actions. These things left me dissatisfied, did not represent my values or who I really am."
4. *Healing Through Authentic Friendships.* "Therefore, as a result of my sexual experimentation, I realize that it's not really sex that I'm after. What I really want is a healthy emotional connection with other men. Our friendship is important to me as an opportunity to fulfill my natural male emotional needs and to help me complete my heterosexual identity."
5. *An Optional Fifth Step*: *Accountability.* The client may ask the friend to hold him accountable to report any form of homosexual enactment to him. This agreement works best if it goes both ways, with the straight friend disclosing "falls" regarding his own particular struggles.*

When the struggler's story is presented to his friend according to this outline, most heterosexual men seem to understand. When the struggler reveals himself honestly to the mature and caring straight friend, the response is almost always positive.

DAY TWO

What the Client Needs From a Straight Friend*

1) The client needs to be *understood,* not to be patronized; not categorized as "gay," but understood as to the nature of his struggle. The straight friend must truly appreciate and empathize with the challenges of his friend. To accomplish this, the client will need to educate his friend on the developmental pathway, deficits, needs, and desires which are the basis of his same-sex attractions.

2) The client needs to be *accepted*, to see that his disclosure does not modify, qualify, or diminish in any way his fundamental acceptance by the other guy. And he needs his friend's unconditional acceptance to be manifest and clearly demonstrated.

3) He needs to be *supported* by his friend in his continuing struggle. The straight man should be actively encouraging about what his friend is trying to accomplish.

4) He needs a show of continuing interest so that he is able to tell the other guy the truth about his behavior. What he is saying is, "Please ask me about it." Sometimes disappointment arises when the friend shows initial support and understanding but never discusses the situation again. Typically, our clients fear mentioning their condition more than once for fear of "bothering or burdening" the other guy. Therefore, an important step in the process of telling the straight friend is to explicitly ask: "I need you to ask me how things are going." This very explicit request has the advantage of freeing up the communication between the two men. It also gives the straight friend a responsive repertoire.

Each step builds upon the preceding one. The heterosexual friend cannot show continuing interest unless he first *supports* the SSA man; he cannot support unless he first *accepts* him; and cannot accept him until he *understands* him. I have always been amazed at the encouraging and supportive response of straight men to the SSA struggler.

---

* This is an additional comment by myself, Richard Cohen. Having Accountability Partners is very important for many who wish to heal from unwanted SSA. This allows them to share their struggles and victories, being supported by healthy OSA peers and mentors on the path of recovery.

Additional Tips for SSA Strugglers Sharing with Straight Friends

In order to make it safe to share about your SSA struggle with Opposite-Sex Attracted (OSA) friends, consider sharing about your life in various conversations, not in one sitting. Be sure to share from your adult self, not form your needy inner child. Stand in your power. Share in stages. Create mutuality, learning about each other over time. This concept of sharing in stages comes from the previous model of Joe Nicolosi, Sr.:

First conversation: Explain about your *family background*, what it was like for you while growing up at home and in school. After you've shared about yourself, ask him about his personal history. If he is unwilling to share about himself, he's not a safe person.

Second conversation: Explain how these *early experiences influenced/impacted your life—didn't have close relationships with other guys* (without mentioning SSA and resultant experiences). Ask him how his early experiences affected his life. Again, if he is unwilling to share personally, he is not a safe person.

Third conversation: Explain how these *influences led to same-sex attraction and any sexual experiences* you might have had. Ask him to share about how his early experiences affected his adolescent or adult behaviors.

Note:

Men who experience unwanted SSA will need to educate OSA men about the truth of same-sex attraction. *People are afraid of that which they do not understand.* As soon as they "get it," their fears will be assuaged. By sharing your story, and how you developed SSA, you will be turning their fear into compassion.

1. Explain about the causes of SSA (e.g., lack of bonding with same-sex parent, lack of bonding with same-sex peers, hypersensitivity, over-attachment to opposite-sex parent, teased and mocked in school, sex abuse, etc.). Share about what created SSA in your life.

2. Share about the process of healing:
   a. Need support from same-gender friends/mentors.
   b. Need to heal wounds of the past. Tell them what you went through.
   c. Need to fulfill unmet love needs in healthy relationships. Let them know what you need from them.
   d. Negotiate healthy boundaries: when to get together, when you may call, what they're willing to give.

3. It's important that you take care of yourself and not expect others to do this for you.
   a. Do your own work – inner child workbook, meditations, affirmations.
   b. Attend JIM (men only), AIM (men only), and/or New Warrior for men and Woman Within for women, seminars and ongoing groups.

Mentorship of Men Who Struggle with Same-Sex Attraction

© By Steven Donaldson, M.A., L.P.C., and Del Thornton, M.S.W., L.C.S.W.
Mosaic Counseling Associates / March 2003 / Used by permission from the authors.
1818 SE Division Street, Portland, OR 97202 / Tel. (503) 231-0743

The Role of the Mentor

One of the most important needs of a man who struggles with Same-Sex Attraction is a process in which an older and spiritually mature man befriends and walks beside a younger man who struggles with SSA. A mentor is not a therapist and so does not need to have special knowledge of SSA. He should not be in a position of ecclesiastical authority over the mentee. He needs only to act as an adult father figure to an adult son. The purpose of mentoring is to help in healing the father wound of the mentee's childhood.

The Father Injury

Men who struggle with SSA have not achieved a complete internalized sense of masculinity. They feel they lack some essential part of masculinity that other men have. This leaves them feeling unacceptable and ultimately inadequate in the society of men. Although this is a common feeling to all men, men who struggle with SSA apparently feel it more intensely and have established a defense of emotional and/or physical withdrawal from the world of men and masculinity.

These men inevitably suffer from some sort of injury in their relationship with their fathers. Either the father did not achieve his own sense of competence and strength in the world or he rejected the son (covertly or overtly) and failed to share his masculinity with him. [Richard Cohen's note: Third possibility is the son's perception of paternal rejection; if there is a striking character difference between father and son, this sensitive boy may interpret his father's actions as personally rejecting of him.] In either case the boy did not form an intimate relationship with a strong and moral father figure. Since young children never perceive their parents as flawed, the young boy naturally assumes that the reason the father does not seek him out and love him is that he is inadequate in some way. This leaves him longing for affection and attention from his father (or father figure) yet hurt and fearful of further rejection. For the boy who will later develop SSA, he develops a fear of men and a sense of alienation from men.

At a very early age, before choice is a factor, the child begins to protect himself from rejection by defensively detaching from his father, who later comes to represent all men. He tells himself that he doesn't need his father's love or approval; that he doesn't care about his father. At this point the child begins to develop an identity in which he simultaneously rejects masculinity for himself and longs for the love, affection and approval of strong and confident men. The boy dis-identifies with his father. He in essence says to himself, "My father is bad, I don't want to be like him." This often leaves the boy with no one to identify with outside of his mother.

Since parental systems function in unison, where father vacates, mother overcompensates. Often, the marriage is between mother and son based on their shared rejection of father. Since the boy has no one else to depend on he must modify himself in any way necessary to maintain his relationship with his mother. This often includes joining her in devaluing (dis-identifying with) father.

When a young man is left fearful of adult men and not understanding how to interact with them, yet desiring a powerful emotional connection, commonly a fantasy idealization of men emerges. For the young man who will develop SSA, this idealization becomes sexualized. This sexualization begins as a way to create a feeling of safety and stop the panic/fear response that is triggered by things that remind him of his own masculine inadequacy. The sexual fantasy or behavior allows the struggler to have connection with a man without the overwhelmingly frightening obligation to become a man. He forfeits becoming fully male, which he fears he cannot achieve, in exchange for having the love and approval of a man. He becomes sexually attracted to the characteristics of other men that he feels he cannot achieve in himself.

Healthy Development

In a healthy family setting, a boy naturally internalizes masculinity when he is pursued and loved by his father, whom he perceives as strong and moral. It is the father's job to go into the maternal nest and literally take his son away from the security of his mother. Boys are always frightened and cling to their mothers. This fear does not make them mama's boys. It is natural. When the father aggressively claims his son as his own, the boy feels scared on the one hand and excited on the other. He learns to catch a baseball, and he learns to dive into deep water. Each triumph with father forms a powerful bond between father and son. The father's natural pride and interest in his son mirrors the boy's own growing sense of masculine competence. This sense of competence can then be taken into the world of his peers and confirmed further. When the process works, the boy naturally feels like a member of the world of his peers (the society of men). For the man who struggles with SSA, something went wrong in this process. He does not develop a complete internalized sense of masculinity; he does not feel like a member of the society of men. He feels different and alienated from men. One perspective would be to view the act of homosexuality as the young man's unconscious abandonment of the pursuit to become a man. He instead accepts the compromise of having a man love and value him sexually.

The mentor serves to work toward healing this wound. Mentors must understand that this wound will never be healed completely. Even a perfect mentoring relationship will not make up for a lost childhood when an affirming father would have made the real difference.

The Characteristics of a Good Mentor

To be effective, a mentor must have several characteristics. No one can be the perfect embodiment of these characteristics. A good mentor must **demonstrate self-confidence** and **good moral character**. That is, he must have achieved a **sense of masculine competence** of his own.

A good mentor must have **strong gender identity**. That is, he must feel good about himself as a man. This does not mean being super macho. Being super macho is actually a sign of weak gender identification. Evidence of sound gender security includes the lack of defensiveness or the need to prove anything to anyone, and active participation in his masculine roles (e.g. father, husband, provider, ecclesiastical leader, male friendships, and male-typical activities). In addition a male with good gender identification relates respectfully and well toward women. He respects and likes women, and it shows. In essence, he should enjoy every aspect of being a man.

A good mentor will have **good ego-strength**. What this means is that he does not get his feelings hurt easily, and has no problem saying "No." Mentoring can be very trying, and requires tenacity for the long haul. Same-sex attraction does not form overnight, and even with motivated clients it does not go away overnight. The mentor's self-esteem cannot depend on the success of his mentee. He must remain positive, loving, and encouraging, no matter how badly his mentee fails. Men who struggle with SSA can be at the same time emotionally needy and defensively detached. This means they long for emotional contact with men but fear being hurt. At the first sign of abandonment they can become defensive and even reactive, which may be interpreted as condescendence. The mentor can never take the defensiveness personally and must be able to set limits on the emotional neediness.

A good mentor must be **emotionally available**. He must be comfortable with his own feelings and able to share these with the mentee. He must be comfortable with his own weaknesses, failures, embarrassments, and fears and be able to share these with the mentee at times when this type of disclosure would be helpful. He must be able to hear the mentee talk about his fears, anger, feelings of inadequacy, and pain without becoming anxious or needing to minimize or fix them. It is not the job of the mentor to know what the mentee should do, or to fix them. This is very important. The mentor's job is to be present over the long haul and emotionally supportive. The mentor is neither the mentee's moral authority nor therapist and does not need to take responsibility for or direct him in these ways. Men who struggle with SSA badly need both spiritual direction and therapeutic help, but this is not the role of the mentor.

While the mentor must be emotionally available, the mentor should **not lean on the mentee for emotional support**. The mentor relationship mirrors the relationship of a healthy father-son dynamic. In this dynamic, the father provides for the son, but the son does not provide for the father. Fathers get their needs met in the adult world, while children seek their emotional support from their parents.

A good mentor must be **physically affectionate**. Many people believe that being physically affectionate with men who struggle with SSA will exacerbate their symptoms. Nothing could be further from the truth. Men who struggle with SSA are afraid of male affection. It is precisely this fear that makes male affection so intensely sexually interesting. As long as the mentor has a strong gender identity, there is no chance of the encounter becoming sexual. This is exactly the kind of safety the mentee needs to experiment with allowing himself to genuinely love and need non-sexual male affection. The deepest longing of the man who struggles with SSA is not for sex. It is for love and affirmation.

Finally, a mentor must **pursue the relationship with the mentee**. The mentee at the core does not trust that the mentor could ever be genuinely interested in him and at the same time need nothing from him. This is a continuation of the father-child injury. For this reason the mentee will not be the initiator in the relationship. [I, Richard Cohen, do not agree with this statement. I believe that the mentee should be the initiator in the relationship. I believe he needs to ask for what he wants, learning to be assertive in a healthy, masculine manner. That is necessary for his personal growth into manhood.]

This will be re-enacted in the mentoring relationship. In addition, when there is any confusion or conflict the mentee is very likely to assume he did something wrong and withdraw or devalue the relationship. The mentor must remember that the withdrawal from, or devaluing of the relationship is a defense (usually unconscious) against the intense need and longing for the love and affirmation of an idealized male. The mentor must not take anything personally and continue to gently but actively pursue the mentee.

Suggested Activities

Men who struggle with SSA long for a non-anxious connection with men. The mentor needs to take initiative in identifying activities that will be fun for both and yet not too anxiety provoking for the mentee. The mentor should explore common interests such as art, music, theater, cars, or sports. Both can introduce each other to the things they individually enjoy. Over time, the relationship will develop that will allow more risks to be taken without the fear of humiliation.

Some men who struggle with SSA have defensively detached from masculinity so extensively that almost any male-typical activity will trigger a fear/inadequacy response. In the beginning, even watching a basketball game may be too much. Defensive detachment seldom is expressed as fear. A mentee will probably never say, "I'm afraid of appearing stupid if I watch a game with you." They are much more likely to express disinterest such as, "I have never seen the point of football. It is nothing but egotistical male aggression!" The mentor must see through this defense and slowly encourage his mentee to be a part of the world of men. This can only happen over time and when trust is established. It is not necessary for all men who struggle with SSA to become NFL fans. They must however develop to the point that they can attend a Super Bowl party or a church softball game without feeling overwhelmed with anxiety and inadequacy.

Learning to play and be competitive at team sports is often a problem for men who struggle with SSA. They should be encouraged to do so; however, this should be approached with extreme caution. Even encouragement in this area can trigger significant fear, which leads to compulsions to act out. This is often an area of significant childhood injury and avoidance is well established. It is typical for these men to gravitate toward individual sports such as track, swimming, diving, and ice-skating to avoid being a member of a team. They feel inadequate to perform in a situation where other men rely on them in competition. Even minor failures in a team sport can be experienced as devastating inadequacy and overwhelming humiliation. It may be wise to consult the mentee's therapist before approaching this issue.

It is important to include the mentee in your family events. Many men who struggle with SSA come from families with poor dynamics and so have a distorted view of family.

Encourage church-based activities but go slowly. Church callings are important but remember, men who struggle with SSA need the friendship of other men, not a calling to the Primary. In some cases, Church attendance can increase anxiety, which in turn can lead to increased sexual compulsion.

Seek feedback from your mentee. They know what they need. Be open to their suggestions and trust them. If at any point you hurt or disappoint your mentee, sincerely apologize without making excuses. It may be their first experience of humility from an authority figure. This can be very healing.

Consider using your mentee as a home teaching companion. Use their talents. Never evaluate their talents in terms of the masculinity of the activity. All men are created by God, completely masculine. Their preferences, talents, and feelings are completely masculine. Everything about them is completely masculine. The thing men who struggle with SSA lack is an internalized sense (feeling) of masculine adequacy. There is no objective thing that he is lacking. The last thing they need is to have a man they respect infer, even indirectly, that they are in some way less than completely male.

Additional Notes from Richard Cohen:

The mentee may ask the mentor for the following:

1) Healthy touch, including lots of hugs;
2) To spend time participating in his passions, and participating in the passions of the mentor; and
3) To show genuine care and concern for the mentee's well-being on a regular basis through telephone calls, emails, text messages and visits.

It is very important to display affection toward the man healing from unwanted SSA. Gradually, his need for and dependency upon the mentor will decrease as he internalizes these experiences of love.

It is advisable for the mentee to seek several mentors, not just one. Each mentor may have different abilities and qualities to offer the man healing from SSA (e.g., spiritual, financial, athletics, healthy touch, etc.).

Please read Chapter 12 in *Being Gay* for more practical suggestions about the mentoring process.

Affirmations

Home for the client: Create a personal affirmation script for yourself. Please make two lists: (1) things you wish your dad (and/or mom) had said to you, and things you wish they had done with you while you were growing up; and (2) things you wish your peers had said to you, and things you wish they had done with you while you were growing up.

Make two lists:

1. Things you wish your same-gender parent had said and done with you when you were growing up, and
2. Things they wish your same-gender peers had said and done with you while you were growing up.

Make sure that each sentence is in the present tense with only positive words and phrases. There should be no words such as: "not," "won't," "can't," and "shouldn't" in the affirmations. Do not say, "You aren't stupid." It should be turned into a positive. So, if you're not stupid, then what are you? Smart! Reframe it and say, "You are smart." As the therapist or coach, go through their lists thoroughly and make sure each affirmation is stated in a positive manner.

The client should then choose a person to represent the same-gender parent, and several people to represent the same-gender peers. These people can then make a MP3 of all the things the client wished had been expressed to him when he was young. It is important that the persons who record this MP3 share from their hearts, not just their heads. It must impact the soul of the listener. If the same-gender parent is willing to make the recording, she or he must speak with emotion, not just read the words. If the parent is unable to share deeply, it will have little consequence to the client. Therefore, have him or her choose someone else to represent the parent, someone who is capable of expressing their deeper emotions to move the heart of the client. And have the person making the recording leave a silent space of equal length after each sentence, so that the person listening can repeat the sentence to him or herself quietly. Finally, put beautiful music in the background of all the affirmations.

The finished MP3 generally lasts about 5-10 minutes. Have your client use this MP3 ideally once in the morning and once before going to bed. If that is too much at first, then ask your client what is realistic: "Are you willing to use it twice a week?" Start out with a small dosage, have them succeed for several weeks, and then systematically increase the dosage until they are using it twice daily. If they use this affirmation MP3 for one year, it will transform their sense of self-esteem and wellbeing.

When they are listening to the MP3, it is normal for negative feelings emerge. The individual puts the MP3 on hold and expresses his/her feelings freely (i.e. "Why now, why not then? Why do you say you love me? I don't believe you, you…."). Allow them to detox as they listen to the MP3. Eventually, as they express their hurt feelings, over time, they will begin to believe the powerful messages of love and affirmation.

Below are several examples taken from an excerpt from *Gay Children, Straight Parents: A Plan for Family Healing* by Richard Cohen, M.A., PATH Press, 2016.

David: Positive things I wish my father had said and done:

- I love you son.
- I'm proud to be your father.
- David, you are tall and handsome.
- I love you son, and I give you my blessing.
- You are strong, brave, and courageous.
- You exceed my expectations as a son.
- I want to spend time with you.
- David, I appreciate you.
- You are very important to me.
- You are very talented, my son.
- David, you are worthy to be loved.

David: Positive things I wish my peers would say and do:

- David, we are your friends, and you are dear to us.
- We accept you.
- We want to hang out with you.
- We enjoy being around you.
- I'd pick you first to be on my team.
- I would like to be buddies with you.
- You are strong and handsome.
- We look up to you.
- You deserve the best.
- We appreciate you.
- We love you, David.

John's affirmations from his Dad:

- I love you, John.
- I am proud that you are my son.
- John, you are very important to me.
- You are a man just like me.
- You belong to me.
- John, you are unique, and I love you.
- John, I want you to have the best in life.
- I respect who you are.
- I care about what you think and feel.
- I want to spend time with you.
- I want to hug you.
- I am proud of you.
- John, here is the way men walk.
- John, I am with you all the way.

John's affirmations from friends:

- John, you belong.
- You are one of us.
- You are cool.
- We are here for you, man.
- You make a difference.
- You are courageous.
- We need you.

Eric: Things I wish my Dad had said to me:

- How wonderful that I have been given a third son to enjoy and to cherish like no other man ever could. What other man has the privilege of calling you son?
- I am so proud of the unique and gifted young man you are.

- Your body is masculine. Your face is masculine. Your mannerisms are masculine. Your voice is masculine. You are tall and handsome, like all the Howell men. What a great addition you are to the family!
- I accept your creativity and sensitivity as God-given manly traits you have been given. Even though I was not allowed or encouraged to share my feelings while growing up, I recognize that you must do this to be true to yourself. I admire the level to which you feel things, and the way you express them. I love it when you share from your heart. This is how I learn about you!
- You are strong, powerful, and manly, like me. You are a natural leader.
- You measure up in every possible way to my expectations for you. You are intelligent, artistic, athletic, and thoughtful.
- I will take the time that's necessary to teach you how to live in the world of men. This includes sports, business, and how to relate to women.
- You come from a line of great men and fall right into place.
- You are constantly in my heart.
- You are masculine and athletic.
- I will take the time to know you and to relate to you in the unique way that you need. You can trust me, for I am on your side.

Eric: Things I wish peers had said to me. Younger years:

- Do you want to come over to my house and play?
- Can you make it to my birthday party? You would add something really special just by being there.
- Hey, a bunch of us are getting together to play some ball. Can you make it over to the field?

High school and college years:

- Anyone would be lucky to have you as a friend.
- Wow, you are really talented. I admire your architectural drawings and your ability to act and sing onstage. Man, that takes guts.
- I think you're so cool.
- You are really a great guy. I've heard other guys say they think you're cool.
- It would be awesome if we could spend some time together, just hanging out, you know? Just a few of us guys?
- Hey, a bunch of us are going skiing for the weekend. Would you like to come with us?
- Man—how did you get so talented? Will you show me how to draw, write, act, or sing like that?
- Wow, you're a strong guy—you must work out.

Group Process Protocol

I ask each person who is joining the group for a three-month minimum commitment. This makes it safe for the others, so that people are not just coming in and out all the time. This helps build a very trusting environment, where all members feel regarded and safe. I led support groups for over 12 years. We had wonderful times together, and radical healing occurred. They bonded together and many have become life-long friends.

1. **Grounding exercise**: Meditation / bioenergetics grounding exercise / vocalization / transformational breath work / play a game / be creative.
2. **Business**: Announcements / schedule / change format, negotiate group rules, etc.
3. **Circle up for check-in:** each person takes 2-3 minutes to share these four points:
   a. Two feeling words.
   b. One-minute summary of where you are at in the moment.
   c. Clearing: Do you need to work out some issue(s) with anyone in the group?
   d. What do you need tonight? (Some may not know, and that's OK.)
4. **Clearing round (if necessary):**
   a. Data: about what was said or done by a person(s) in the group.
   b. Feelings (simple one-word feelings) about what s/he said or did.
   c. Judgments/opinions about that.
   d. Ownership of projection.
   e. Need from the relationship.
   f. What you are willing to give to the relationship.
5. **Individual process work:**
   a. Facilitator leads each person's work. If peer-led group, take turns facilitating. Mankind Project (www.mkp.org) offers Guts Training. Divide the time by the number of people who wish to work or get help.
   b. Two kinds of work: Process or questions. Depends on the level of each participant.
   c. Process work—use various therapeutic interventions: Bioenergetics (have pounding pillows, tennis racquet, and gloves), psychodrama, voice dialogue, role play, psychodrama, inner child, etc. Goal: Help each participant work through his/her issue(s) and experience his/her power. Create solutions for present-day issue(s).
6. **Holding time**:
   When I led groups, we finished with an exercise of healthy touch (please read the section on Healthy Touch that follows). I put beautiful music in the background, and each person got held for approximately 10 minutes, then switched partners (total 20 minutes). It was safe a container and so beneficial and healing for all group members.
6. **Check-out circle:** Each person share two simple feeling words.

Feelings Wheel

Based on Nonviolent Communication by Marshall Rosenberg, Ph.D. May be duplicated for personal use and for teaching Nonviolent Communication. Graphics and organization of feelings and needs wheels by Bret Stein. artisantf@hotmail.com Revised 1/1/11

Feelings are <u>internal</u> emotions. Words mistaken for emotions, but that are actually thoughts in the form of evaluations and judgments of others, are any words that follow "I feel like ..." or "I feel that ..." or "I feel as if ..." or "I feel you ...", such as:

Abandoned	Attacked	Abused	Betrayed	Blamed	Bullied	Cheated
Coerced	Criticized	Dismissed	Disrespected	Excluded	Ignored	Intimidated
Insulted	Let Down	Manipulated	Misunderstood	Neglected	Put down	Rejected
Unappreciated	Unloved	Unheard	Unwanted	Used	Violated	Wronged

*Feelings Wheel used by permission from Bret Stein based on Nonviolent Communication (NVC).

Stage Two: Grounding (Cognitive Therapy)

1. Continue with all tasks of Stage One:
   a. Continue to journal: Identify triggers and create positive alternatives.
   b. Continue with the support network.
   c. Continue to build self-worth and experience value in relationship to God.

2. Cognitive therapy: *Ten Days to Self-Esteem* by David Burns
   a. Do one lesson every two weeks. Bring in homework to review.
   b. Do additional Daily Mood Logs (DML) – 3-4 extra per week after Step Four.

3. Learn communication skills:
   a. Sharing oneself ("I" statements, conflict resolution, etc.).
   b. Listening skills (paraphrasing, thought and feeling empathy).
   c. Reality checks: Ask questions when in doubt. "Are you upset with me?"

4. Journaling: Identify triggers that lead to sexual desires or acting-out behavior(s).

5. Begin inner child work after completing *Ten Days to Self-Esteem*.
   a. *Recovery of Your Inner Child* by Lucia Capacchione (use a sketch pad and crayons and/or colored pencils).
      Do one chapter (beginning with Chapter 2) every two weeks. Bring in homework to review.
      Note: Never make false promises to your inner child.
   b. Inner child meditation MP3 twice-three weekly.
      https://www.pathinfo.org/digital-downloads
      https://pathinfo2016.sellfy.store/p/vwik/
   c. Use other meditations and affirmations intermittently.
   d. Get a doll and use it for sharing with your inner child.

Cognitive Therapy

Ten Days to Self-Esteem
(David Burns, Harper Collins, New York, 1993, 1999)

ABC Model:

- **A**ctivating Event
- **B**elief System
- **C**onsequential Feelings

It is not an event that causes us to feel bad; it is our belief system or interpretation of the event that creates a negative response. The Greek philosopher Epictetus said, "Men are not disturbed by things, but by the view they take of them."

Negative Thought Processes and Distorted Thinking

1. All-or-nothing
2. Overgeneralization
3. Mental filters
4. Discounting positives
5. Jumping to conclusions
6. Magnification/minimization
7. Emotional reasoning
8. "Should" statements
9. Labeling
10. Blaming

Daily Mood Log

Step One:	Upsetting Event
Step Two:	Record Your Negative Feelings
Step Three:	Triple-Column Technique
	Negative Thoughts → Distortions → Positive Thoughts*
Step Four:	Go back and revise how you are feeling now

*A positive thought must be affirming, valid, realistic, and put to lie the negative thought.

DAY TWO

Communication Skills – Effective Listening

1. **Maintain eye contact:** When standing or sitting across from another person, be sure to look her straight in the eyes. This creates your first connection, and lets her know that you are attentive to what she is saying.

2. **Join together.** Rather than give advice or your opinion, stand in her shoes. As you listen, seek to understand her viewpoint. This will take practice as you need to quiet your own thoughts and opinions. Join in her world.

3. **Observe**. Take note of her body language, tone, and words. Research has shown that body language and tone generally say more than the spoken word. Observe her posture, her gestures, and her facial expressions. Are her arms crossed around her chest, or relaxed at her side? Is her face joyful or upset? Listen to the tone of her voice. Is she saying one thing and yet speaking another message through her tone and with her body language? Listen with your eyes, your mind, and your heart.

4. **Practicing reflective listening:**

    As suggested by Dr. Harville Hendrix, here is a threefold technique to teach the art of reflective listening:

    First: Mirror or paraphrase his communication. After listening to a few sentences, you may say,

    "If I heard you correctly, you said that you were upset that I do not greet you with a hug and a kiss when you come home from work. Did I get it? Is there more?"

    Continue to listen and paraphrase, listen and paraphrase every few sentences. If he goes on for too long, gently interrupt and say, "Dear, if I heard you correctly, you said…" If you get something wrong, or forget something, don't worry, he will correct you. After his sharing is complete, then summarize all that he spoke:

    "In summary, what I heard you say was that you get upset if I don't hug and kiss you when you come home from work. You really need that each night because you work very hard to provide for our family. All you need is for me to honor you in this way. Then you will feel so much better and loved. Is that the essence? Did I get it right?"

    If he says, "Yes, but you forgot …" Then after he finishes, paraphrase this thought and say, "Is that it?" When he says, "Yes," then you move to the next phase.

    Please do not put your thoughts, feelings, or inflection into the communication when you paraphrase. It is fine to 100% disagree with the speaker. However, you need to *join* with him and reflect what you heard. In this way, he will feel understood and respected.

    Second: Validate his thoughts. Here you imagine how he is thinking based upon what you just heard. It is difficult to separate thoughts and feelings; do your best.

"You make sense to me because you worked hard all day to take care of us and simply want me to validate you with affection. Is that it? Did I get it?"

Here you have to imagine how he *thinks*. You are validating his thoughts. After you finish say, "Is that right?" If it's wrong, don't worry; he will correct you. Then paraphrase what he says and ask, "Is that right?"

If he affirms your understanding of his thinking, then you finish with:

Third: Empathize with his feelings, using simple feeling words (you may refer to The Feelings Wheel).

"Given all that, I imagine you feel hurt, frustrated, and sad. Are those your feelings?"
Wait for him to confirm or amend your suggested simple feeling words.
"Yes, but I also felt upset and mad."
Finish with validating his new feeling words. "I see, you also felt upset and mad. Is that it?"
"Yes, thank you for listening and understanding me. I appreciate you very much." You have successfully heard what he was saying.

During reflective listening, you do not have to agree with what the speaker is saying. The important thing is to hear and validate him. Most of the time, we do not need advice; we just need to be heard. When you are paraphrasing, make sure *not* to interject with a sarcastic tone. As best as you can, use the same tone as the speaker. If you use a sarcastic tone, this will invalidate everything he shared. Remember, you don't need to agree, just listen and paraphrase. This takes a lot of practice and patience. As one of my clients brilliantly stated, "I would rather be in relationship than be right."

Reflective listening is learning to walk in the other person's shoes, seeing life through his eyes. And, if you wish to respond to what he just shared, you must ask his permission when you finish the three-step reflective listening process. "Would you like to hear my thoughts?" If he says "Yes," proceed. If he says, "No," then that's it. The communication loop is complete.

5. **Use the magic words**: "Thank you, (person's name), tell me more." If you are too upset by his words, and you cannot paraphrase what he is saying, then simply say, "Thank you (his name), tell me more." This is such a simple, yet effective listening skill. Try it and you will see how great it works with family, friends, co-workers, and your boss.

6. **If all else fails, KYMS**: Keep Your Mouth Shut and just listen without comment. Be a silent witness. You can always add, "Thank you, tell me more." Use KYMS when temperatures are hot, especially yours!

7. **Silence is golden**: Silence is one of the greatest gifts you can give another person. You do not need to fill the empty moments with words or questions. Just "be" with her. It will allow her to know that you are "there" for her, and it gives her the opportunity to go deeper.

8. **Don't look at your watch while she is talking:** Do it when you are speaking.

DAY TWO

Communication Skills – Effective Sharing

1. Use "I" statements, not "You" statements. Own your thoughts, feelings, and needs.
    Do not say: "You shouldn't speak to me that way."
    Say: "I don't like it when you speak to me that way."
Speak in the first person:
    Do not say: "You upset me when you did…"
    Say: "I get upset when you…"

Important use of "I" statements: In the USA, we are taught from elementary school to speak in the second person, that it is selfish to begin sentences with "I think…" or "I believe…" or "I feel…" We are also taught to write in a similar manner.

Listen to the news every evening, or an interview with a celebrity or politician, or someone who just experienced loss. Here are several real life examples of what you may hear: "You get hurt, and you just don't know what to do. You are beside yourself with fear." "You win an Oscar and you are so surprised." "You heard that a neighbor was killed, and you are so shocked."

Once again, we are taught to speak and write in the second person. This disconnects us from our somatic experiences—our own thoughts, feelings, and needs. Therefore, please begin to shift your awareness to speaking and writing in the first person. For example, "I was very hurt when I heard that my neighbor was killed. It shocked me. I am so sad." "I won the Oscar! I was genuinely surprised." "I got hurt and didn't know what to do."

Each time you use an "I" statement instead of "You" statements when referring to your own experience, you step into your personal power and begin to know thyself more intimately. Begin to listen to yourself when you are sharing with others. Soon you will become aware of when you are speaking in the second person, "You" instead of "I." Slowly change and own your thoughts, feelings, and needs. "I think…" "I feel…" I need…" This is not selfish, but self-full. You are becoming a more powerful man or woman.

2. Optimum effective communication:
    a. Eye contact.
    b. Physical touch—with family, friends, and other close relationships.
    c. Responsible language—"I" statements, not "You" statements.

If you have something negative or sad to tell someone, hold his or her hands. This acts as a grounding conduit between you and the other person. Three optimum ways to communicate are with the eyes, words, and touch (holding hands, hands on her shoulders, etc.). Women in business have an advantage when they want to close a deal. They may touch a man on his shoulder, arm, or hand and say, "Please buy my (product name)."

3. Conflict resolution: Here is a five-step protocol to express your thoughts, feelings, and needs when you are upset about what someone said or did (modified from the Mankind Project procedure).

First: Present the facts—what she said or did that caused you to have a strong reaction. Make it specific to this one event. Please do *not* say "You always…" or "You never…" or "Everybody says…" or "Everybody thinks…" Keep it focused on this one-time event, what she said or did. Example: "This morning before you left for work, you got angry and yelled at me."

Second: Acknowledge your feelings—use simple feeling words (sad, mad, glad, afraid, etc.). Example: "When you raised your voice to me this morning, I felt scared, mad, and upset."

Third: Identify the judgments and beliefs that you have about what he said or did. Example: "When you raise your voice with me, it reminds me of my father's angry outbursts. I become like a naughty little girl."

Fourth: State your needs, desires, or wishes. Example: "I do not deserve to be spoken to in such a manner. When you are upset, would you please speak to me in a civil tone, or ask me to hold you so that I may comfort you. I appreciate that very much."

Fifth: State what you are willing to give to make the relationship work. Example: "I know that I can get upset and lose my temper as well. Therefore, let's both commit to not taking our feelings out on each other. I will ask you to hold me when I'm upset, or I will withdraw from the room to calm down. Please agree to do the same. Thank you."

Be mindful *not* to preach in the third step. No sermons on the sofa. Own your reactions to what he said or did. Make simple requests and offer the same. This conflict resolution protocol works in all personal and professional relationships. Like all communication skills, it takes lots of practice. Try using this and the other skills when things are going well, so when tempers are hot, you will be able to use it more easily.

4. Sandwich technique:
First: State how you feel about the relationship.
   "I really care about you."
   "I love you."
   "I value our relationship."
Second: State the difficulty that you have with the individual. State what outcome you would like to see.

"Recently, you have been screaming at me a lot. That hurts me deeply. I feel unloved, unimportant, and rejected. I think you are under a lot of pressure, and I'm taking the blame for your frustrations. Please deal with your feelings more responsibly. Do not take them out on me. I am willing to help you in a positive way, but not be your punching bag."

Third: State once again how you feel about the relationship.
"I love you and I am committed to our relationship."

In this way, you sandwich the problem (meat of the sandwich) in between your real feelings of love (the bread). It makes it easier for the other person to receive your sharing. Again, please be responsible in all communication, using "I" statements instead of "You" statements. "I" statements mean that I take responsibility for how I think, feel, and what I need. "You" statements try to make others responsible for your wellbeing.

> *It is not the situation or person that upsets us. It is our unresolved wounds that are being resurrected in the present that cause distress.* We must learn about our core issues, take care of ourselves properly, and communicate in responsible ways.

5. When sharing, use "and" as a conjunction, instead of "but."
   "I think what you said is important, *and* I have a different opinion."

   Now feel the difference between these two sentiments:
   "I love you *but*…"
   "I love you *and*…"

What a difference the "and" makes! When you use "but" as a conjunction in most sentences, you annihilate all the good that you shared previous to the "but." After hearing "but," the listener will shut down and their walls will come up. Be sure to use "and" as a conjunction in all your personal and professional communications. This includes texting and emails.
"You're a great man, but your temper scares me."
"You're a great man, and your temper scares me."

6. Reality check: If you think someone is thinking something about you or another person, then ask them if this is correct or not. For example, "Are you upset with me?" "Did you mean (such and such) when you said (such and such)?" Alfred Hitchcock's 1941 movie *Suspicion* is predicated upon a wife's fear that her husband is trying to kill her. Spoiler alert: Her hypothesis was found to be untrue at the end of the movie.

How many unnecessary arguments between spouses, friends, colleagues and co-workers could be avoided if we only asked for clarification about what someone said, or what we thought they meant when they said something. I have experienced that our judgments are wrong at least 90% of the time. Please use a simple reality check to test your hypothesis. "Did you mean (such and such) when you said (such and such)?" If the person tells you her truth, great, then it clear. If she decides to mask her real thoughts and feelings (that you judge she is really harboring in her mind and heart), you must leave it there. You cannot make anyone say or do what they are unwilling to say or do. The good news is, most people will share their truth with you.

Do not make assumptions. When I assume anything, I make an "ass" out of "u" and "me." Instead use a "reality check" if you think someone is upset with you. Here is an example of a reality check: "Were you angry with me when I saw you in the kitchen this morning?" A reality check is a litmus test about a belief or judgment that you have about another person. It helps objectify perceptions.

7. Expectations kill: Do not expect others to know what you need. It is important to learn to express your needs, rather than expect others to know what you want (expecting them to mind-read). Infants and toddlers expect us to know what they need because they are totally dependent upon the parent or caregiver for survival. As adults, we must learn to express that which we need rather than assume or expect others to know what we want, need, or desire.

Journaling

If the client masturbates and/or acts out sexually on a regular basis, then have him keep a journal in order to:

- Identify the triggers that lead to unwanted desires / behaviors.
- Use the HALT diagnosis: Hungry, Angry, Lonely, Tired.
- Resolve issues in healthy ways.
- Create positive alternatives.
- Use inner child drawing and dialoguing.

The HALT diagnostic tool is a simple way to identify causes for unwanted masturbation and/or sexual activity.

Hungry/Hurt—There may be physical hunger which turns into sexual desires. Additionally feelings of rejection experienced in personal or professional relationships may lead to emotional hungering for or lusting after another person, and resulting in masturbation/porn, sexual hookups, or use of substances to self-medicate.

Angry—Unexpressed feelings may become eroticized. When we suppress and then repress our feelings, i.e., anger, frustration, sadness, etc., abracadabra the desire to masturbate or have sex emerges.

Lonely—Legitimate needs for intimacy that go unmet may be experienced as sexual desires. Once again, isolation equals misery/death.

Tired—Stress factors kick in and the desire to take care of oneself by using sexual habits may arise.

For those seeking to resolve compulsive masturbation/porn and unwanted sexual behaviors, I suggest starting and using a Sex Journal on a regular basis. It will help the client understand his/her inner thoughts, feelings, and needs, and to learn about the triggers that may stimulate unwanted sexual behaviors. A trigger is any activity, event, or situation that will lead one to act out sexually and/or become emotionally distressed. Journaling helps achieve some distance from the intensity of the experience. By doing this either before or after s/he have acted out, soon s/he will learn what triggers the unwanted behavior. Then s/he may take positive action steps to resolve the issue, i.e., express feelings with a sympathetic witness, give and receive healthy touch, volunteer and help others, resolve conflicts with loved ones or co-workers, exercise, etc.

Inner Child Healing

Recovery of Your Inner Child
(Lucia Capacchione, Fireside Book by Simon & Schuster, New York, 1991)

1. Non-dominant hand drawing and dialogue.
2. One chapter every two weeks.
3. Use the inner child meditation MP3 several times weekly.
4. Use doll or pillow to share with and listen to your inner child.

Chapters

1. Meeting your inner child.
2. Embracing the vulnerable child.
3. Accepting your angry child.
4. Finding the nurturing parent within.
5. Invoking the protective parent.
6. Encountering your critical parent.
7. Healing the wounds of childhood.
8. Letting your child out to play.
9. Celebrating your creative child.
10. Discovering your spiritual child.

Seven Stages of Development

Stage	Time	Activity	Needs	Learns
Bonding	0-6/9 months	Cries	Mirroring	Being Trust Hope
Exploring	0-6/9 months 18/24months	Explores	Protection	Doing Self-Motivation Will
Separation	18/24 months -3 years	Rebels	Acceptance/ Limits	Thinking Independence Will
Socialization	3-5/6 years	Questions	Answers	Identity Power Purpose Cause-Effect
Latency	5/6- 12/13 years	Doing Arguing	Rules Reasons	Skills Structure Negotiation Competence
Adolescence	12/13- 18/21 years	All of the above in a more mature form		Identity Sexuality Separation Autonomy
Adulthood	18/21 years- rest of life	Recycle through all stages in ways that support specific adult tasks		Independence Interdependence Fidelity

Source: Jon and Laurie Weiss, *Recovery from Codependency*, used by permission from the authors.

Three Stages of Healing Your Inner Child

1. **Self-Parenting**
   a. Listen to thoughts, feelings, and needs.
   b. Be a good parent: Time, touch, and talk.
   c. Healing behaviors.

2. **Spiritual Parenting**
   a. Prayer, meditation, study.
   b. Experience value as son/daughter of God.
   c. Healing of memories with spiritual mentor.

3. **Mentoring or Re-parenting**
   a. Heal homo-emotional and hetero-emotional wounds.
   b. Mentoring relationships.
   c. Developing healthy same-sex friendships and participating in activities.

Day Three

1. Read *Being Gay* Chapters Six, Eight, Ten, and Twelve
2. Read *Focusing* by Eugene Gendlin
3. Read *Embracing Ourselves* by Hal and Sidra Stone
4. Read *Door of Hope* by Jan Frank
5. Read *Unwanted: How Sexual Brokenness Reveals Our Way to Healing,* Jay Stringer

Class Syllabus:

Stage Three: Healing Homo-Emotional and Homo-Social Wounds (Psychodynamic)

1. Root Causes: Process of Grieving, Forgiving, and Taking Responsibility
2. Attend Healing Seminars
3. Focusing Protocol and Practice
4. Voice Dialogue Protocol and Practice
5. Body-Centered Therapy Protocol

Break

6. Body Image Wounds – Mirror Exercise
7. Holding Protocol
8. Bioenergetics – Use of Anger in the Healing Process, *Bioenergetics* by Alexander Lowen
9. Role Play
10. Psychodrama
11. *EMDR: Eye Movement Desensitization Reprocessing* by Francine Shapiro
12. Process Training Protocol

Stage Three: Healing Homo-Emotional/Social Wounds (Psychodynamic Therapy)

1. Continue all tasks of Stages One and Two.
   a. Continue to journal: Identify triggers and create positive alternatives.
   b. Continue with the support network.
   c. Continue to build self-worth and experience value in relationship to God, using affirmations.
   d. Use Daily Mood Logs to slay negative self-thinking.
   e. Use good communication skills.
   f. Use inner child drawing and dialogue/meditation.

2. Discover and heal the root causes of homo-emotional/homo-social wounds.
   a. Attend healing seminars (the individual may attend some of these seminars prior to Stage Three). This order is suggested:
      - Journey Into Manhood (JIM): www.brothersroad.org
      - New Warrior Weekend: www.mkp.org
      - Adventure In Manhood (AIM): https://familystrategies.org/adventure-in-manhood
   b. Identify homo-emotional and homo-social wounds.
      - Refer to evaluation: Father wound, male peer wounding, sexual abuse, etc.

3. Begin the process of grieving, forgiving, and taking responsibility.
   Step One: Recall the wounding experience(s).
   Step Two: Re-experience the feelings (feel to heal), grieve with others, experience healthy love.
   Step Three: Discover the messages/mental constructs developed as a result of the wounding experience(s).
   Step Four: Take your power back, create new mental constructs, and make new choices in life and in love.
   a. Need healthy same-gender mentors and friends from the support network who are able to "be" with the individual while grieving the many losses of his/her past. He or she needs to be blessed by those who experience the fullness of their gender identity, and have healthy love to give and share:
      (1) SSA men on the path of healing.
      (2) Heterosexual friends who know about the struggle and supports him.
      (3) Heterosexual friends who don't know about his struggle and supports him.
      (4) Heterosexual mentors (the more the better).

b. Mentor other men/women (SSA and OSA).

c. Work through abuse issues: anger, grief, and forgiveness.
   (1) Read *A Door of Hope* by Jan Frank (Thomas Nelson Publishers, 1995).

d. Develop an understanding of post-traumatic stress disorder (PTSD).
   (1) Read *Walking the Tiger: Healing Trauma* by Peter Levine (Berkeley, CA: North Atlantic Books, 1997).

e. Develop an understanding of the addictive family system.
   (1) Read *Another Chance: Hope and Health for the Alcoholic Family* by Sharon Wegscheider-Cruise (California: Science and Behavior Books, Inc., 1981).

f. Focusing.
   (1) Read *Focusing* by Eugene Gendlin.
   (2) Practice the six-step method to identify feelings and resolve present day conflicts.

g. Voice Dialogue.
   (1) Read *Embracing OurSelves* by Hal and Sidra Stone
   (2) Practice voice dialogue method.
   (3) Learn to know yourself by identifying the different parts of your inner personality.

h. Healthy/healing touch: Work on energy blocks and grounding techniques to melt the protective armor that has developed around your body.
   (1) Begin bioenergetics work. Read *Bioenergetics* by Alexander Lowen (New York: Penguin, 1975.
   (2) Healthy massage by an OSA licensed massage therapist.

i. Healing body image wounds.
   (1) Draw picture of man/woman you admire (with non-dominant hand).
   (2) Draw picture of yourself (with non-dominant hand).
   (3) Stand in front of a mirror, and share how you feel about each body part.
   (4) Begin process of healing each wound.

j. Process Training Protocol

Therapeutic Approaches to Healing (these are just a few):

- Focusing
- Voice Dialogue
- Body-Center Therapy Protocol
- Inner Child
- Journaling
- Bioenergetics
- EMDR
- Psychodrama
- Role Play
- Healing Prayer
- Healthy Touch
- Process Training Protocol

DAY THREE

Focusing

(from *Focusing*, Eugene Gendlin, Bantam Books, New York, 1981. Used by permission from the publisher.)

Focusing is a body-oriented process of self-awareness and emotional healing. It is as simple as noticing how you feel and then having a deeper conversation with your soul. Focusing starts with a familiar feeling in your body that relates to something that you are currently experiencing. Focusing is the process of listening to your body in a gentle, accepting way and hearing the message that your inner self is sending you. It's a process of honoring the wisdom that you have inside you. The results of listening to your body are insight, physical release, and positive life changes. You will understand yourself better, feel better, and act in ways that are supportive of your life's mission.

The discovery of focusing

In the early 1960s, Professor Eugene Gendlin at the University of Chicago began research into the question "Why is psychotherapy helpful for some people, but not others?" He and his colleagues studied tapes of hundreds of therapy sessions. They recorded the entire course of therapy, from the first session to the last, with many different therapists and clients. Then they asked the therapists and the clients to rate whether the therapy had been successful, and they also used psychological tests to determine if there had been a positive change. If all three agreed—therapist, client, and independent test—then that course of therapy was used in the study. The results were two groups of tapes: successful therapy vs. unsuccessful therapy.

The researchers then compared the tapes to see if they could determine what created the difference in results. They first listened to the therapist on the tapes. Common sense suggested that there would be something about the therapist's behavior that would determine whether therapy was successful or not. Surely the therapists in the successful therapy were somehow more empathetic, genuine, accepting, or brilliant. But in fact there was *no significant difference* in the therapist's behavior. In both sets of tapes, the therapists were essentially the same. All the therapists were doing their best—and some clients were getting better, while others were not.

Then the researchers listened to the clients on the tapes, and that is when they made a fascinating and important discovery: There *was* a difference between the successful clients and the unsuccessful ones.

What they heard was this: At some point in the session, the successful therapy clients would *slow down their talk, become less articulate,* and begin to *grope for words* to describe something that they were feeling at the moment. If you listen to the tapes, you would hear something like this: "Hmmm. How would I describe this? It is right *here*. It's . . . uh . . . it's . . . not exactly anger . . . hmmm." Often the clients would mention that they experienced this feeling in their bodies, saying things like, "It's right here in my chest," or "I have the funny feeling in my stomach." So the successful therapy clients had a vague, hard-to-describe body awareness that they were directly sensing during the session. Dr. Gendlin then found a way to teach this powerful and effective skill of emotional healing, and he called it "Focusing." Focusing is a natural skill that was discovered, not invented. It was discovered by observing what people are doing when they are changing successfully. In other words, *what you feel, you can heal.*

Six Steps of Focusing

(from *Focusing*, Eugene Gendlin; revised by Richard Cohen)

1. **Clear a space.** Focusing is a process of listening to something inside you—within your body and soul—that wants to communicate with you. And yet, like a shy animal, it may first need to discover that you are trustworthy and that you have created a safe place for it, before it can deliver its message. Put everything else to the side. Imagine putting your other life issues on bookshelves or in filing cabinets to the side. This clears a space for this one issue.

2. **Felt sense.** Learn to be in relationship with your feelings (practice by using the Feelings Wheel). Being in relationship with your inner experience allows you to be *with* your feelings, not in them. Pick one problem and find out where in your body you are experiencing that feeling or sensation (e.g., chest, stomach, solar plexus, arms, neck, groin). It may be more than one place. Take time and be "in touch" with each feeling. Identify where you are feeling the feeling(s). Then choose the feeling that is the strongest.

3. **Get a handle.** What is the quality of the felt sense? Give it a name or phrase (e.g., sad, mad, glad, afraid, hungry for love, lonely, hate you). Take time. It may change its name several times. Be patient, be a good listener. Be a good parent. Your soul is speaking. Once you have identified its name …

4. **Resonate.** Go back and forth between the word/phrase and the felt sense. Make sure they correlate. If the name doesn't match the feeling/felt sense, then change it until you find a match. Take your time. After you find a perfect match (name/phrase with the felt sense), then sit with that for a minute. Just be quiet.

5. **Ask the question(s): "What is it about _____ that feels so uncomfortable?" (The ____ is the word/phrase name of the felt sense). OR "What is it about the whole issue that makes me so _____?"** Now listen. First the head will come up with many answers. It's never the head that holds the deeper truth. Allow your mind to speak. Simply allow it to run its course. Your deeper truth will come from below your neck, from deep within your gut/soul. Be patient. Keep repeating the question directly to the felt sense. Listen a bit more. This may take time. Be a good parent to your soul. Eventually the answer will come from within. You will know when you're there when you get a deep "Ah hah!" You'll know when you get it. There is usually a deep breath of relief that comes with the "Ah hah!" The body holds all of our truths.
After you experience the "Ah hah!" response, then ask: "What do you need?" Then wait and listen. Perhaps it just needed to share and that was sufficient. Perhaps it has a specific need. Listen like a good parent. DO NOT MAKE FALSE PROMISES. You can commit to do something now or later, within the realm of your abilities, no more or less. You can create a visualization at the moment to bring healing to this part of your soul. Be attentive. Let your body lead. Then be a good parent/CEO. Finally, bring this sequence to a natural conclusion.

6. **Thank your body and the inner parts that have shared with you.** This is the time to thank and appreciate your body process for what it has given you. Remember that the essence of focusing is to have a good relationship with your inner self, to get back "in touch" with your soul.

DAY THREE

Voice Dialogue

Embracing OurSelves, Hal and Sidra Stone, Nataraj Publishing, California, © 1989.

1. Name the different voices/energy patterns.

2. They interact with each other—primary personality and disowned selves.

3. Each primary self has an equal and opposite disowned self, less developed.

4. Think of psyche in terms of balance—complimentary opposites.

5. Protector/Controller (P/C) is the Boss!

6. We are born vulnerable, without shields, and then we build walls of defense.

7. P/C observes people and the environment to determine which behavior works best in which circumstance and with whom—the purpose is to protect us from harm.

8. Do not criticize/judge/condemn P/C—join with it—define its purpose, mission. It always has your best interest in mind.

9. P/C is the conservative part of our personality.

10. We have liberal voices, too. The goal is to live in balance.

11. First get to know the P/C. It operates our ego structure.

12. Voice dialogue helps us reclaim our natural instinctive energies.

13. Embrace the disowned parts, or they will do us and others harm by driving us to do what we don't want to do.

14. **As long as our disowned parts remain unconscious, we project onto the world our negative viewpoints.**

15. Voice dialogue gives access to the different sub-personalities.

16. Higher self is the CEO of our inner family.

17. Learn about your internal sub-personalities.

18. Remain non-judgmental; honor both sides in order to find your truth and deepest needs.

19. This takes time, so be patient. Awareness is the goal.

Voice Dialogue

Embracing OurSelves, Hal & Sidra Stone 1989, © Nataraj Publishing*

[Opening questions to ask:]
"Close your eyes and find out where you are feeling in your body … Identify what the feeling is, and give it a name(s) … Once you have found where it is, and what it is, then please move to another place in the room, and let that part of you take over your whole body. Feel it from head to toe. Allow your body to take the shape of that feeling, as if it were a sculpture of what it feels like."

[The person now moves to another place in the room.]
"Let the energy come in, welcome it, and accept it as it is."
[Pause] [If it's a painful part, say, "I know it might be painful, but please, just stay with it, and let it in. I'm with you. You are not alone."]

[Pause after each question. Wait for response. Be with silence.]
"How are you (feeling) today?"
"Who are you?" "What is your name?"
"What role do you play in _____'s life?" "What is your job/your purpose?"
"Where did you learn how to do your job? Who taught you?"
"When did you come into _____'s life; at age 3, 5, 7 years old … later/earlier?"
"Does _____ listen to you now?" "From 1-100%, how much of the time does s/he listen to you?"
"Is there anything you want/need from _____?" [KEY QUESTION]
"What's in the way of you getting what you want/need?"
"Is there another part of _____ that does not want you to get it?"
"What would happen if you got what you wanted?"
"What is at risk if you let go of or give up your personality?"

[If another part shows up, or speaks up during the session, ask that part to wait until you finish with this particular personality.]

"Is there anything else you want _____ to know, or is there anything you need right now?"

"I would like to thank you for showing up and speaking your truth. I acknowledge the important part you have played in _____'s life. You have great meaning for him/her. Thank you … Now, would you please take a deep breath, and then go back to the place where _____ was sitting and reintegrate into his/her body. Thank you."

[Person re-centers himself/herself. Have them take several deep breaths, then come back to present time, or move into another personality.]

[After the session is over, review with the person the different personalities that came out, what they represent, and what was learned in this session.]

* Questions amended by Richard Cohen from Rich Menges's Voice Dialogue training.

Shame and Attachment Loss: The Practical Work of Reparative Therapy

Joseph J. Nicolosi, Sr. Copyright © 2009. Used by permission from InterVarsity Press

This therapeutic opportunity arises when: 1) the client reports past homosexual enactment, and/or 2) when the client begins a therapy session mired down in the gray zone (see below).

1) **In the beginning of the session, the client should cognitively revisit the scenario with the therapist, discussing what specific events led up to the incident. Together, client and therapist retrace the preceding self-states, which are:**
   a. Assertion (where we want the client to be – directing their energy outward)
   b. Shame (where client goes after he is hurt or wounded) → we want this to lead to grief work
   c. Gray zone (the scenario before he is about to sexually act out)
   d. Homosexual enactment (sex with other men or self-sex with pornography/sexual fantasy)
- Both occasions (homosexual enactment or the gray zone) offer the client the opportunity to recall and identify the critical events that led to his abdication of the assertion self-state.

2) **Assist the client's recall of the preceding assertion-shame conflict that created his present mood.**
- Often times, the client will not recall what put him in his present mood, or he may not have recognized the conflict that led him into the gray zone as a problem until the therapist helps him realize it. In the early stages of treatment, the client usually has no idea he is in the gray zone, and he may resist the challenge to recall the assertion-shame conflict that preceded it, most commonly by simply forgetting. Thus, it is important for the therapist to help the client retrace the entire day (or even several days) before homosexual enactment occurred to determine when the client got out of the assertive self-state (this is sort of like detective work).
- It is rare that the client has the capacity to move from the "dead state" of the gray zone directly into an experience of his attachment loss, because the gray zone is a defense mechanism against feeling the pain of shame that preceded it, which if fully felt, will lead back to grief. Most often, rather than feeling genuine grief, the client would rather dwell in the gray zone, eventually getting himself out of his paralysis through homosexual enactment.

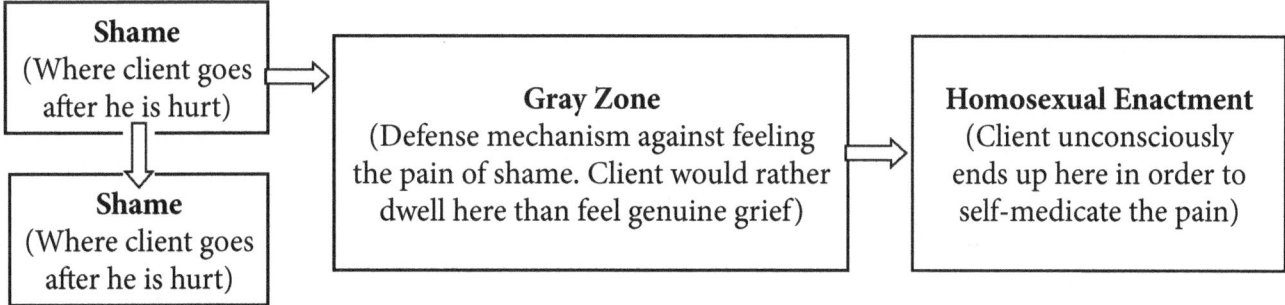

3) **Utilize the assertion-shame conflict as the identified conflict for body work (See Body-Centered Therapy Protocol: Working the Two Triangle Sequence)**
- Success in these steps results not only in the client's affective shift out of the gray zone (and renewed contact with the therapist) but also offers a lesson in identifying a past assertion-shame conflict, experienced as a shame moment, and by extension, the client will learn how to avoid future homosexual enactment by identifying the feelings and getting back into assertion.

Body-Centered Therapy Protocol: Working the Two-Triangle Sequence

Shame and Attachment Loss: The Practical Work of Reparative Therapy
Joseph J. Nicolosi, Sr. © 2009. Used by permission from InterVarsity Press.

1. Identify the client's conflict:
    a. In some cases, this may be a difficult task for the client who cannot recall specific conflicts in the present – his whole life may be a series of conflicts that constantly reinforces shame, so the therapist must sometimes help him identify when and where the conflict occurred that put him in a certain mood.
2. Help him explore his feelings over the conflict:
    a. Ask the client: What feelings are associated with this conflict? How are you feeling about this?
    b. Let the client explore the feeling and any other feelings that emerge. Don't rush through this sequence (to get to the *triangle of persons*) – let the client express all the feelings he is experiencing. When he identifies all of his feelings over the conflict, ask him which feeling is the strongest?
3. Help the client find the bodily sensation of this feeling:
    a. Ask the client: What is the sensation associated with this feeling? Please describe the sensation (e.g., emptiness in the chest is usually sadness; tightness in the chest is usually fear; queasy in the abdomen is usually anxiety; tingly or burning in the arms may be anger; welling behind the eyes is sadness or loss; dropping, sinking, or a heavy feeling in the center chest, sometimes dropping to the upper abdomen can also be sadness).
    b. Note: Anger and sadness go back and forth, with one emotion moving into another.
    c. This is where resistance is most likely to occur – feeling the sensation is uncomfortable for the client, so defenses may come up. Intellectualization, humor, frustration, impatience, even argumentativeness may occur.
    d. If the client is having a hard time feeling the bodily sensation, remain silent for a minute and let him just sit with it.
    e. The main goal is to help the client identify the strongest bodily sensation he experienced during the identified conflict. Try to keep him on his feelings and sensations in his body around the conflict.
4. When the client really comes into an understanding and feels the sensation, move him into the *triangle of persons* and ask him: "Have you ever felt this same feeling and sensation before – does it evoke something from your past?" *Note: We have found that asking the client, "What age do you feel right now?" and then "What is happening to that (insert age) boy right now?" is helpful, as it helps the client stay with their feelings.*

5. If the client remembers an incident, let him tell the story, and then ask him to go into the body again and remember this same feeling and describe it – feeling and sensation – ask: "Are these the same feelings?"
6. Continue to have empathy with the client's pain, which can be quite overwhelming for him. It's common for the client to experience tears and sobbing at this point (this is grieving and is very helpful).
7. When the therapist has reflected back empathy and the client's feelings go into the meaning transformation phase and review: ask the client, "What did you learn here? What did you accomplish?" Have the client discuss the conflict and what feelings and sensations came up and how it evoked painful memories from the past. Discuss how these two are related to each other.
8. Therapist then takes the client into the Double Loop: Affirm what the client shared, the work he did, and say that you think it's great that he can share these feelings with you. Ask him something like: "Do you feel like I understand you? How do you feel about me right now? How do you feel about what we did today?"
   a. This final part is integral—because the client has historically received double-binds from parents and other significant others that wounded him (e.g., father, older brother, male peers etc.) when he tried to express his hurt. Affirming the client in sharing these deep, painful memories releases him from the feelings of shame he experienced and still experiences when he feels these conflicts.

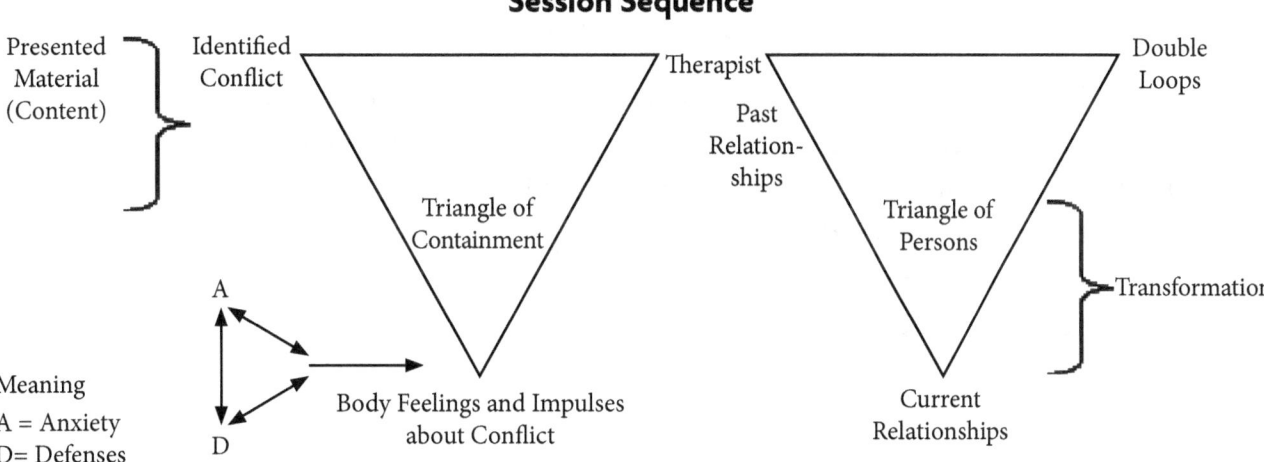

The *triangle of containment* is designed to keep the client contained within the three points of the triangle—the identified conflict, the therapist, and his own body-based feelings and impulses. At the same time we work to extinguish the anxiety and defenses of persons and meaning transformation.

The *triangle of persons* gives understanding to the emerging emotions and impulses as they relate to past and current relationships, including the client-therapist relationship.

[This worksheet was developed by Christopher Doyle, M.A.]

Healing Body Image Wounds: Reclaiming Your Healthy Masculine/Feminine Body

1. **Define the wound:**
    a. Be specific about each body part.
    b. Start from your head and work your way down to your feet, or
    c. Start from your feet and work your way up to your head.
    d. Include each part of your body that you feel bad about.

2. **What happened to create the wound?**
    a. Be specific about each event regarding the specific body part.
    b. Allow each part to speak/share its truth.

3. **What did you come to believe as a result of the wound(s)?**
    a. Be specific about each body part:
        1. Belief about yourself.
        2. Belief about others.

4. **What do you need to heal the wounds?**
    a. Create healing activities/rituals.
    b. Employ different therapeutic approaches to heal each body part.

5. **What do you believe now about your body part? About yourself? About others?**
    a. Replace the negative with a positive—create affirmations for the different parts of your body.
    b. Repeat this often, looking into the mirror and honoring yourhealthy, masculine/feminine, strong, handsome/beautiful body.
    c. Grieve as necessary.
    d. Celebrate your sexuality.

DAY THREE

Healing Body Image Wounds—Mirror Exercise

This exercise is to determine specific body image wounds and begin the process of healing.

1. Have the client stand in front of a full-length mirror.
2. As he looks at himself in the mirror, say to him, "Please begin either at the top of your head or at the bottom of your feet, and describe how you feel about each body part."
3. Depending upon the amount of time you have, he may wish to go into the history of particular body parts (e.g., "My brother beat me up when I was 5 to 10 years old. He hit my face and stomach. I can still feel the hurt in both of those places." "I was sexually abused when I was 8 years old." "One of my neighbors, who was about 5 years older than me, had me perform oral sex on him. I still feel that horrible feeling in my mouth." "I hate my penis. I think it's too small. My older brother used to laugh at me and joked about the size of my dick. I was so self-conscience in gym class. I didn't want to shower with the other guys. I thought they all had bigger dicks than me." "I am too fat. I hate my body. I always wanted to be thin, but all the dieting failed." "I'm too skinny; I don't like my chest or legs. They are so frail looking. I want to be more buff.").
4. After he is finished, you may ask if he needs assistance at this time to work through any of the issues revealed. He may not require this at the time; it's entirely up to him and the allotted time. You may use a variety of techniques: Voice Dialogue, Focusing, Psychodrama, Role Play, Bioenergetics, and/or Healing Prayer.

Another way to do this exercise is within a group. Have the men pair up, stand in front of each other, and share about how they think/feel about their body parts. Take turns, moderating the time. Then circle up and have volunteers share how that was for them. Support anyone who is in a great deal of pain and needs to grieve. Be sure to leave enough time for this exercise, or return to it the following week(s).

Homework:

At home, suggest that the client stand in front of a full-length mirror without clothes on, and allow each body part to speak its truth by imagining that he is the voice of that particular body part (similar to Voice Dialogue work). Start from the head or feet. Continue until each part has had a chance to share.

After detoxing each time, he begins to speak loving, affirmations to each body part (e.g., "You are the most perfectly formed feet. You are great just the way you are. I thank you for supporting me all these years. You are strong, handsome, and powerful." "You are my perfect, powerful, and masculine chest. I love you just the way you are. I think you are great. God created you, and I enjoy your presence in my life.").

Have the client write out positive affirmations for each body part and bring them in to share with you (and/or the group). If he has trouble creating positive affirmations, please help him create these. [**NOTE**: If a particular client is more narcissistic, and has a habit of masturbating in from of the mirror, this exercise is not to be given to him.]

Healthy Touch in the Healing Process

It is very important to understand the significance of healthy touch in the healing process, as many men and women who experience unwanted same-sex attraction (SSA) are touch-deprived. Why have they been touch-deprived? Basically, there was a disruption in attachment between them and either their same-sex parent and/or their same-sex peers. Often many of them were over-attached to their opposite-sex parent and/or opposite-sex peers. Therefore, in the process of reclaiming one's sense of true gender identity, there needs to be a resolution of this attachment need in healthy, same-gender, non-sexual relationships.

Touch will need to be administered with great compassion, sensitivity, and understanding at the right times and by the right people. Otherwise, it can reinforce unhealthy patterns in relationships. The one to offer healthy touch must be secure in his or her sense of gender identity. The ideal candidates for this are happily married men and women. If the individual's parents are available, willing, and healthy, they are the best administers of this gift of healthy touch. If however they are unavailable, unwilling, or unhealthy, then it is ill advised to have them be the bearers of touch for the man or woman in recovery.

I would like to discuss the application of healthy touch in the healing process by covering the following topics:

- Development of healthy gender identity
- Four stages of healing
- Three stages in the mentoring relationship
- Proper self-care: avoiding codependent relationships

DEVELOPMENT OF HEALTHY GENDER IDENTITY

Regarding healthy male development, a boy will bond with his mother in the first stage of life: from birth to one or one and a half years of age. In the second stage of development, he will need to bond with and play with his father. This generally begins during and after the toddler years, when the boy can walk and talk. Horseplay, wrestling around, and other physical activities help create father-son secure attachment and connection. They may also play ball together and engage in other sports activities. Through time spent together in shared activities of healthy male bonding and physical touch, the boy becomes imbued with a sense of his own masculine identity. With this foundation, he begins to broaden his social sphere, playing with relatives and neighborhood and school boys. Research has shown that boys who played with their dads in the early years of development are more socially adept and fit in with their same-age peers.

"Studies of three- and four-year-old children conducted by Ross Parke and Kevin MacDonald provide evidence to this link between father's physical play and how children get along with peers. Observing children in twenty-minute play sessions with their dads, the researchers found that kids whose fathers showed high levels of physical play were most popular among their peers … Across the board, researchers have found that children seem to develop the best social skills when their dads keep the tone of their interactions positive and allow kids to take part in directing the course of play" (John Gottman, *The Heart of Parenting*, Simon & Schuster, 1997, p. 171).

Before and during puberty, boys experience a "body longing" stage between the ages of nine to fourteen. This is when they punch each other, wrestle, horseplay, hit each other on the butt, and put their arms around or on each other's shoulders. Sports and other activities help fulfill this homo-social need for male bonding. These experiences then allow him to feel like one of the guys: "I belong, I fit in, I'm competent."

Touch needs for many boys are fulfilled during sports activities, where it is considered acceptable and not "queer" or "gay" to display physical affection. Why is touch so important for the healthy development of one's gender identity? It is a prerequisite to heterosexuality. We know that during the preadolescent stage, boys further develop a sense of their own gender identity—comfortable being a boy among other boys. In essence they are rubbing up against each other as a form of bonding with the masculine. These behaviors reinforce masculine identification and provide a rite of passage into heterosexuality, except for those who were left out, who were perhaps non-athletic, more sensitive, and more artistic.

Magically, when puberty hits, the athletic boy typically develops strong heterosexual attractions. His interest is then in girls, craving intimacy and attention from them. They become bored with the familiar and are attracted to the mysterious, the unknown—the feminine.

When all of this happens naturally, it is beautiful. However, most who develop same-sex attraction are/were touch-deprived. They missed either the homo-emotional (father-son) and/or homo-social (same-gender peers) bonding, and then those core needs became sexualized during puberty and/or young adulthood. Homosexual desires therefore represents arrested psychosocial and psychosexual development. Same-sex-attracted men then learn to associate touch and sex because of insecure bonding and lack of attachment, either from homo-emotional and/or homo-social wounding.

Regarding healthy female development, first she bonds with her mother. After she learns to walk and talk, she will begin to separate and individuate from her mom, yet continue to gender-identify with her (whereas the boy must individuate from mom and then gender-identify with his dad or a male role model). Throughout her early years of child development, the daughter must view her mom as her gender role model of femininity, wanting to emulate her example. "I want to be just like Mom." If her mom is in an unsatisfying marriage and the daughter views her mother as ineffectual, then she will often detach from her mother and therefore deny her own sense of femininity.

In healthy female development, next she will expand her radius of social relationships with other girls in the family, neighborhood, and school. Here she begins to gain a sense of her own identity, being her unique self in the presence of other girls. She contributes, she shares, she plays, and she learns about the value of relationships and friendship. As men are often activity-centered, girls are more relational-centered. Here is where female bonding takes place, through healthy homo-social relationships.

Again, if this bond and connection is not experienced with either Mom and/or other girls, during and after puberty, those natural needs for secure attachment will become sexualized. The underlying meaning of same-sex attraction (SSA) is to achieve successful bonding with those of the same gender, which never occurred during the normal stages of child and/or adolescent development.

Core needs for bonding must be met. They are non-negotiable. That is why they are not called wants but *needs*. They must be met, or the individual may spend the rest of his or her adult life looking to fulfill those needs in inappropriate ways (i.e., fear of intimacy with others, preoccupation with sex through pornography, compulsive masturbation, multiple sexual partners, over-religious life, and performance-based behaviors).

Again, core needs must be fulfilled in healthy relationships. This is a God-given prerequisite for healthy growth and development into manhood or womanhood. Therefore, let us look at the four stages of healing from unwanted SSA.

FOUR STAGES OF HEALING

In *Being Gay: Nature, Nurture or Both?*, you may read a detailed analysis of the four stages of healing unwanted SSA. In this treatment plan, it clearly defines the parameters and guidelines for healthy touch in the various stages of healing. Here is a brief overview:

In Stage One the individual seeks to heal from unwanted same-sex attraction. He begins to remove himself from homosexual activities and relationships. Now he needs to create a new support network of healthy men and women in his life. This becomes his new family of choice, consisting of healthy same-gender relationships instead of unhealthy, co-dependent homosexual relationships. The support network may consist of, but not be limited to, the following: support groups, others on the path of healing from unwanted SSA, Opposite-Sex Attracted (OSA) peers who know about his struggle and love and support him, OSA peers who don't know about his SSA and love and support him, and OSA mentors who pour into his life. It is very important for men and women healing from unwanted SSA to obtain as many OSA peers and mentors as possible. Men must heal with other men, and women must heal with other women, as same-sex attractions represent a gender identity deficit in their body and soul. Therefore, the more OSA peers and mentors in his life, the better.

Also, he begins to define himself as a child of God, no longer identifying as gay, bisexual, or transgender. Simultaneously, he begins to use positive affirmations on a regular basis as a means of releasing toxic mental constructs. Instead of thinking, "I'm not good enough," "I'm worthless," "God and others don't like me because of my SSA," he begins to formulate more positive thoughts about himself: "I am valuable," "I am forgiven," "I am loved just for who I am." If the individual has a particular spiritual belief, he then develops a personal relationship and connection with God. This time, it is one of intimacy between a loving parent and child—again, being loved for who he is, SSA and all.

In Stage Two, she will continue to deepen the relationships with those in her support network, continue to use affirmations to develop a sense of self-worth, continue to experience intimacy with a loving God, and then begin to deal with faulty thought processes and get in touch with her feelings and needs. The purpose of Stage Two is to create more successful interpersonal and professional relationships in the present, not waiting for the removal of SSA before she experiences peace and fulfillment in her life. The sense of inner peace and successful relationships need to be accomplished in the here and now, not at some future time, and well before she is able to go back and begin to heal the wounds of her past.

In Stage Two, she begins to challenge negative thought patterns, the blaming of others and herself. She will use specific cognitive therapeutic approaches to slay "stinking thinking" and replace it with positive and rational responses. After successfully learning how her thoughts may betray her feelings, and gaining success in turning the negative response into a positive response, she will need to learn effective communication skills. Now she develops the ability to express her thoughts, feelings, and needs in constructive and healthy ways in all relationships, both personal and professional.

Also, in Stage Two, she learns more skills for proper self-care, learning to be assertive in a positive manner, learning to identify the triggers that lead to unhealthy desires, and gaining numerous techniques to become more successful and fulfilled in her everyday life. Finally, she begins the work of healing her inner child. This part is critical in order for her to become a good parent to her own soul and not look to others to "save her," to be "Ms. Right" and fill her loneliness. The one special person she needs to find is her *Self*, and of course, her personal relationship with God.

Throughout Stage Two, as she becomes more in tune and in touch with her own soul—thoughts, feelings, and needs—the relationships with those in her support network deepen. She shares freely with her friends in the healing process, she gains support from her OSA peers, and she is continuing to experience healthy touch and affection from her OSA mentors, e.g., arm around the shoulder, healthy hugs, and support while grieving.

In Stage Three, he will begin the process of addressing homo-emotional and/or homo-social wounds, i.e., father wound, peer wounds, sexual abuse, body image wounds, cultural wounds, etc. One by one, he will face, trace, and ultimately erase the pain that was associated with each unhealthy relationship and/or situation. This is the process of grieving, forgiving, and taking responsibility.

During this time, he will need the support from his OSA peers and mentors. Naturally, as he faces these painful memories, he will begin to grieve. Part of the grieving process is being supported. Sometimes, he will need to be held as he releases years of heartaches and pain. Other times he will need a "sympathetic witness," as Dr. Alice Miller spoke about in her landmark book *The Drama of the Gifted Child*, a person to simply be with the individual as he re-experiences the pain and grieves the losses of his past.

The experience of being held while grieving generally takes place in Stage Three of the healing process. The wondrous element of this experience of being supported is where lasting and true freedom may occur. First, we recall the painful event(s) of the past. Next we re-experience how it felt, the powerlessness, the pain, the question "Why?" And then, when supported—either physically or simply by someone's presence—we ask the important question "What did I come to believe about myself and others as a result of this experience?" From this revelation generally comes a sense of release, relief, and a deeper freedom than ever experienced. This is when the truth begins to set us free, for we then "know" the truth as we perceived it from this traumatic experience of our past.

The use of healthy touch administered in a time of deep grief is a source of comfort and support. It is as natural as holding a child when she scrapes her knee. It is as natural as taking care of your son when he is hurting.

Some in the process of healing have sought to find the right one, the one and only, the "Mom" or "Dad" who would set things right. This, unfortunately, is wrong and only serves to delay the healing process. For, as you have seen in this brief description of the stages of healing thus far, the person must first become the ideal parent to his own soul, and not look outside of himself for that proper self-care. It first must begin within. Of course, as deep grief occurs, he needs to experience support from family and friends. However, this isn't the same as looking for that one special person to meet all of his needs; that in and of itself mirrors the pursuit of a homosexual relationship. This is both unrealistic and counter-therapeutic.

In Stage Four she addresses the resolution of hetero-emotional and/or hetero-social wounds, i.e., father wound, brother/relative wounds, sexual abuse, male peer wounds, and so forth. Again, the process of grieving continues, aided by the support of healthy opposite-sex and same-sex mentors and friends. Healthy touch will be very delicate if she had incurred any kind of abuse by men. *The antidote is similar to the disease itself. What was born out of broken relationships must be healed in healthy relationships.* If she was sexually abused, she will need to grieve, rage, and express the full range of her emotions about the travesty that occurred in her past, all in the presence of a "sympathetic witness." Next, she comes to forgive the perpetrator (this will take time and needs to be addressed throughout the healing process). Then, she needs to discover what she came to believe about herself and others as a result of her experiences. She also needs to learn how to establish healthy boundaries in relationships, gaining the wondrous ability to say "No," standing strong in her power. Finally, she needs to restore what was lost, a healthy sense of intimacy with men. For this, she will need loving, safe, and healthy male mentors to offer the gift of healthy touch, e.g., hugs, arm around the shoulder. If this important experience is bypassed, she will continue to fear intimacy with men, allowing her past to create an intolerable present and future.

This is a very brief description of the four stages of recovery and the use of healthy touch in the process of healing. During Stages Three and Four is when the need for support is paramount. Therefore, it is imperative for the woman or man in recovery to establish a strong network of support from Stage One. Thus, when the time comes to work through the deeper issues of their past, they have already established loving relationships with many OSA peers and mentors. Healthy touch and compassion are a natural extension of these close relationships.

Not every man and woman in the process of recovery from unwanted SSA has the same need for healthy touch. This will depend upon several factors:

(1) Some are touch-oriented by nature, as this is their primary love language.
(2) Some are more demonstrative depending on their ethnic and cultural background—some cultures are more acclimated to touch, while others are more reserved.
(3) Some experienced varying degrees of detachment from same-sex parent and/or same-sex peers.

All of these variables, and more, will determine how significant the need for touch will be in the healing process.

THREE STAGES IN THE MENTORING RELATIONSHIP

In *Being Gay*, chapter twelve discusses the role of mentoring in the healing process. "Mentoring is an attachment model whereby two people participate in a relationship mirroring the parent-child paradigm" (p. 200). It is advised that the individual find at least three OSA mentors, as each one will be able to offer different gifts, e.g., spiritual teacher, sports mentor, financial advisor, emotional support, etc. It is highly unlikely that one person would be able to fulfill all the needs of the individual in recovery; therefore, the more the better.

"Four areas need to be addressed in the process of mentoring: (1) break down the walls of detachment, (2) develop healthy patterns in relationships (socialization), (3) re-educate neurology with healthy touch and activities, and (4) connect with God, self, and healthy parenting" (p. 204). "The therapist or counselor should not be the mentor. The therapist may help train mentors; however, it is ill advised for him to stand in as the mentor" (p. 203).

Again, if the same-gender parent is available, willing, and healthy enough, he or she is the best candidate. If they are unavailable or unhealthy, then the individual must pursue other mentoring relationships. In chapter twelve, I address both the roles and responsibilities of the mentor and the adult-child. Healthy touch is just one part of this restorative relationship. Again, most often the gift of healthy touch will be employed when the individual is in a state of deep grief, to support him or her as they move through the wounds of the past. Placing an arm around his shoulder, holding her while she grieves, is similar to the support we would give our own child.

Because she or he did not successfully bond with the same-gender parent, they will work through various stages in the mentoring relationship: Dependence → Independence → Interdependence. First, the client will rely heavily upon his mentor. There will be times of romantic feelings of being "in love" with him, and then times of "I can't stand you." This is the stage of tearing down the walls of defense around his mind and heart. This conflictual process will eventually lead to a deep bond of trust and love. After working through this messy stage, he will learn to stand on his own, as an empowered son of God, knowing how to take care of himself in healthy ways. Finally, he will be capable of mutuality, both giving and receiving love. He has processed through the wounds of his past, received support while grieving, learned proper self-care, and developed many healthy same-gender relationships. He stands as a man among men. She stands as a woman among women.

After he grieves with a "sympathetic witness," which may occur on repeated occasions as necessary, he begins to internalize healthy love. The extreme need for healthy touch will wane as he lets go of the past and strengthens his sense of manhood (gender identity) in the present.

Proper self-care: Avoiding codependent RELATIONSHIPS

Many who experience unwanted SSA are in strong pursuit of healthy touch. There are reasons behind this need. The greater the detachment from feelings, thoughts, and needs in the present, and the greater the detachment from the unresolved wounds and unmet needs of the past, the greater or more intense the drive will be to obtain touch in one form or another. If someone is constantly looking for Mr. or Ms.

Right, it is wrong! No one will be able to satiate that empty space within. That has to be healed over time, working through each issue with the loving support of God and others. Yes, many will come alongside her on the journey to wholeness; however, she must first know herself before she can expect another human being to fulfill a specific need that she might have.

Follow the four-stage protocol of healing. Develop many healthy same-gender relationships. It is not advised that one person be the sole source of healthy touch in the life of a man or woman coming out of homosexuality. First, they need to be a healthy parent to their own soul. Second, if they have a spiritual perspective, God needs to be their loving parent and source of comfort. Finally, the individual will need to experience meaningful and restorative relationships with healthy OSA mentors and peers … restoring the years the locusts have eaten. Again, what was born out of broken relationships must be healed in healthy relationships.

If someone was sexually or physically abused, it will take much time and patience to work through these issues and allow safe people to offer the gift of healthy touch. Proceed carefully and prayerfully to release the pain and receive love in healthy ways, from healthy men and women.

Please realize that there is a danger in seeking comfort from other SSA men or women because both are wounded in similar ways and have the same unmet needs. That is why it is ideal to seek support and comfort from OSA men for the men, and OSA women for the women.

CONCLUSION

The gift of healthy touch is just one piece of the puzzle to heal from unwanted SSA. As written, there are four stages in the journey that demand much patience, effort, and persistence. I encourage everyone not to overlook the importance of touch in the healing process. Why? What you resist persists. Those who constantly deny their inherent need for healthy touch oftentimes end up acting out sexually, or white-knuckling it through their recovery. Without addressing and fulfilling basic needs for healthy touch, one will most likely live a frustrating life.

I worked through unwanted same-sex attraction. I was blessed by healthy men who held me in their arms as I relived and released the pains of my past. As a husband and father, I have given the gift of healthy touch to all three of my children. Today, they are flourishing in the world. As a psychotherapist of thirty-five years, I have witnessed the benefits of healthy touch in the lives of countless men and women.

Personally and professionally, I believe that the gift of healthy touch is an integral and instrumental part of the healing process that is too often overlooked. We need to separate and clearly distinguish between sex and healthy touch. Many in this country, and throughout the world, are over-sexed because they are undernourished. The skin is the largest organ and most neglected part of our body. Regarding the five senses, we can live without seeing, hearing, smelling, and tasting. But without touch, infants cannot survive, and adolescents and adults cannot thrive. Read ***Healing Humanity: Time, Touch, and Talk*** for more information.

Use of physical touch in the "Talking Cure": A journey to the outskirts of psychotherapy, Verena Bonitz, American Psychological Association, © 2008, Psychotherapy, Theory, Research, Practice, Training, Vol. 45, No. 3, 391-404.

https://www.scribd.com/document/48292116/Bonitz-2008-Use-of-Physical-touch-1

Exploring the use of touch in the psychotherapeutic setting: A phenomenological review, James E. Phelan, Psychotherapy Theory, Research, Practice, Training, American Psychological Association © 2009, Vol. 46, No. 1, 97-111.

https://www.academia.edu/33514359/Exploring_the_use_of_touch_in_the_psychotherapeutic_setting_A_phenomenological_review

Healthy touch demonstrated by Richard Cohen and his youngest son, Alfred.

* Read Chapters Ten and Twelve in *Being Gay: Nature, Nurture or Both?* and Chapter Eight in *Gay Children, Straight Parents: A Plan for Family Healing.*

Bioenergetics

Bioenergetics, Alexander Lowen, Penguin/Arkana, New York ©1975, 1976, 1994.

1. Wilhelm Reich was the originator of this therapeutic approach. It was later developed by Alexander Lowen and called Bioenergetics (p. 13).
2. **Armoring = patterns of chronic muscular tension in the body that serve to protect us against painful and threatening emotional experiences; they shield us from dangerous impulses within us and from those who would attack us (p. 13).**
3. A symptom is overt expression of repressed trauma (p. 14).
4. We develop neurotic symptoms (p. 14-15).
5. **Muscular armoring or chronic muscular tension helps us maintain balance and bind the emotions that cannot be discharged (p. 15).**
6. Process of healing (p. 19):
   - 1st Step: Breathe easily and deeply.
   - 2nd Step: Experience the emotions locked in the body.
   - 3rd Step: Release muscular tension that blocks one's ability to feel.
7. Deep breathing and the release of muscular tension may cause many negative, painful emotions to flow or bodily spasms (p. 19).
8. The use of physical pressure facilitates the breakthrough of feelings and recovery of memories (p. 26-27).
9. **Energy blocks in the body are structured patterns of behavior that represent an unsatisfactory resolution, a compromise of childhood conflicts (p. 34).**
10. This creates a neurotic and limited self (p. 34).
11. **Process of healing: Work backward into the client's past to uncover the original conflict(s) and find ways to handle life-denying and life-threatening situations that forced the individual to create bodily armor and defenses (p. 34).**
12. Only through reliving the past will an individual become alive again and true growth will ensue in the present (p. 50).
13. **A person's past is in his or her body (p. 54).**
14. Bioenergetics is a therapeutic technique to help a person get back together with his body and to help him enjoy life to its fullest (p. 44).
15. Just as a woodsman reads the history of a tree from a cross-section of the trunk, so a bioenergetics therapist reads a person's life history from his body (p. 57).
16. **The goal of therapy is to increase one's capacity to give and receive love (p. 89).**

[PLEASE NOTE: Only a trained Bioenergetic therapist is qualified to use appropriate touch with her or his client to facilitate healing.]

Role Play (Gestalt)

1. Client speaks to the person s/he felt hurt by.
2. Therapist plays the role of that person.
3. May switch chairs so the client may respond as the perpetrator.
4. Switch back and forth until the client experiences a natural resolution.

Healing Prayer / Theophostic Prayer

1. Pastoral Care Ministries: Leanne Payne (www.leannepayne.org)
2. Theophostic Prayer Ministry: Ed Smith (www.theophostic.com)
   - Go back to the original episode of wounding.
   - Re-experience the feelings.
   - Ask the Holy Spirit to reveal "What did I come to believe about myself and others from that experience?"
   - You will *know* the truth, and the truth will set you free (John 8:32).
3. Ruth Carter Stapleton: *The Gift of Inner Healing*
   - Go back to the original episode of wounding.
   - Bring Jesus and the Holy Spirit there to heal the experience.
   - Grieve and release the pain.

EMDR

(*Eye Movement Desensitization and Reprocessing*, Francine Shapiro and Margot Forrest, Basic Books, New York, 1997)
Explanation from EMDR.com website: http://www.emdr.com/q&a.htm#q1

"Eye Movement Desensitization and Reprocessing (EMDR) is a psychotherapy treatment that was originally designed to alleviate the distress associated with traumatic memories (Shapiro, 1989a, 1989b). Shapiro's (2001) Adaptive Information Processing model posits that EMDR facilitates the accessing and processing of traumatic memories to bring these to an adaptive resolution. After successful treatment with EMDR, affective distress is relieved, negative beliefs are reformulated, and physiological arousal is reduced. During EMDR the client attends to emotionally disturbing material in brief sequential doses while simultaneously focusing on an external stimulus. Therapist directed lateral eye movements are the most commonly used external stimulus but a variety of other stimuli including hand-tapping and audio stimulation are often used (Shapiro, 1991). Shapiro (1995) hypothesizes that EMDR facilitates the accessing of the traumatic memory network, so that information processing is enhanced, with new associations forged between the traumatic memory and more adaptive memories or information. These new associations are thought to result in complete information processing, new learning, elimination of emotional distress, and development of cognitive insights. EMDR uses a three pronged protocol: (1) the past events that have laid the groundwork for dysfunction are processed, forging new associative links with adaptive information; (2) the current circumstances that elicit distress are targeted, and internal and external triggers are desensitized; (3) imaginal templates of future events are incorporated, to assist the client in acquiring the skills needed for adaptive functioning."

DAY THREE

Process Training Protocol

The following list of therapeutic protocols is taken from our Process Training Protocol seminars.

Disclaimer, Principles, and Ground Rules for Process Work

Disclaimer

The facilitation of these processes is reserved for mental health professionals, i.e., master's level professional counselors, social workers, marriage and family therapists, psychologists, and/or certified coaches. The correct use of these processes is the sole responsibility of the facilitator. S/he is responsible for maintaining the safety and confidentiality of all participants. By using this manual, facilitators agree to take full responsibility to protect and provide a safe environment for all participants in their care. Facilitators and participants also agree to hold PATH, its staff and board members harmless in the unlikely event that a client is harmed in any way by any of the processes described in this manual.

Principle of Process Work

Generally, the presenting problem is not the real issue. The individual is stuck and cannot identify the real cause(s) of their issue(s). The solution is hidden in their unconscious, or shadow parts. If s/he is ready and willing, help her or him go deeper. *The only way out is through.*

Ground Rules for the Group

- Have participants sign a non-disclosure and liability release form before any work begins.
- Create a safe environment.
- Make sure there are clear ground rules & guidelines/boundaries:
    - Two kinds of work:
      1) Questions to be discussed
      2) Processing their issue(s), i.e. psychodrama, bioenergetics, role-play, voice dialogue, inner child, grief work, etc.
    - Group members support the person who is working.
    - Nobody interrupts his/her process.
    - If someone is moved by their work, they are welcome to grieve, get angry, and express their own emotions as long as it does not disturb the person who is working. They may seek support from their neighbor, or approach a co-facilitator for assistance.
    - People may volunteer to assist the person working. When requested, they may say "Yes" or "No" freely. No need to feel guilty or please others in the process work of others.
    - Participants may not harm themselves, another person, or destroy furniture during process work.

Presenting Issues:

1) Anger at spouse, parent, child, self, God, institution, boss, friend, etc.
2) Hurt and pain by partner, parent, caregiver, friend, boss, teacher, etc.
3) Guilt and shame.
4) Low self-esteem, i.e. feel bad about self, don't belong, don't fit in, feel different, etc.
5) Resentment, bitterness, pain, anger, hurt towards someone living or dead.
6) Fear of others, i.e. physical intimacy, sexuality, relationships.
7) Affairs: relationships outside marriage with the same or opposite sex person(s)—means of avoiding real issues within self-and/or the relationship.
8) Confusion: about sexuality, relationships.
9) Stuck, don't know what is happening, what s/he is feeling, what to do.
10) Trust.
11) Addictions.
12) Body Image.

Different Types of Process Work:

- You may use different protocols for one person's process.
- There is more than one way to approach any issue(s).
- The more experience you have, the more intuition you'll acquire and know which protocol(s) work best for different types of people with different presenting issues.
- Less is more. Don't try to do too much. KISS: Keep It Simple Stupid.
- Facilitator makes sure to ask the person working if they want people to support them. **Important note:** Most of us are not accustomed to getting or asking for support in our lives. Therefore, you may need to encourage and/or coach them how the support would look. For example, two people may stand behind the person with their hands on his/her shoulders, encouraging them, or they may stand in between the individual and perpetrator, or they may embrace the person while s/he is sharing with the perpetrator or other person, howeverx they wish to receive the support. Important point: it is good for them to receive support while sharing their "truth."
- When each process is complete: 1) de-role all parts, 2) clear/clean the energy in the room: clear the negative energy from the room, pillows, and any other objects used; then bring in positive energy, healing light to all objects and persons, i.e. give the person the option to offer up all hurts expressed with a prayer, and 3) see if the client needs further support; ask volunteer(s) to help her/him (Optional: facilitators may also create a designated space for the participant to be taken care of after their work is complete. They may request that a volunteer hold them, listen as they process further, or continue to grieve as necessary).

Types of Processes

Anger / Hurt & Pain / Guilt & Shame / Resentment / Fear / Confusion / Trust

When each process is complete, de-role, clear/clean the energy in the room, and ask client if s/he needs anything, i.e. to be held, etc.

Line-ups:

1) Line-ups either across the room or front to back. If the individual was abused by multiple persons, line them up back to front (original abusive person in the back, most current abusive person in the front of the line), or across the room (left to right in the same manner). Then the individual stands in front of each abuser (beginning with the most current one, sharing her/his truth, speaking from their heart/gut/soul. The intention is to release as much hurt, pain, guilt, and shame as possible—and thereby knock down each perpetrator.

2) Best to start with the present-day perpetrator, and work their way backwards to past abusers. In this way, they will see the pattern emerge—how they allowed themselves to be hurt over and over again, resurrecting the original wound.

3) The client must knock each one down with his/her intention/power: *the process of emotional detoxification*. In a group setting, the people surround the process, making a circle and divided into two groups: 1) support the person working with encouraging and loving words: "I believe in you," "You can do it," "We love you," "Get it out," "We are here for you," etc.; and 2) other groups say negative words: "You're weak," "It's all your fault," "You'll never be free," "You're a victim and deserved it." These emulate the voices one hears in their mind.

4) This continues until all the perpetrators are knocked down (not physically), by the individual's intention and emotional/mental release. Perhaps after they are finished, they may wish to be held by persons representing their ideal Mom and/or Dad.

Role-Play Perpetrator: (two ways)

If someone is "on it" with his/her spouse, or any intimate relationship, it is most often due to unresolved relationship wounds from the past. Several approaches:

1) Have client begin to express her/his thoughts and feelings with their spouse; then put the original abuser in between the client and spouse and have the client speak to each one (if s/he gets stuck in cyclical blame, here are two ways to assist):
   a. Have the client speak to the person they have unresolved issues with, i.e. "Dad, Dad, Dad…" S/he can do this with her eyes open or closed.
   b. Have her/him close her/his eyes and give the feeling a sound (this will bring them much deeper, into core wounding). This will work only if the person is ready. Don't force or push.

2) Set up a psychodrama with members of their family of origin, and current person(s) s/he is upset with (perhaps another psychodrama with their new family).

a. Client chooses volunteers to represent each person from their past/present and assigns roles;
b. Client then speaks to each one. Again, from this process, s/he will begin to see a pattern and connection between past and present-day relationships…
c. The client may stand in the position of each person from their family of origin, and/or their new family—giving a voice to how the client believes each person felt/thought.
d. When finished, De-Role:
   - Client says, "I know you are not (for example) my Dad, you are John. Thank you for helping me. I am very grateful."
   - John says, "I am not your Dad, I am John, and I love and appreciate all you did just now."
e. Finally, clean out the room of all the hurtful emotions; the client either prays or simply releases all those negative feelings, and then fills himself and the entire room with love.

Role-Play Parent's Parts:

1) Assign different roles of the parents to three different people—1) good parent, 2) bad parent, and 3) his wounded inner child (note: oftentimes, the wounded/bad parent will get on his knees and represent to the adult child).
2) Have different people play each part (note: very religious participants think it is wrong to get angry at their parent(s), so you must remind them that this is not reality, but about their own healing. You may also remind them that God was angry 1/3 of the time in the Old Testament, thus, the expression of anger is not wrong. Finally, make sure you reinforce that their honoring the "good parent" allows them to speak of the bad parts more effectively).
3) The individual then speaks to the three different parts of their parent, working out issues with each part of the parent's personality. De-role and clear the space afterwards.

Anger / Hurt & Pain / Guilt & Shame / Resentment / Fear / Trust

Awakening the dead: (2 ways)

1) Speak to the loved one who is deceased to bring closure. Create an imaginary grave with the loved one under a blanket and the client lays down by their side; or
2) You may also have the deceased person speak, imagine how s/he thinks and feels to see their loved one in so much pain, and not letting go; you may also do role-reversal with the client in the grave, and then switch the role back and forth for the client to speak back and forth to their deceased loved one. When finished, de-role and clean the space.

Anger / Hurt / Unresolved Issues / Resentment / Affairs / Confusion / Stuck

Anger work: (5 ways)

Releasing anger and pain. Several different types of anger release (present to the client these options):

1) First, give the client gloves to protect their hands. Bioenergetics: use pounding pillows while the perpetrator stands on the other side; perpetrator says what s/he would have said to the client in

the past (client feeds them the lines before beginning bioenergetics; the client gets her/his anger out during this process.

2) Held back by two men (linking arms around the person's arms); the client speaks to the perpetrator as perpetrator says what s/he would have said in the past.

3) Throwing symbolic guilt, shame, pain, hurt, and/or fear back to the perpetrator (can use crumpled up paper or telephone book pages for this exercise).

4) Client holds the perpetrator closely—standing up holding (not embracing); if the client needs to scream, just shift his/her face to the left or right side of the perpetrator, never into the perpetrator's face or directly into his/her ear. Have the client breathe into the anger, hurt, pain…level down until they hit bottom by giving the feelings a sound (instead of verbalizing words).

5) Have the client use a towel to scream in at first to take away the shame of screaming. When the process is complete, de-role, clean, and have a good parent(s) there if the client needs to be held by a "safe" person(s).

All Issues

Psychodrama / Role-Play / Role Reversal:

1) Have the client choose volunteers to represent members of her/his family of origin. S/he places the characters in formation spatially as it felt like growing up.

2) Client then stands in her/his position. See how it feels there… And/or have someone play the client's position.

3) Client then observes the family system and shares. You may ask, "What does it feel like seeing your family of origin?" "How was it for you growing up in this family?"

4) Observe the constellation of relationships between parents and children. You may ask questions to the client based on these relationships, or lack of relationships.

5) Finally, "How does this reflect your present-day relationships?" When the client is finished relating to the family of origin, create solutions, "How do you wish to be in these relationships?" "Place yourself and others in the positions you ideally wish to be." Have the client move individuals in the family system where s/he wants each person to be. When the process is complete, de-role, clear/clean the energy in the room, and see if the client has further needs (to be taken care of by a volunteer).

Inner child:

1) Have the client choose a volunteer to represent her/his inner child.

2) Client then shares with her/his inner child, how they think and feel about her/him, i.e. their hurts, loneliness, anger, powerlessness, etc. (perhaps have the client choose a specific age or ages to address).

3) Client is welcome to embrace her/his inner child during and/or after sharing. If it seems right, have them switch roles: client then becomes the inner child, and the inner child stands in the position of the adult.

4) After this, switch back and client shares one final time with his/her inner child. When the process is complete, de-role, clear/clean the energy in the room, and ask the client if s/he wishes further support.

Voice Dialogue:

1) Use basic Voice Dialogue protocol, allow particular part to manifest and share, or;
2) Splits—split the different parts of the personality into separate roles. Have the client choose volunteers to play each role. Client then gives each personality phrases that this part would usually speak. Let the client listen to each part, and see how it feels … Allow the client to respond to each part, how s/he thinks and feels about their role in her/his life.
3) If time permits, use role-reversal: Let the client exchange positions with the split part and respond to what the adult just said. Then switch back and let the adult do final sharing with the split. Do this with each part if there is time.
4) Honor their defenses/roles; find their truth. The solution will come from the process.

When finished, de-role, clean/clear, and get further support as needed.

Changing Inner Processes (CHIP):

Make five pieces of paper and mark each one: 1) Issue, 2) Thoughts, 3) Feelings, 4) Heart's Desire, and 5) Draw a Heart on the final piece of paper.

Below are the positions of each piece of paper. Get a piece of rope and place it in between Thoughts/Feelings and Heart's Desire. This will symbolize letting go of the "Issue" and crossing over to the Promised Land!

1) Person stands on "Issue" and describes the presenting problem. Then ask her to share her thoughts about the issue. She then stands on "Thoughts." Often she shifts easily, quickly from "Thoughts" to "Feelings." If so, have her move to the appropriate place.
2) After she has processed her thoughts and feelings about the issue, ask her, "What is your heart's desire? What do you want/need?" Let her share. Ask, "Are you ready to leave behind/let go of the issue and live in the solution to fulfill your heart's desire?" Sometimes she will be ready, other times not. Don't push or coerce in any way. It's her process, and if she's stuck, so be it. Let her stay behind the invisible line with her issue, thoughts, and feelings.

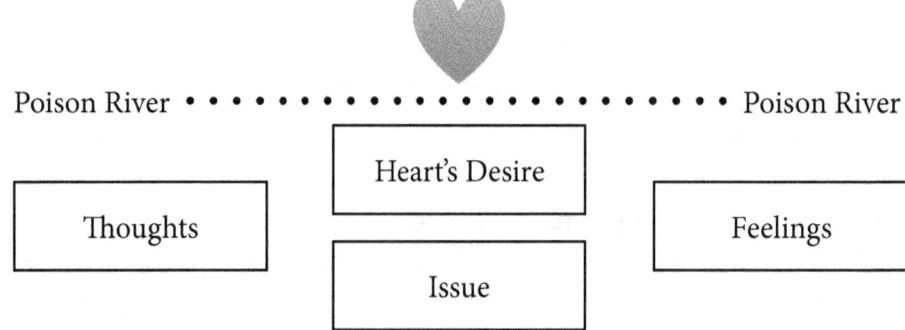

3) However, if she is ready/willing to step over the line and leave this all behind, have her take a big step to her "Heart's Desire," as if she's stepping over the poison river, or a final curtain of that phase of her life. Ask her to share clearly how it feels to be in her heart's desire.
4) When she's done, she sits down or stands on the final paper with the Heart. Have her sit or stand there, experiencing how it is to live in this new place, new way of being. When she's complete, give an appropriate assignment as a result of the work.

Unresolved Issues / Low Self-Esteem / Fear / Confusion / Stuck / Guilt & Shame

Gauntlet:

Either breakthrough, break out, fight for something, i.e. getting his balls back, getting her power back.

1) Form two lines of about 8 volunteers (four on each side), link arms across.
2) Have someone stand at the end of the human chain, representing the person who took the client's power, i.e., mother, father, or perpetrator. The perpetrator may hold something symbolizing the client's lost power, i.e., hold two oranges representing client's balls.
3) The client has to break each link of the chain to achieve breakthrough, taking back her/his power. After breaking through the human chain, the client takes pack his power, (balls) from the perpetrator, however, the perpetrator doesn't just hand over the "balls." Client fights for them.
4) During the process, the group represents the two internal voices of the client, both positive and negative: "You can do it," "You're great," "You can break through," "Take your power back," "You're strong and courageous," etc. Other group: "You're stupid," "You're a wimp," "You're weak and insecure," "You have no power," etc.
5) After the client breaks through, have him declare his new power. Stand in the middle of the room (on a chair) and make a declaration, i.e. ,"I am a powerful man. I am free," etc. When the process is complete, de-role, clear/clean the energy in the room, and see if s/he needs any further support from a volunteer.

Low Self-Esteem

Listening to a Shy Person:

1) Have the client sit on a chair, and the group sits on the floor around her/him.
2) Everyone just listens to what s/he has to share as they speak their truth.
3) This is very good for quiet people, those who haven't been "heard" before in their lives. The group is just a "sympathetic witness," being there to support her/his sharing. This is a very powerful process for a shy person who seldomly shares.

Low Self-Esteem / Stuck

Getting Your Power Back:

1) Client stands on a chair in the center of the room and speaks from his/her power.
2) If someone is co-dependent and afraid of standing up for herself, have her stand on a chair and proclaim who she is: "I am a daughter of God. I have infinite value. I won't take your crap any longer. I deserve much better. I demand it," etc.
3) Finally, have the client look into a full-length mirror and speak to herself, affirming her value.

All Issues / Resentment / Blaming / Victim

Carrying Baggage:

If the person is "carrying" a lot of issues, blaming other(s), and seems unwilling to give them up, then fill a bag (pillowcase) with heavy objects.

1) Have the client name each issue as he places it in the bag.
2) When finished filling the bag with presenting issues, have the client walk around the room, carrying the pillowcase over his/her shoulder, experiencing the physical/emotional/mental burden this creates in his/her life.
3) Ask the client: "Is this working for you?" "What's at risk of giving up carrying these issues?" "What's in your way of letting go?"
4) Give the client time to process his/her thoughts, feelings, and responses. See if s/he is ready to let go. If so, do some ritual to bury the issues that are in the bag...

Stuck, Blaming, Complaining, Frustration, Disempowered

Three Positions for Married Couples Communication

1 – Higher Self
2 – Critical Parent
3 – Wounded Child

Write out these three titles on separate pieces of paper for each spouse. Have them stand across from each other. Explain the different positions first: (1) Higher Self is the part of us that is connected to God, self, others, and experiences unconditional love; (2) Critical Parent is the part of us that is judgmental and derives from introjections, messages received from our parents, authority figures, moral leaders, and cultural messages, i.e., you are worthless, you are "good for nothing," you are stupid, your body is ugly; and (3) Wounded Child is the part of us that internalized past hurts that still remain lodged deep in our soul: feelings buried alive never die, and negative messages stick to our psyche until extracted.

When each spouse shares with the other, they move from one position to the other. It is imperative that s/he identifies what position they are sharing from. This will help them become more responsible and powerful in their communication. Equally, they will eventually stop blaming each other and learn to become more responsible to offer unconditional love and express their needs in healthy ways.

Low self-worth / Blaming / Stuck / Body-Image Wounds

Mirror Work:

If someone has low self-worth, poor body image, use a full length mirror.

1) Have him stand in front of the mirror, look at himself, and speak to the part(s) that he doesn't like.
2) Authenticity and honesty is critical. Encourage him to take it all out…speak his truth…of self-hatred, etc.
3) If it's appropriate, after he's finished, have him stand in front of himself (where the mirror was), and respond to what he just said. Let his body part(s) share how they feel.
4) After this, have him go back to his position, look in the mirror once again, and respond to what his body part(s) just said. Bring an appropriate closure and assignment to develop healthy self-worth…affirmations, etc.

Frustration / Anger / Pulled in all directions

Pulling your strings:

If someone is constantly complaining about or blaming someone else for their problems, use the towel with rope attached to it.

1) Have the client choose a volunteer to represent the abuser, and then the client gives him words/phrases that the abuser would often speak.
2) Then place the towel with strings around the abuser, and the client is holding onto the strings. Have the abuser start moving around the room, speaking his lines, while the client is holding on. Round and round they go, and the client continues to hold on.
3) You may say to the client while this is happening, "What's at risk for you to let go?" Listen to what he says. Then, when it seems right you may ask, "Are you ready to let go?"
4) When he separates from the abuser. Have the client face him and speak his truth. Finish by giving an assignment for continued growth (moving from codependency to healthy self-care). De-role, clean/clear, support.

Conflict Resolution Protocol

[Modified from Mankind Project & Marshall Rosenberg's *Nonviolent Communication*.]

When someone is triggered by another person, below is how to work through it:

First: Present the facts, the data—what she said or did that caused you to have a strong reaction. Make it specific to this one event. Please do *not* say "You always…" or "You never…" or "Everybody says…" or "Everybody thinks…" Keep it focused on this one-time event, what she said or did. Example: "This morning before you left for work, you got angry and yelled at me."

Second: Acknowledge your feelings—use simple feeling words (sad, mad, glad, afraid, etc.). Example: "When you raised your voice to me this morning, I felt scared, mad, and upset."

Third: Identify the judgments and beliefs that you have about what he said or did. Own your triggers/projections. Example: "When you raise your voice with me, it reminds me of my father's angry outbursts. I become like a naughty little girl."

Fourth: State your needs, desires, or wishes. Example: "I do not deserve to be spoken to in such a manner. When you are upset, would you please speak to me in a civil tone, or ask me to hold you so that I may comfort you. I appreciate that very much."

Fifth: State what you are willing to give to make the relationship work. Example: "I know that I can get upset and lose my temper as well. Therefore, let's both commit to not taking our feelings out on each other. I will ask you to hold me when I'm upset, or I will withdraw from the room to calm down. Please agree to do the same. Thank you."

1) Two players in a clearing: client and witness (person who the client is upset with).
2) The Facilitator asks the witness to repeat/paraphrase exactly what he hears the client say after the Data, Feeling, and Judgment steps. The witness need not say anything else during the clearing process. It is important that the client feels heard.
3) The most important piece in a clearing is for the client to discover and identify the shadow creating the emotional charge within him, and then to own and withdraw the projection. This helps the client see what he is projecting onto others, whether it is his wife, a parent, or the man he is clearing with.
4) The Facilitator is also responsible for keeping the clearing clean and concise. A clearing is not an opportunity for a man to spew on another.
5) If the facilitator feels that the client is spewing on the witness and not holding the intention of becoming clear about what he is projecting, the facilitator is to pause the clearing. He points this out to the client and asks him whether he is willing to proceed with the intention of owning his projection(s).
6) Once these steps are completed, the facilitator asks the client if he is clear. If he says "yes," the clearing is over and both men sit down … no need for the witness to share or respond. This was the work of the client.
7) After the client sits down, if the witness needs to do a clearing, he has that option and chooses a volunteer to share with. The facilitator uses the same clearing protocol with him.

Teach HALT Technique:

In an escalated state, e.g., wanting to act out sexually, going into a rage, wanting to use substances…either call someone and use the HALT diagnostic tool, or journal using HALT:

Hungry/Hurt: Hungering after someone or something (to fill the emptiness), hurt by someone
Angry: Upset with someone or something; unexpressed feelings turned inward sour
Lonely: Legitimate needs to give and receive love; keep your love tank filled
Tired: Overstressed; life imbalanced—too much work, not enough play and/or proper self-care

Blessing, Nurturing, Rebirth, and Stretching

Part II of Anyone's Work: Blessing

1) Those around the circle, and/or those who participated in the process, may step up and share with the individual who did his/her work.
2) Share how s/he thinks/feels about this person, how their work affected him/her and their life.
3) They can form a line, or go around the circle.

Part II of Anyone's Work: Nurturing

1) Ideal parents hold the individual (if possible)
2) Group rocks the person (sing "How could anyone" or another nurturing song); or
3) Same-gender mentor holds this individual.
4) After working through painful issues with their parents, they have the option to receive healthy love from ideal mom and dad, or to be nurtured by a specific individual (mentor), or to receive nurturing from the entire group.
5) The facilitator may ask the individual what he or she wants, or intuit what is best. When the process is complete, de-role, and then clear/clean the energy in the room and/or if the client continues to be held, have client/mentor/ideal parents move outside the circle, and move on to the next person who wishes to work.

Part II of Anyone's Work - Give him/her a Stretch:

1) After a process is complete, you may ask the client to make/create a "stretch" for himself (or you assign a "stretch").
2) A stretch is some simple, measurable activity that will help enhance their personal growth, something that may also be a bit challenging.
3) You may ask if someone would serve as their accountability partner, so they may check-in and share about their progress regarding the "stretch."

Summary of Types of Processes (quick referencing guide)

Ask client if s/he wants/needs support. Clean environment afterwards: release negative emotions…fill up with light, love, and truth.

- **Line-ups**: horizontal or vertical, client knocks out each person with his/her intention, while group encourages
- **Role-Play w/ Perpetrator**: spouse is "on it" with partner—put perpetrator in between, have client repeat perpetrator's name, i.e. "Dad, dad, dad," and then ask client if s/he wants support
- **Role-Play Parent's Parts**: line up 1) good parent, 2) bad parent, and 3) wounded inner child
- **Awakening the Dead**: 1) speak to dead person; 2) get in grave and breakout; 3) role-play w dead person
- **Anger Work**: 1) Bioenergetics w perpetrators on the other side, 2) hold back and speak to perpetrator, 3) throw back negative feelings to perpetrator (use paper, etc.), 4) hold perpetrator, scream and/or share
- **Psychodrama / Role-Play / Role Reversal**: re-enact family system / client views drama / role-reversal: have client play different parts /client create solution, rearrange different roles
- **Gauntlet**: two lines interlocked, client has to breakthrough, group shouts pro & con, client reclaims power (balls)
- **Listen to Shy Person**: everyone sit around and listen/witness/affirm
- **Get Your Power Back**: client stands on chair in center, proclaims his truth, reclaim his power from perpetrator
- **Inner Child**: someone role play IC / client speaks to IC / role-reversal / embrace IC
- **Voice Dialogue**: traditional or splits—separate parts; people play each role; give them phrases to speak; client speaks to each part
- **Carrying Baggage**: use pillowcase, fill while naming each wound/resentment carrying around, then decide how to resolve/ask client "Is this working for you?" Help him/her find solution—transition to another protocol, i.e. IC, anger work, getting power back, CHIP, etc.
- **Three Position for Married Couples**: (1) Higher Self, (2) Critical Parent, and (3) Wounded Child. Establish three parts for each partner, and have each one share from the appropriate position, one at a time.
- **Clearing Protocol**: data/feelings/judgments & projections/wants-needs/giving
- **CHIP**: 5 pieces papers for each step, and rope to separate issue/thoughts/feelings from the steps four & five: 1) issue, 2) thoughts, 3) feelings, 4) heart's desire, and 5) heart: how it feels to live in heart's desire.
- **Mirror**: for body image wounds…look into the mirror, let body parts speak their history/truth—grieve…
- **Blessing**: after process, go around circle and people bless the person who did his/her work
- **Nurturing**: ideal parents hold the client; group holds and lifts up the client, rocking back and forth, singing "How Could Anyone" by Shaina Noll, or same gender mentor holds the client
- **Pulling Your Strings**: use towel and rope, client pulled by perpetrator…
- **Give Stretch after Process**: one thing to work on as result of their work

Day Four

1. Read *Getting the Love You Want* by Harville Hendrix
2. Read *How to Get a Date Worth Keeping* by Henry Cloud
3. Read *Five Love Languages* by Gary Chapman

Class Syllabus:

Stage Three: Healing Homo-Emotional and Homo-Social Wounds (Psychodynamic)

1. Alcohol and High-Stress Family Issues
2. Sexual Abuse Issues

Break

Stage Four: Healing Hetero-Emotional and Hetero-Social Wounds (Psychodynamic)

1. Healing Mother-Son/Father-Daughter Relationships and Hetero-Social Wounds
2. Process of Grieving, Forgiving, and Taking Responsibility
3. Five Love Languages
4. Understanding Healthy Male-Female Relationships
5. Preparing Former SSA Men and Women for Dating and Mating

Alcohol and High-Stress Family System

Another Chance: Hope and Health for the Alcoholic Family, Sharon Wegscheider-Cruse, Science and Behavior Books, 2nd ed., California, 1981, 1989.

1. **Dependent: Shame → Anger**

2. **Codependent/Enabler: Anger → Helplessness**

3. **Hero: Guilt → Competence**

4. **Scapegoat/Rebel: Hurt → Defiance**

5. **Lost Child: Loneliness → Rejection**

6. **Mascot: Fear → Hyperactivity**

DAY FOUR

Sexual Abuse

Handbook of Clinical Interventions in Child Sexual Abuse, Susan Sgroi et al., The Free Press, Simon & Schuster, Inc., New York, 1982.

Impact Issues:
1. Damaged goods syndrome
2. Guilt and shame
3. Fear
4. Depression
5. Low self-esteem
6. Anger and hostility → Hyperactivity
7. Inability to trust
8. Blurred role boundaries and role confusion
9. Pseudo-maturity and failure to accomplish developmental tasks
10. Poor social skills

Symptoms:
1. Weight problem
2. Migraine headaches
3. Preoccupation with sex
4. Problems with authority
5. Memory loss (psychic numbing)
6. Confusion over sexual orientation
7. Confusion over gender roles
8. Drug and alcohol addiction
9. Suicidal ideation
10. Marital problems
11. Phobias (panic attacks, etc.)
12. Potential to become an abuser

A Door of Hope, Jan Frank, Thomas Nelson, Inc., Tennessee, 1993, 1995.
1. **F**ace the problem
2. **R**ecount the incident
3. **E**xperience the feelings
4. **E**stablish responsibility
5. **T**race behavioral difficulties/symptoms
6. **O**bserve others/educate yourself
7. **C**onfront the aggressor (when appropriate)
8. **A**cknowledge forgiveness
9. **R**ebuild self-image and relationships
10. **E**xpress concern and empathize with others.

Stage Four: Healing Hetero-Emotional / Social Wounds (Psychodynamic Therapy)

1. Continue all tasks of Stages One, Two, and Three.
    a. Continue to journal: Identify triggers and create positive alternatives.
    b. Continue to build a healthy Support Network.
    c. Continue relationship with God/use affirmations.
    d. Use Daily Mood Logs to slay negative self-thinking.
    e. Use good communication skills.
    f. Use inner child drawing and dialogue/meditation.
    g. Use focusing and voice dialogue.
    h. Heal body-image wounds/receive healthy touch.
    i. Strengthen new mental pictures/constructs/imprints for healthy living.
2. Identify mother-son/father-daughter and hetero-social wounds, and work through each issue. Process of grieving, forgiving, taking responsibility.
   Step One: Recall the wounding experience(s).
   Step Two: Re-experience the feelings (feel to heal), grieve with others, experience healthy love.
   Step Three: Discover the messages/mental constructs developed as a result of the wounding experience(s).
   Step Four: Take one's power back, create new mental constructs, and make new choices in life and in love.
3. Develop healthy, healing opposite-sex relationships: Learn about the character and needs of the opposite sex; affirm his/her sense of gender identity.
    a. Elders (happily married men/women).
    b. Family member mentors.
    c. Spiritual mentors (from Church/Synagogue/Mosque/Temple).
4. Understanding healthy male/female relationships.
    a. Preparing men and women for dating:
        (1) Bibliotherapy
            - *Getting the Love You Want* by Harville Hendix
            - *How to Get a Date Worth Keeping* by Henry Cloud
            - *Conscious Dating: Finding the Love of Your Life in Today's World* by David Steele (Great principles, and he is Pro-Gay)
    b. Same-sex mentors
        (1) Teach about the opposite sex from one's gender's perspective.
        (2) Encourage and educate about dating.
    c. Create a relationship map/vision (dating apps).

DAY FOUR

Dating and Mating for Former SSA Men and Women

1. **Former SSA men and women are often nervous about dating.**
   a. Those who have worked through their unwanted SSA and are ready to date are like teenagers. Their nervousness is to be expected.
   b. Help them to understand that they are now passing through adolescence. It is natural and normal to be nervous—welcome to the teen years of growth, and emotional adolescence!

2. **They need male and female mentors to help them navigate through the waters of dating and understand the opposite sex.**
   a. Ask respected same-gender friends about dating, what women/men like, and how to act around them.
   b. Ask respected opposite-gender friends/mentors about dating, what women/men like, and how to act around them.
   c. *Getting the Love You Want* by Harville Hendrix. Understand the "unconscious marriage," why we are attracted to specific types.
   d. *How to Get a Date Worth Keeping* by Henry Cloud (Christian author) Understand the meaning of dating (not to marry, but to get to know people and be known).
   e. *Real Love / Real Love in Marriage* by Greg Baer, M.D. Understanding the meaning of real love in relationships and marriage.

3. **Blocks to successful dating:**
   a. Unresolved relationship with opposite-sex parent and/or other hetero-emotional/hetero-social wounds (abuse, etc.).
   b. Men heal their mother wound / women heal their father wound; otherwise, they will project those issues onto their future spouse.
   c. No one can genuinely love another person unless he first loves himself.

KEY: Do not push the individual to date before s/he has dealt successfully with his or her SSA and OSA issues.

Five Love Languages

The Five Love Languages ©, Gary Chapman, Northfield Publishing, Chicago, 1995, 2004. Used with permission from the publisher.

Gary Chapman describes five basic types of love languages. Each person has a different love language that she or he prefers. Of course, it is best to experience all five. However, everyone has a primary and secondary love language. Here is a brief summary of the five love languages.

Love Language 1: Words of Affirmation

1. Verbal compliments.
   a. Appreciate their BEING, or who they are (i.e., their qualities and attributes). For example: "You are such a wonderful man." "I appreciate your generous heart." "You are a very sensitive and gifted man." "You're such a masculine man." "You're such a beautiful and feminine woman."
   b. Appreciate their BEHAVIOR, or what they do (i.e., their behaviors that you like). For example: "You look sharp in that suit." "I really appreciate your taking out the trash." "I admire your working so hard at school."
2. Words of encouragement. See the world through the eyes of your child. Learn what is important to them. "Son, it's great you're in the school play. I know you'll do a wonderful job."
3. Words of affection. "I love you." "You mean so much to me." The tone is important, especially to a sensitive child.
4. Testify to others. Speak affirming words about your child in front of family members and other people. Tell them how wonderful your child is.
5. Written affirmations. Write affirming notes, letters, texts, or emails to your child.

Love Language 2: Quality Time

1. Togetherness. Focus your undivided attention on your son or daughter and what they like (not what you like).
2. Quality conversation. Use sympathetic dialogue and good listening skills, focused on what your child is saying—their thoughts, feelings, and needs. Do not analyze or problem-solve, just use reflective listening skills.
3. Learn to share your thoughts, feelings, and needs without judgment of the other. Use "I" statements, not "You" statements. Teach and instruct rather than preach and lecture, which are immediate turn-offs. Note: If you are opposite personality types—Dead Sea (does not like to share) and Babbling Brook (cannot stop talking)—then it is important to establish regular sharing times to create balance in the relationship.
4. Quality activities. Provide wonderful memories that last a lifetime (for example, camping, fishing, hiking, attending a play or concert, or going on a trip together). Participate in your child's interests.

Love Language 3: Receiving Gifts

1. Gifts are meant to be an expression of love from the heart. They are visual symbols of love for the other person.
2. Find out what your child likes. Investigate their desires and interests.
3. Gifts may be purchased or made. Spending on a child whose love language is receiving gifts will fill their love tank.
4. Make rituals or ceremonies to place value on the giving of your gifts, whether for birthdays, special events, or just surprises. Gifts are an expression of your love, not just a material object.
5. Give the gift of yourself. Your physical presence is a powerful gift, especially in times of crisis.
6. Receiving gifts is unearned grace.
7. Note: Gifts should not be given out of guilt. That is counterfeit giving.

Love Language 4: Acts of Service

1. Do something special with/for your child (for example, build something together, teach them a skill, do homework together, work on their car). This is an investment of time, effort, and thought.
2. Teach your child to make requests, not demands. Do things they cannot do for themselves, or teach them something they do not know how to do but would like to learn.
3. Ask your child to make a list of things they would like you to do for them.
4. A child's criticism is a clue to his love language (for example, "I really wish you would teach me to throw a ball"). It is never too late to spend time with your child—whether they are 14 or 54.
5. Do not be a doormat and let your child walk all over you. They will not respect you if you do. Kids need bonding and boundaries, love and limits, and then they will feel safe and secure.
6. Overcome stereotypes. Dad, oftentimes these are sensitive boys, so first you may have to join them in their activity before you invite them into yours. Dean Byrd gives excellent counsel to dads with young boys who like to play with dolls: "Get down on the floor and play with him and his dolls. After joining in his world, then he will be more willing to participate in yours." It works.

Love Language 5: Physical Touch

1. Physical touch communicates emotional love.
2. Babies must be held, kissed, rocked, cradled, and caressed in order to survive.
3. Adolescents and adults need lots of healthy touch in order to thrive.
4. Healthy non-sexual touch may consist of holding hands, hugging, putting your arm around their shoulder, and more.
5. Touch = emotional intimacy and love. Be flexible. Follow your child's cue. Adult children may want to receive hugs and/or may want and need to be held.
6. Healthy touch will help create secure attachment, especially for those who experience SSA. Sons need their dads, and daughters need their moms.
7. Many men and women who experience SSA are hungry for healthy touch. They are touch-deprived and end up going into the "gay" world to get their needs met.

Developing Heterosexual Attractions

Jeffrey W. Robinson, Ph.D. Used by permission from the author (http://www.theguardrail.com/home).

Seven Blocks to Heterosexual Attractions (for men)

1. Moral Anxiety
   a. Not allowed to have sexual thoughts about women.

2. Performance Anxiety
   a. Afraid I won't be able to function sexually with a woman.

3. Heterosexual Incompetence
   a. Clueless about opposite-sex relationships.
   b. Haven't developed understanding about women.

4. Homosexual Flooding
   a. Occupied with thoughts, desires for a man.
   b. No space in psyche for Opposite-Sex Attractions (OSA).

5. Beliefs
   a. Beliefs about SSA prevent heterosexual feelings from developing.
   b. Kinsey Scale says I'm ___ (0-6).
   c. Heterosexuality is not something that I can do/be.
   d. I believe that people are born with SSA.

6. Heterosexual Perfectionism
   a. I'm SSA and can only get aroused by a beautiful, perfect woman.
   b. I can only go with a perfectly beautiful woman.
   c. I can't date unless she's marital material.
   d. Individual is clueless about how to go about dating and developing OSA.

7. Heterosexual Disgust
   a. Many SSA men find the female body yucky, disgusting.
   b. Some have obsessive compulsive disorder (OCD), are overly clean, and find a woman's body dirty.
   c. Some think about a woman from a moral perspective and have anxiety.

These 7 concepts are not deeply embedded in the psyche. They are overt, perceptible ways of thinking, not deep psychological constructs. Therefore, they can be changed.

Four Ways to Increase Heterosexual Development in SSA Men

Work to diminish sexual thoughts of men. Create a new path in your mind about women.

1. Systematic Desensitization
   a. Counselor allows the client to discuss his fears, thoughts, and anxiety.
   b. Discuss romance and sexuality.
   c. Show pictures of the female body, and explain how things work.
   d. One step at a time, relax and expand intimacy step by step.

2. Cultural Participation
   a. Like learning a second language, you can't just read or study it; you need to participate by speaking the language with others, immersing yourself in the language.
   b. We are influenced by our social involvement: Have one fifth of social network be SSA healing buddies, and four fifths should be OSA men and women.

3. Here and Now Focus
   a. Be in the moment. Relax. Don't have any expectations about what will happen in the future. Just enjoy the here and now.
   b. Do your best and don't care about mistakes.
   c. Practice is needed to learn how to be with a woman.
   d. Focus on the person, not anything else.

4. Learn to be a Loving Person
   a. Porn and lust are one-dimensional.
   b. These objectify men or women, so both are wrong.
   c. Reduce anxiety by loving the person for who she is.

Criteria for Marriage

1. Successful track record of not acting out homosexually.
2. Reduced SSA, masturbation, and porn.
3. Significant level of OSA.
4. Demonstrated ability to keep a commitment to one person (woman).
5. Deep commitment to God and His Word; spiritual life in order.

Conscious Dating © MP3

David Steele, 2006. Used by permission from the author.

Five types of relationship coaching: (1) Readiness Coaching, (2) Attraction Coaching, (3) Pre-Commitment Coaching, (4) Couples Coaching, and (5) Bliss Coaching.

Fourteen Dating Traps and Solutions

1. Marketing Trap
    a. Trap: Making yourself more appealing, and not showing or being the real you.
    b. Solution: Present yourself as you really are; be authentic.

2. Packaging Trap
    a. Trap: Focusing on appearance, wealth, external details of others.
    b. "She's so hot." "He's rich." Unhealthy view of others—objectifying them.
    c. Solution: We all have some packaging requirements; emphasize character.

3. Scarcity Trap
    a. Trap: Thinking there is a limited supply of partners.
    b. "I'll take what I can get." You settle for less.
    c. Dating is not a numbers game; it is just about finding the right one for you.
    d. Solution: Go after your first choice (requirements), and don't settle for anything less.

4. Compatibility Trap
    a. Trap: Even if you get along, it doesn't mean you'll be able to sustain a long-term relationship, that you are compatible.
    b. Having fun doesn't mean you will be a good couple.
    c. Solution: Requirements must be met; your needs are non-negotiable.

Four Steps for Conscious Dating:

1 – Scout:	Find people to date.
2 – Sort:	Dates are good possibilities if they meet your requirements.
3 – Screen:	Learn more about the person.
4 – Testing:	Compare your requirements with your experience.
	(You must know your requirements before you begin dating.)

5. Fairytale Trap
    a. Trap: Thinking that your partner will magically appear.
    b. This is childlike thinking—not realistic at all.
    c. Solution: Take personal responsibility to find your potential partner—you be the chooser.

6. Date to Mate Trap
   a. Trap: Thinking that dating is about mating, that it's about coupling.
   b. Don't be result-oriented, feeling pressure to make it work.
   c. Solution: Identify which stage you're in (see Four Steps on the previous page). Have fun. If you're ready to make a commitment, make sure this person meets your requirements. Then have a pre-commitment period to see if the relationship will last.

7. Attraction Trap
   a. Trap: Defining a relationship as good because you are attracted to each other.
   b. Paradox because need attraction for a good relationship, but that's only one component of a relationship.
   c. Your requirements must be met.
   d. Unconscious choices based on attractions usually lead to failed relationships
   e. Solution: Use the Four Steps for Conscious Dating, to choose consciously.

8. Love Trap
   a. Trap: Interpreting sex and emotional attachment as "love."
   b. This is not enough, because the person must meet your requirements and needs.
   c. Solution: Screening, no red flags before entering into a relationship, then pre-commitment period to test the relationship.

9. Sex Trap
   a. Trap: Interpreting good sex as love.
   b. Women use sex to get love, and men use love to get sex.
   c. Some use sex as the main requirement of compatibility (this doesn't work).
   d. Solution: Consciousness of requirements, needs, and wants. Sexual attraction is good but it is just one part of the relationship.

10. Rescue Trap
    a. Trap: Thinking a relationship will solve your life challenges: emotional loneliness, financial woes.
    b. Not taking responsibility for your life; looking for a partner to solve it.
    c. Solution: Define your life vision and be successful in fulfilling that. Be in a position to want a relationship, not need someone to rescue you.

11. Co-Dependent Trap
    a. Trap: Focusing life on someone else, needing to be needed.
    b. Not getting what you need because you are unworthy and incomplete in yourself.
    c. Solution: Define the vision and requirements of a relationship. Ask for what you need. Establish healthy boundaries. Be the chooser.

12. Entitlement Trap
    a. Trap: Thinking you deserve to be taken care of, relying on a partner to make you happy.
    b. Pretty or wealthy people think this way.
    c. Solution: Take responsibility for the relationship; define your purpose and vision.

13. Virtual Reality Trap
    a. Trap: Believing that what you see is what you get—based on impression, not knowledge.
    b. Thinking the person will change.
    c. Solution: Making a commitment period is important. Discover who the person really is. Say "No" to things you don't want. You need to experience 100% commitment to make the relationship succeed.

14. Lone Ranger Trap
    a. Trap: Thinking your sole focus is finding a partner.
    b. Not cultivating friendships and family relationships.
    c. Just looking for a partner, feeling lonely, thinking you have to do it all by yourself, feeling bad about being single.
    d. Solution: We all need many types of relationships. You must be successful with family and friends. Have them help you find a potential partner.
    Men need good female friends, and women need good male friends. They can be good scouts for you. Get support from others.

Ten Principles of Dating

1. *Know who you are and what you want.*
   Understand your values, relationship requirements, and vision for the relationship.
   In a recipe, all the ingredients are necessary. The same is true in a relationship. You need 100% of your requirements to make it work. Identify your needs. Two types:
   (1) Functional Needs: Things to make a good relationship (money, job, etc.); and
   (2) Emotional Needs: What you need to feel loved (calls, hugs, etc.).
   Wants are icing on the cake; they make life fun and can change.

2. *Learn how to get what you want.*
   Attitudes about self and others.
   Four levels of attraction venues: (1) public setting, (2) single events, (3) special-interest settings, and (4) highly aligned communities (religious, etc.).

3. *Be the chooser; take initiative.*
   Know yourself so you choose who you want, or else you will risk a wrong relationship.
   How to be a chooser: (1) Awareness of your choices, (2) Identify choices, and (3) Make productive choices to achieve a positive outcome.

Seven things to do to be a chooser (CRAP GAP):
- **C**reative, new ideas.
- **R**isk taker: Failure is part of life, so don't take it personally.
- **A**ssertive: Ask for what you want; say "No" when you need to.
- **P**ro-active, not reactive.
- **G**oal oriented.
- **A**ssume abundance.
- **P**ositive: Anticipate success!

Robert Bennett said, "We choose our joys and sorrows long before we experience them." Take control of choosing. Life is the sum result of all conscious and unconscious choices.

4. *Balance heart with head.*

    Not just emotional and/or physical attraction.

    Easy to confuse sex and attachment.

    Visions, values, goals, and requirements are imperative.

5. *Be ready for commitment.*

    Ready to enter a committed a relationship.

    Have a stable and fulfilling life already: work, health, finances, and emotions.

    Type of dating: (1) recreational dating (not ready for a commitment yet), (2) committed dating (looking for a partner), and (3) mini-marriage (try it out; see if it's right for both).

6. *Use the law of attraction.*

    Develop yourself, and create the life you want.

    If you build it, s/he will come.

    Like attracts like, the law of attraction.

7. *Gain relationship knowledge and skills.*

    Don't expect things to come with ease; the entitlement concept is unrealistic.

    Must learn, study, and practice—get relationship coaching.

    Date for fun and practice.

8. *Create a support community.*

    Relationships survive and thrive in a community; they improve the quality of your life.

    Isolated singles may create isolated couples—birds of a feather flock together.

    Like attracts like. Ask for support from friends and family; have them help you find a partner, or make suggestions.

9. *Practice assertiveness.*

    Enforce boundaries; say "No."

    All your needs and values are valid and important. Do not minimize your needs.

    There are no small needs. This is how intimacy is created.

10. *Be a successful single.*

    Live fully in the present; don't think about the outcome.

    Like attracts like; happy, successful people attract the same.

    Don't act out of desperation.

These principles help create successful relationships. Use these tools and strategies to create your ideal relationship. Live the life you want.

Website to order this MP3 and other resources: www.consciousdating.com

DAY FOUR

Conscious Dating: Finding the Love of Your Life in Today's World

David Steele, RCN Press, California, © 2007. www.consciousdating.com
Used by permission from the author.
(Note: David Steele affirms "gay" relationships; this book contains many invaluable insights into becoming and finding the right partner.)

- If you are not happy with your life or yourself, a relationship will not fix it.
- Know who you are and what you want.
- Unmet needs will break up relationships.
- Core needs are non-negotiable.
- Clarify your needs for a partner.

Relationship Readiness Quiz for Singles:

To assess your readiness for a committed relationship, rate yourself in each of the following ten areas. Try to be objective and honest with yourself. We recommend asking close friends and family members for their opinions as well.

1. I know what I want: I have a clear vision for my life and relationships. I can envision my perfect life in rich detail that feels strong, very real, and keeps me motivated.
2. I know my requirements: I have a written list of at least ten non-negotiable requirements that I use for screening potential partners. I am clear that if any are missing, a relationship will not work for me.
3. I am happy and successful being single: I enjoy my life, my work, my family, my friends, and my own company. I am living the life that I want, and I am not seeking a relationship out of desperation and need.
4. I am ready and available for commitment: I have no emotional or legal baggage from a previous relationship. My schedule, commitments, and lifestyle allow my availability to build a new relationship.
5. I am satisfied with my work/career: My work is fulfilling, supports my lifestyle, and does not interfere with my availability for a new relationship.
6. I am healthy in mind, body, and spirit: My physical, mental, or emotional health does not interfere with having the life and relationship that I want. I am reasonably happy and feel good.
7. My financial and legal business is handled: I have no financial or legal issues that would interfere with having the life and relationship that I want.

8. My family relationships are functional: My relationships with my children, ex, siblings, parents, and extended family do not interfere with having the life and relationship that I want.
9. I have effective dating skills: I initiate contact with people I want to meet, and disengage from people who are not a match for me. I keep my physical and emotional boundaries, and balance my heart with my head concerning potential partners.
10. I have effective relationship skills: I understand relationships, can maintain closeness and intimacy, communicate authentically and assertively, negotiate differences positively, allow myself to trust and be vulnerable, and can give and receive love without emotional barriers. (pp. 176-178)

Ten Relationship Attitudes

1. I will be happy by having goals and letting go of attachment to outcomes.
2. I strive to live and "be" in the present.
3. I love, accept, and trust myself.
4. I focus on connecting, not results; a partner is someone to love, not an object or a goal.
5. I strive to be authentic, being fully honest with myself and others, and aligning my words, values, and actions.
6. I strive to live my life with intentionality, making choices conscious of my goals and consequences.
7. I strive to take the necessary risks, overcome my fears, and stretch my comfort level to reach my goals.
8. I assume abundance; all the opportunities and resources that I need will appear.
9. I take responsibility for my outcomes by taking initiative in my life and relationships.
10. What others judge about me is about them; I strive to let go of what others think and not take it personally. (p. 210)

How to Practice Assertiveness

1. Be self-aware: Be aware of your thoughts and feelings, and realize when a situation doesn't work for you.
2. Own your needs, issues, thoughts, and feelings: Take responsibility for asserting your needs. Don't expect your date to read your mind, and then make the person wrong when he/she doesn't.
3. Be positive: Adopt an attitude that your date/friend means well and might not know if something is a problem for you. Be optimistic that by being assertive your need can be met (until the evidence proves otherwise).
4. Communicate effectively: Let your date/friend know your issue; communicate your issue clearly and request what you need.
5. Handle defensiveness gracefully: It's normal to feel defensive when someone corrects your behavior. Have compassion and patience when this happens. Be firm but understanding.
6. Take risks: Be prepared to risk conflict—and even the relationship—to resolve the issue and get your needs met. (p. 236)

What are your boundaries?

We all have needs and boundaries. *A boundary is the line between what is comfortable and what is not comfortable for you in a relationship.* Many of us think a boundary is like a fence or a limit, but this is not just about protecting oneself. It's about being respected and being respectful. Having boundaries is important in every relationship we have—with family, friends, and children—not just in romantic relationships. (p. 236)

- *Know your requirements, needs, and wants.*
- *Unmet needs create issues.*
- *All of our needs are valid.*
- *There is no such thing as a small need.* (p. 237)

Relationship Readiness Assessment for Singles (pp. 260-266)

This assessment will help you identify specific goals for being a successful single.

I. My Vision, Values, and Life Purpose
   1. I have a vivid "vision" of what I want for my life and my relationship.
   2. I am clear about my values and live by them.
   3. I have clearly defined my life purpose and put it into action daily.
   4. I know where and how I want to live.
   5. I have written goals and an action plan to help me achieve my vision.
   6. I am living my life fully and in alignment with my vision, values, and life purpose.

II. My Requirements
   7. I know what I will not tolerate in a relationship and don't tolerate these things.
   8. I know what I can't live without in a relationship and don't settle for less.
   9. I know what values I must share with a partner.
   10. I am clear about what personality traits and qualities I most value in a partner.
   11. I am clear about what interests/activities I must share with a partner.
   12. I have a written list of requirements and will not enter a relationship if even one is missing.
   13. I know that only I can be responsible for my own life and happiness.

III. My Needs
   14. I am clear about what I need for a relationship to function for me on a daily basis.
   15. I am clear about what I need emotionally to feel loved in a relationship.
   16. I am clear about my boundaries and how to enforce them to get my needs met.
   17. I ask for what I need and want, and take responsibility for the outcome.
   18. I do not expect a relationship to meet all my needs and make me happy.
   19. I have a support system to supplement meeting my social and emotional needs.
   20. I have inner strength that helps me be self-reliant and proactive about my needs.

IV. My Relationship History and Patterns
   21. I understand what did and didn't work for me in previous relationships.
   22. I understand which positive and negative relationship patterns I risk repeating.
   23. I am aware of the traits of my parents that drive my partner choices.
   24. I am aware of specific traits of my parents in myself.
   25. I am aware of habits, patterns, and values I have inherited from my family.
   26. I understand my past patterns of choosing partners.
   27. I understand my past relationship attitudes, choices, and actions/behaviors.

V. My Emotional Issues
   28. My past relationship experiences do not impact my present relationships.
   29. I have forgiven my parents for my past and present unmet needs.
   30. I have let go of relationships that were damaging to me.
   31. I have forgiven people who have hurt me.
   32. I have sought forgiveness from people whom I may have hurt.
   33. I am able to forgive myself for my past mistakes.
   34. I trust that everyone does the best they can at all times.
   35. I am aware of, and own, my emotional issues when they arise in a relationship.

VI. My Communication
   36. I do not gossip or talk about others.
   37. I clearly communicate what I want and need; I don't make people guess.
   38. I deal positively with misunderstandings and disagreements when they occur.
   39. I own my judgments and accept differences with others.
   40. I do not get defensive and take personally the things that people say about me.
   41. I make requests rather than complain.
   42. I regularly practice active listening, give validation, and express appreciation.
   43. I am careful about what I promise and keep my word.

VII. My Community
   44. I am aware of how I come across and affect others.
   45. I am surrounded by caring people.
   46. I add value to everyone in my community.
   47. I spend my social time with healthy, happy, able people.
   48. I have positive relationships with my parents, siblings, children, and ex.
   49. I have a close circle of friends and we gather regularly.
   50. I take extraordinary care of the people I have chosen to love.
   51. I am a member of two or more communities (hobby, spiritual, professional, etc.).

VIII. My Lifestyle
- 52. I am satisfied with my work/career.
- 53. I support my present lifestyle and am preparing for my future security.
- 54. I have no financial or legal problems.
- 55. I am happy and successful being single.
- 56. I am living the life that I want as a single person.
- 57. I am ready and available for commitment.
- 58. I am healthy in mind, body, and spirit.

IX. My Dating Patterns
- 59. I take initiative and responsibility for choosing who I want in my life and don't wait to be chosen.
- 60. I have clearly defined guidelines for sexual involvement that I adhere to.
- 61. I am authentic and do not present myself inauthentically to attract a partner.
- 62. I am able to communicate my issues and needs to dating partners.
- 63. I balance my heart with my head and make careful relationship choices.
- 64. I do not interpret infatuation, attraction, attachment, and/or good sex as "love."
- 65. I do not expect a relationship to "rescue" me from emotional or financial problems.

X. My Relationship Plan
- 66. I understand and use the Law of Attraction (like attracts like).
- 67. I scout, sort, and screen potential partners effectively.
- 68. I am clear whether I am seeking a short-term recreational relationship or am ready to seek a long-term committed relationship.
- 69. I effectively disengage from prospective partners who are not a fit for me.
- 70. I use my community support system to scout for me.
- 71. I am actively involved in activities and groups of people highly aligned with me.
- 72. I am balancing my partner search with investing in myself and living my vision.

Order this book on Amazon / Barnes & Noble

Summary: Preparing Men and Women for Dating and Mating

- Make a list of requirements and needs.

- Create a relationship vision.

- Seek mentoring from elders, OSA friends, and those in the spiritual community:
  - Same-gender mentors.
  - Opposite-sex mentors.

- Resolve opposite-sex issues.

- Love oneself.

- Enjoy dating as a process.

- Former SSA men and women are now emotional teenagers.

Day Five

1. Read *Gay Children, Straight Parents* by Richard Cohen
2. Read *After the Ball* Summary (summary included here)
3. Read *How to Meet the Press* (summary included here)

Class Syllabus:

1. Twelve-Step Protocol for Parents/Families with SSA Children:
   Assisting Parents, Family Members, and Friends Whose Loved Ones Are SSA

2. Syllabus for Parents Support Group

3. Counter-transference: Therapist's Shadow Work

Break

1. Taking Care of the Therapist/Ministry Leader/Clergy/Coach: Preventing Burnout

2. Socio-Political Issues and the Gay Rights Movement: Their Impact Upon Our Religious Institutions, Schools, Children, and Therapeutic Practices

3. Media Training: How to Meet the Press – TV, Radio, and Newsprint

4. Family Healing Session (FHS) Protocol

Protocol for Family Members, Friends, and the Religious Communities Who Have SSA Loved Ones

Gay Children, Straight Parents: A Plan for Family Healing
Richard Cohen, PATH Press, 2016. Used by permission from the publisher.

Introduction

1. Shock, sadness, grief, loss, and more—all feelings that parents may experience when they find out their child has SSA.

2. They did not create their child's SSA. SSA is always the result of many contributing Factors—environmental, psychological, and temperamental.

3. Fear others may find out: family members, friends, spiritual community members.

4. Teach the parents that change ensues when healing occurs: When the wounds are addressed, and the unmet love needs fulfilled in healthy same-gender relationships, the child will experience the fullness of their gender identity and heterosexual desires may occur.

5. SSA is about not belonging, not fitting in, and feeling different from others of the same gender. SSA is about internalized emotions of detachment from oneself and from others. Therefore, it will take time to undo the years of feeling this way.

6. Socialized indoctrination about being "gay"—Innate and immutable mythology of homosexuality; born this way and cannot change.

7. Seven stages of coming out:
    1 – Causes of SSA.
    2 – Same-sex attractions begin.
    3 – Conflict over SSA.
    4 – Need for belonging.
    5 – Indoctrination.
    6 – Identity acceptance as gay, lesbian, bisexual, transgender, non-binary, etc.
    7 – Coming out process.

8. Beware of what your child is taught about the process of change:
    1 – This therapy leads to suicide and depression.
    2 – It doesn't work and creates more harm.
    3 – This is rejected by most mental health organizations.

4 – Those who promote this therapy are homophobic and anti-gay.
   5 – Those who believe in this are part of the religious right.

9. Therefore, do not push your child to "change" or go through sexual orientation therapy without their personal desire to do so.

10. *This is a battle of love, and whoever loves the most and the longest wins!*

11. Stages for parents to go through:
    1 – Educate yourself about SSA.
    2 – Educate yourself about the homosexual movement.
    3 – Realize that you are now entering your child's world.
    4 – Join with your child/loved one—listen, and use good communication skills.
    5 – Establish trust, do things together, attend their meetings.
    6 – Seek professional help: therapy, seminars, family healing sessions.
    7 – Pray the right kind of prayers (read Step Three).

12. Don't repeat your moral views about homosexuality. Once is sufficient.

13. Part of SSA is oppositional behavior because of defensive detachment from same-gender parents/peers, which resulted in a wounded heart and soul.

14. Marriage is never the solution for SSA. First, they must heal their own gender identity, then they can be successful with someone of the opposite sex.

15. God will do the changing. Your job is to love ceaselessly, in all its forms.

16. The goal of this 12-step treatment plan is to create intimacy and secure attachment between father-son, mother-daughter, and to set love in order with the opposite-sex parent.

17. Take care of yourself and your relationship along the way. This is a marathon, not a sprint. Receive God's love; take care of each other. Create a community of love to surround you and your SSA child.

18. Enjoy the journey—it will transform you and your family!

Gay Children, Straight Parents: A Plan for Family Healing

Richard Cohen, M.A., Bowie, MD: PATH Press, 2016

Section One: Personal Healing

Step One: Take Care of Yourself

Step Two: Do Your Own Work

Step Three: Experience God's Love

Section Two: Relational Healing

Step Four: Investigate the Causes of SSA

Step Five: Utilize Effective Communication Skills

Step Six: Make Things Right between You and Your SSA Child

Step Seven: Discover Your Child's Love Language and Participate in Their Interests

Step Eight: Same-Gender Parent: Display Appropriate Physical Affection

Step Nine: Opposite-Gender Parent: Take Two Steps Back

Section Three: Community Healing

Step Ten: Create a Warm and Welcoming Environment in Your Home, Place of Worship and Community

Step Eleven: Boyfriends, Girlfriends, Ceremonies and Sleepovers

Step Twelve: Find Mentors and Mentor Others

© Richard Cohen, M.A., 2023

DAY FIVE

Summary of the Key Points from *Gay Children, Straight Parents:*

Section One: ***Personal Healing***

Step One: Take Care of Yourself
    a. Deal with your guilt and shame.
    b. Gut reactions: "Yuck" factor.
    c. Five stages of grieving.
    d. Create a support system.
    e. Welcome to your child's world.
    f. Stop self-accusation and/or accusing others.

Step Two: Do Your Own Work
    a. If you want your loved one to change, change yourself.
    b. Lead by example.
    c. Do exercises in *Ten Days to Self-Esteem*.
    d. Do exercises in *Recovery of Your Inner Child*.

Step Three: Experience God's Love
    a. Pray the right kind of prayers.
    b. Three Ss of visualization.
    c. God will do the changing.

Section Two: ***Relational Healing***

Step Four: Investigate the Causes of SSA
    a. Ten causes of SSA.
    b. Write an evaluation of why you believe your loved one has SSA.
    c. Create a treatment plan based on their wounds/unmet love needs.
    d. Movie therapy.

Step Five: Utilize Effective Communication Skills
    a. Good listening skills.
    b. Good communication skills.

Step Six: Make Things Right between You and Your SSA Child
    a. Express regrets.
    b. Bonding and boundaries.
    c. Ask about his/her history of SSA.
    d. Make an affirmation MP3.
    e. Write a letter.
    f. Attend healing seminars.

COUNSELOR TRAINING PROGRAM MANUAL

Step Seven: Discover Your Child's Love Language and Participate in Their Interests
  a. Words of affirmation.
  b. Quality time.
  c. Receiving gifts.
  d. Acts of service.
  e. Physical touch.
  f. Sharing literature.

Step Eight: Same-Sex Parent: Display Appropriate Physical Affection
  a. It's a gender identity issue.
  b. Display physical affection and expect rejection.
  c. Stages of parent-child bonding.

Step Nine: Opposite-Sex Parent: Take Two Steps Back
  a. You are now the co-pilot.
  b. Help create bonding between the child and same-sex parent.
  c. Affirm your child's gender identity.

Section Three: Community Healing

Step Ten: Create a Warm and Welcoming Environment in Your Home, Place of Worship, and Community
  a. Educate your family, friends, and spiritual community.
  b. Help find same-gender friends for your SSA loved one.
  c. Educate your religious leaders about SSA.
  d. Join or create a support group in your area.

Step Eleven: Boyfriends, Girlfriends, Ceremonies, and Sleepovers
  a. Embrace your child's boyfriend or girlfriend.
  b. Attend a commitment ceremony or not?
  c. Sleepovers: The rules.

Step Twelve: Find Mentors and Mentor Others
  a. Roles and responsibilities.
  b. Mentor SSA strugglers in your community.

Conclusion

1. SSA has nothing to do with sex; it's a gender identity issue.
2. Write a personalized treatment plan, and put it into action day by day.
3. Feel and be real in order to heal. Lead by example: Heal yourself.
4. Succeed small rather than fail big; take one step at a time.
5. *Whoever loves the most and longest wins!*

Syllabus for a Parents Support Group

I facilitated online Parents Support Groups for years. Here is the syllabus so that you may see how I led these groups, and the many homework assignments required of the parents. Research demonstrates that those who do homework assignments in therapy heal quicker. I tell the parents, *"It is imperative for you to change your perspective—from changing your child to changing yourself, your relationship with your partner (if still married), and the dynamics of your family system."*

Note: All group participants will need their own copy of *Gay Children, Straight Parents: A Plan for Family Healing* (GCSP).

Week 1: Introduction:

1. Introduce yourself, first names (5-7 minutes maximum per family, depending on how many couples/individuals are present):
2. Where do you live in the world?
3. Ages of your child or children?
4. A bit about your family situation and SSA child?
5. What you want to learn and gain from this class/support group?

- Review the entire syllabus and then email the participants The Feelings Wheel for them to practice (you may download The Feelings Wheel from our website: https://www.timetouchandtalk.com/time).
- Homework:
    1) Practice using The Feelings Wheel daily: share with your spouse two feeling words and what's behind your feelings.
    2) Read the Introduction and Step One from *Gay Children, Straight Parents* (GCSP).
    3) Do the exercise in Step One about sharing with your SSA child (dealing with your guilt and shame), both husband and wife. Do ***not*** do this exercise with your SSA child. This is for you to expunge the toxic guilt and shame from your soul. Do the exercise with your spouse or a trusted friend.

Week 2:

1. Two feeling words check-in (each participant).
2. Share about the homework: What did you learn from reading the Introduction and Step One? Let each person share succinctly, depending on the number of participants.
3. Did you do the exercise about sharing your guilt and shame regarding your SSA child? How was it for you? (Repeat the exercise as often as necessary.)
4. How are you taking care of yourself and the relationship with your spouse (if they are still married)?
5. Teach about the major points in the Introduction and Step One.

[As the facilitator, be mindful of those who talk a lot and those who do not share. Be sure to keep a balance between these two types. Ask the more quiet ones to share, and ask the more talkative ones to give opportunity for others to speak. Additionally, keep the balance between positive feedback and those who may tend to share only negative things.]

- Homework:
    1) Practice sharing two feeling words daily with your partner, and what's behind your feelings?
    2) Read Steps Two and Three of GCSP.
    3) Make a list of members of your Support Network. Begin to develop a Support Network if you don't have one. We will create an e-list of the parents in our group if you wish to share with and support each other.
    4) Purchase *Ten Days to Self-Esteem* by David Burns and *Recovery of Your Inner Child* by Lucia Capacchione. Start to do the exercises in either one of these books. Share your homework with your spouse. Take your time, do one chapter every two weeks. These are not just books to read, but workbooks.

Week 3:

1. Two feeling words check-in (each participant).
2. Share about what you learned in Steps Two and Three of GCSP.
3. How is your homework coming along? Developing your Support Network?
4. Did you begin to do the exercises in *Recovery of Your Inner Child* (after finishing inner child exercises, begin doing *Ten Days to Self-Esteem*)? How was that for you?
5. Teach about the major points in Steps Two and Three (GCSP). Also, teach about the Ten Causes of SSA.

- Homework:
    1) Practice sharing two feeling words daily with your partner, and what's behind your feelings?
    2) Do the creative visualization exercise: email your three S-statements to me so that I may review them (see page 62 of GCSP for the details about the three Ss.)
    3) Continue doing the exercises from the Inner Child or Ten Days books.
    4) Read Step Four of GCSP.

Week 4:

1. Two feeling words check-in.
2. How is it going with using your visualizations (3-Ss)?
3. What did you learn in Step Four of GCSP?
4. How is it coming along with the exercises from the Inner Child and/or Ten Days book?
5. Review Step Four of GCSP as necessary.

- Homework:
    1) Practice sharing two feeling words daily with your partner, and what's behind your feelings?
    2) Make a list of what you believe contributed to your child's SSA? (GCSP pp. 70-75)
    [Each parent does this independently and then they share their lists with each other. Finally, they make a combined list of why they believe their child experiences SSA.]

3) Begin to create a treatment plan for your child: based on their wounds that have not healed and unmet love needs (examples of the Treatment Plans are at the back of GCSP).
4) Visit 4 websites: 2 pro-LGBTQ+ / 2 pro-healing. For example:
   Pro-LGBTQ+ websites include:
   https://www.hrc.org
   https://www.glsen.org
   Pro-healing websites include:
   https://www.pathinfo.org
   https://www.therapeuticchoice.com.
5) Continue doing the exercises from the Inner Child or Ten Days books.

Week 5:

1. Two feeling words check-in.
2. Share about your homework: creating the evaluations and starting to make your treatment plans.
3. What did you learn from viewing the LGBTQ+ websites, and the healing websites?
4. What issues have come to your attention that you need to personally address?
5. How are the exercises coming along from the Inner Child or Ten Days books?

- Homework:
   1) Practice sharing two feeling words daily with your partner, and what's behind your feelings?
   2) Continue working on your treatment plan for your SSA child.
   3) Make a schedule of activities; make goals SMART: Simple, Measurable, Achievable, Realistic, Timely.
   4) Read Step Five of GCSP.

Week 6:

1. Two feeling words check-in.
2. What did you learn from reading Step 5 of GCSP or anything else during the week?
3. How is it going with creating your treatment plan?
4. How is it going with the Inner Child or Ten Days exercises?
5. Review Step Five from GCSP, Communication Skills: sharing and listening.

- Homework:
   1) Practice sharing two feeling words daily with your partner, and what's behind your feelings?
   2) Practice effective listening and sharing skills with your spouse, child/children, friends, work colleagues. Practice using the communication skills a minimum of 3 times per week.
   3) Continue working on steps from your treatment plan. Celebrate each victory!
   4) Read Step Six of GCSP.

Week 7:

1. Two feeling words check-in.
2. How is it going with the communication skills for effective sharing and listening?

3. What did you learn from Step Six in GCSP?
4. Discuss Step Six of GCSP and the exercises.
5. How it's going with your treatment plan?

- Homework:
    1) Practice sharing two feeling words daily with your partner, and what's behind your feelings?
    2) Write Affirmations for your child (each parent does this individually). Email them to me to check.
    3) Write a Letter to your child expressing regrets and asking forgiveness (each parent writes their own letter)—not in the context of SSA or gender confusion. Do not share this with you child (yet).
    4) Continue exercises in the Inner Child or Ten Days book.

Week 8:

1. Two feeling words check-in.
2. How is it going with developing your Affirmations and writing the Letter?
3. How's it going with the Inner Child or Ten Days books?

- Homework:
    1) Practice sharing two feeling words daily with your partner, and what's behind your feelings?
    2) Watch movies, e.g., "Man of the House" (old version with Chevy Chase and Farrah Fawcett) and "Life as a House."
    3) Same gender parent joins with child in an activity of their child's choice and will share about it in the next class.
    4) Read Step Seven from GCSP and define your child's love language and interests.

Week 9:

1. Two feeling words check-in.
2. Share something that was challenging or helpful.
3. What did you learn from Step Seven of GCSP?
4. Each parent shares how it is going—changing their family system/dynamics.

- Homework:
    1) Practice sharing two feeling words daily with your partner, and what's behind your feelings?
    2) Read Steps Eight and Nine in GCSP.
    3) Continue working on the Treatment Plan and doing the exercises from the book.
    4) Continue exercises from the Inner Child or Ten Days books.

Week 10:

1. Check-in with two feeling words.
2. Share something that was challenging or helpful, and what you learned from Steps Eight and Nine of GCSP.

3. How are the exercises coming along from the Inner Child or Ten Days books?
4. Is the opposite-gender parent backing up and supporting the same-gender parent in bonding with his/her child?
5. How is the same-gender parent doing in getting closer to the SSA child?

- Homework:
    1) Practice sharing two feeling words daily with your partner, and what's behind your feelings?
    2) Read Steps Ten, Eleven, and Twelve in GCSP.
    3) Continue doing the exercises from GCSP.
    4) Continue doing the exercises from Inner Child and Ten Days books.

Week 11:

1. Two feeling words check-in.
2. Share something that was challenging or helpful.
3. What did you learn from Steps Ten – Twelve in GCSP?
4. How are the Inner Child or Ten Days exercises going?
5. Teach from Steps Ten, Eleven and Twelve in GCSP.

- Homework:
    1) Practice sharing two feeling words daily with your partner, and what's behind your feelings?
    2) Finish writing your Treatment Plans for Family Healing—Short Term & Long Term Goals (examples at the end of GCSP).
    3) Make a list of people who can love your child: particularly same-gender siblings, relatives, friends and members of your spiritual community.
    4) If you found the book helpful, please go to Amazon and write a positive book review of *Gay Children, Straight Parents: A Plan for Family Healing*. Many thanks☺

Week 12:

1. Two feeling words check-in.
2. Review your Treatment Plans (based on causes and needs—examples at the back of the GCSP book).
3. What are the most important things you have learned from the book and your journey this far?
4. Where do you go from here?

Be sure to have the parents share something positive during each session. It is easy for them to just express negative things. Therefore, have at least one or a few parents share small victories each class. This will hopefully inspire the others. Finally, you may organize a Parents Group over a much longer duration of time. As you just read, this was a very intense 12-week course. It could easily be a 20-week Parents Group. It's entirely up to you. Additionally, you may restart the group and they may begin it all over again. There is so much to learn and implement in this book/program.

Two stories from parents who participated in our classes:

A Daughter's Homecoming, *Gay Children, Straight Parents,* 2016, pp 132 – 136.

We found out about Sarah's SSA when she was nineteen years old but didn't discuss it much after that. When she went to college, Sarah told us that she was having an affair with another girl in her youth group from the time she was fourteen. We responded negatively, thinking that homosexuality was worse than murder. We also believed that homosexuality was a choice. We thought she had chosen this herself.

Instead of compassion and sympathy, we responded in judgment. We told her, "You'll go to hell. This is sinful behavior." We had various arguments after that. She moved out and closer to the gay community downtown. She felt much better with them. There she was accepted.

We spent four years in that situation. We helped her out financially, but were at odds about everything else. There was no connection. She revealed to us later that she just wanted us to drive down there, especially mom, and pick her up and take her home. She told us that she had gone through the most brutal experiences of her life while living in the gay community. She said, "Mom and Dad, you threw me to the wolves!" We know that she hasn't told us everything, yet. She felt abandoned and left alone by the two people she loved and needed the most. She even contemplated suicide but didn't because she thought it would hurt us too deeply!

She was truly a child looking for love in all the wrong places because we didn't understand her in the ways that she needed at the time. We didn't love her as God loved her. We told her how we wanted her to be and how we needed her to conform to our demands. And it sent her straight into the arms of the sad gay world. We would be friendly one minute, then get angry the next and say things like, "Why are you living this horrible lifestyle?" We were critical of her and her friends and never socialized with them.

Several years ago, we were going to buy a house. The Spirit of God moved us to ask her if she wanted to live with us. She said she would if her girlfriend could live there too. Somehow we agreed. That was the beginning of reestablishing our relationship. But it lacked relational substance. We were still locked into the mindset that this was rebellious and chosen behavior. This produced anger and judgement, and caused us not to connect in the ways that she needed. We continued to neglect her essential needs for love.

Our church was very judgmental about homosexuality. We didn't feel comfortable to speak with anyone about this, so we ended up leaving. We felt alone, in pain and anguish. We quit going to church and tried desperately to find a place where we belonged.

A big break came when her girlfriend charged our credit card for thousands of dollars! Our daughter had the strength to throw her out of the house. We asked Sarah to see a counselor who was a friend of ours from church. She finally agreed to see him once and then began having regular sessions.

In late 2004, we said we must do something because we were in deep despair. I (Dad) went to my office one Saturday morning. I found in my desk drawer, among a group of papers, a letter to the editor I had kept for years that mentioned homosexuality. I had this piece of paper for so long it had turned brown! I believe this was divine intervention. In that article it mentioned PFLAG and PFOX. I eventually went to the PFOX website and spoke with the director. She told me about Richard Cohen. That was the beginning of our enlightenment.

Before Christmas of that year, we were going around in circles and getting nowhere. It was hurting our marriage. Our hearts had darkened until we met Richard. Then we participated in the Parents Class and attended one of Richard's Healing Seminars. The suffering and pain of the SSA strugglers at the seminar opened our eyes. We saw them crying and realized that our daughter felt the same way!

During the past eight months, we have progressed more than in the last six years. Last night, our daughter called saying, "I feel so much pain. Can I come over and share with you?" This would never have happened before. The turning point was realizing the truth about homosexuality. We finally understood that our daughter never chose to have same-sex attraction. We came to realize that SSA resulted from many of her life experiences and perceptions about events.

The truth lifted the veil of ignorance from our minds and allowed our hearts to love our daughter the way that she needed. The truth has set us free. Sarah recently said, "I haven't felt your love in six years. I feel closer to you now than ever before."

When we understood that she wasn't born this way and did not choose to have SSA, we were able to move from anger and judgment to compassion and love. This was the greatest lesson we learned in the parents classes and by attending Richard's healing seminar. There we witnessed the wounded hearts of so many men and women who struggle with SSA. We gained such a greater appreciation for our daughter.

Author's Note: Please read more of their story in *Gay Children, Straight Parents* (pages 132-136). Today, Sarah has been married to her husband for 14 years and they have three beautiful children. Their family is blossoming.

One Couple's Journey, *Gay Children, Straight Parents*, 2016, pp 161 – 165.

My wife and I are Lutheran pastors. We attended a presentation that Richard made two weeks after our son told us, with much anguish and many tears, that he was attracted to the same sex. Although we believed that people were born that way, we did not want it to be so for him, because of the potential persecution and agony that he would undoubtedly endure in living out his inborn sexuality. But we never admitted to either one of our children that we had not been able to reconcile our belief with the Scriptures.

We went to hear Richard talk about understanding and healing homosexuality. We sat near the back so we could leave "if things got too weird." His impassioned testimonial about his thirty-year struggle with unwanted SSA touched our hearts and minds on a level never before experienced. Though we initially squirmed when he said, "No one is born with SSA, and people can change," this made sense of a lot of what we had experienced as a family while raising our son and daughter. As we left the hall, we were speechless.

We purchased *Being Gay: Nature, Nurture or Both?* and that night we went home and haltingly shared this radical new learning with our son. He was furious at our interest in this approach and extremely angry that we would even consider a new direction, but thankfully, he was willing to listen.

My wife and I read the book and found our family's reality described on most of its pages. How blind we had been! We had all wholeheartedly bought into the "born that way and can't change" myth. We realized, in fact, that this myth had permeated our seminary education and theological underpinnings. These new ideas challenged that myth. We also discovered a loving truth that accurately makes sense of the Scriptures. We knew that God was indeed a God of love and possibility, and not a God of ignorance or avoidance. We had avoided facing the truth that we could not reconcile with the Scriptures, but we also knew that love was the answer and not prideful judgment or shame. We had been uncomfortable with particular groups, churches and denominations that had called homosexuality a sin and said that it could be "prayed away." We knew that wasn't quite right either.

Although our son was very angry that we had done a 180, he was willing to read the book, and we could tell that he was finding meaning in some of the things that he was reading. Of the ten different potential variables mentioned in the book that cause SSA, we realized that we could relate to eight of them. We decided to proceed to the Washington, D.C., area for a Family Healing Session with Richard. We were so grateful that our son was willing to attend.

It was one of the most incredible experiences in our lives. Though we have always cared for each other with a fierce love, we realized through family therapy that the dynamics of our relationship as husband and wife and pastor and pastor had profoundly affected our children. In particular, it had contributed to our son's same-sex attraction. Furthermore, some of our wounds and childhood needs were excavated, and we began to see how these influenced our son's detachment from me and overattachment to his mother.

I began to come to terms with the fact that I had a distant relationship with my father. Because of that, I tend to remain at a distance or emotionally unavailable. That was my preferred method of coping as a child and later as an adult. My wife realized that she had come from a long line of matriarchs and that, in some cases, men were subtly emasculated. She had also experienced abandonment and rejection as a child, which led her to be a needy adult. She realized that she had inadvertently expected our son to take care of some of those needs. Family therapy exposed some of our blind spots and changed our lives in ways we never before imagined.

Although it was difficult at first, my wife took a backseat with regard to our family. At times she would be silent at the table and that allowed my son and me to converse in a way that we had not done before. As for me, I began to concentrate on being emotionally present. I practiced active listening and tried not to react, but rather paraphrase and respond with questions. *I realized that it was more important for me to be in relationship with him than to be right all the time.*

My own heart and self-care have been of foremost importance in the healing process. I was parented in unhealthy ways while growing up. Now I am getting in touch with my own inner child, and he is teaching me important lessons. I am learning to more fully celebrate the process of becoming the man that God created me to be. My wife is keenly aware of becoming the woman that God created her to be as well. We realized that our son's bravado in sharing his same-sex attraction was the release our family needed to begin the process toward healing and wholeness.

We finally got real with each other, and this allowed our son to begin to express his childhood wounds and unmet needs. He began to share his hell with us. He told us what it was like to sustain peer rejection and criticism. We knew he had a sensitive spirit and that both of our children were confused about male and female gender roles within the family. My wife and I are now taking responsibility for our past failures and our family is healing.

As part of our family treatment plan, I held my son several times a week. Most often, he just sat there, not wanting to be in my presence or arms. But I determined to win him back! In all honesty, it was exhausting. And there were many setbacks along the way. After one year of doing this, he found a boyfriend. So I thought, this isn't working. And I quit holding my son.

After one week he came to me and said, "Dad, I feel so hurt that you gave up on me and stopped the holding." I was shocked. I was humbled. And I determined not to quit this time, no matter what. And so we resumed our weekly holding sessions. Even though he still had a boyfriend, I fought hard to win him back. In time, that relationship did fall apart.

Our son graduated high school and went on to train with a professional theatrical company. He was steeped in the "gay" world but extremely unhappy. And then a miracle occurred. He met a wonderful group of men and women from a church that surrounded him with incredible love and affirmation. They invited him to move into a house with other youth group members. And so he did. More and more, while receiving the same-gender peer affirmation and attention he had never experienced in his life, we saw the walls around his heart melting day-by-day. Our son was coming alive; in fact he was blossoming and his faith rekindled for the first time in years.

Now he is determined to heal from his SSA. He himself requested another Family Healing Session to resolve the remaining issues he has with us and within himself. Recently he came home and has been sharing his newfound faith and freedom with his close friends. He even stood before the church congregation and shared his testimony of transformation. This new reality is a blessing beyond measure.

We are still dealing with our feelings of anger over the myth and how it ruins so many lives and robs so many people of their true personhood. We are grateful that we can harness some of that anger and channel it toward helping other people realize that *change is possible*. My wife and I are coming to terms with our new learning and reflecting on the way that the myth affected our family, our theological education, and our church family. We have hope. Our family is now experiencing newfound joy, healing and wholeness. Thank God.

Author's Note: What a remarkable story of changing the family culture, and taking responsibility for each family member's personal healing. Now their son has been married to a beautiful woman for eight years, and they have two gorgeous children. Dreams do come true!

Conclusion to GCSP

1. SSA has nothing to do with sex; it's a gender identity issue.
2. Parents write a personalized treatment plan and put it into action day-by-day.
3. Feel and be real in order to heal. Lead by example: Heal yourself.
4. Succeed small rather than fail big; take one step at a time. Celebrate each victory.
5. Whoever loves the most and the longest wins!

I know that I did not specifically address the transgender, non-binary, and other LGBTQ+ identities. I tell the parents to utilize the same principles from this book. Tell the parents: "Do not, do not, do not try to talk your child out of identifying as transgender or non-binary. It will not work." They must be unconditionally loving and utilize all the exercises from this book.

OK, here is my truth, and I don't mean to disappoint anyone. Over the past 35 years working with parents who have SSA and/or LGBTQ+ identified loved ones, the percentage of those who achieve the goal of helping their children come out straight or revert to their innate gender identity is very low. Why? Most parents want their kids to change without working to change themselves, their dysfunctional relationship(s), and the family dynamics. Has anyone been successful in changing his or her spouse or partner? Of course not. The only person we can change is ourself, and that's a lifelong odyssey. The good news is that parents who work on themselves, become closer as a couple, and change the family dynamics succeed. That's the formula for positive results. Once again, SSA is not the issue—it is a mask for a hurting heart and unmet love needs.

As you have seen, *Gay Children, Straight Parents* is a book filled with exercises and homework assignments. As a therapist, we lead by example. We must continuously work on ourselves to heal our own issues, improve our marriages (if we are married), and lovingly care for our children. Marriage and parenting are the most difficult jobs on earth. If we are not taking care of ourselves and our relationships, we have no business being in the helping profession!

DAY FIVE

Counter-Transference

1. **Transference**: When the client is reminded of his/her past, they transfer their unmet psychological wounds and unmet needs in the present onto the therapist, coach, pastor, or ministry leader. It's like being in a biological time machine, or emotional time warp.

2. **Counter-Transference**: When the client triggers your psychological wounds and unmet needs, your emotional time warp or biological time machine kicks in. For example, you may become attracted to a particular client. He carries the energy of someone that you have unresolved issues with. Or you get angry with a particular type of person: "Why don't they just get over it and do what they have to do?" "Why is he so emotional?" Impatience, anger, lack of compassion, and sexual desires indicate an unconscious part of your character is being awakened. This is an opportunity for your growth, if you are aware of what is happening.

3. What are your core wounds?
    a.
    b.
    c.
    d.
    e.

4. What are your deepest unmet needs?
    a.
    b.
    c.
    d.
    e.

5. It is important to be aware of and define your shadow parts and unresolved issues. When triggered, you are then able to self-regulate and take care for your soul during the session, and follow up with proper self-care afterward.

    What are your weaknesses and vulnerabilities?
    a.
    b.
    c.
    d.
    e.

6. Family therapist Carl Whitaker stated, 'Good therapy occurs when transference and counter-transference are happening simultaneously.'

7. Keys:
    a. Define your core issues.
    b. Be conscious when your (core) issues arise.
    c. Do not project those issues, wounds, needs onto the client.
    d. The "devil" will use your weaknesses against you.
    e. Physician, heal thyself: Do your own healing work.
    f. Do not attempt to get your needs met through or with your clients.
    g. Get your needs met in healthy, loving, reciprocal, adult relationships.
    h. Your clients are not your friends, even though they may think that way.
    i. The gift of discernment is very important to develop: Is it mine, theirs, or someone or something else?
    j. Seek God, asking for wisdom, protection, guidance, and abundant love.

8. Additional issue: Should you cry when a client shares painful experiences?
    Basic principle: Whatever is in the best interest of the client.

You may like to read the following article:

Transference: Are You a Biological Time Machine?
Michael G. Conner, Published in *The Source*, June 2001; revised February 2007.
http://www.crisiscounseling.com/articles/transference.htm

DAY FIVE

Taking Care of the Therapist/Coach/Counselor: Preventing Burnout

1. Know your weak and vulnerable areas; know your unmet love needs.
   These will be triggered by clients who hold similar wounds/needs or someone who carries the energy of your perpetrator(s).

   You must define your weaknesses. Otherwise, they will unconsciously get in the way of your working with clients (and your personal growth).

   On a spiritual level, the "devil" will use your weaknesses, vulnerabilities against you (whether it's a father wound, peer wound, mother wound, body image issue, sexual abuse issue, etc.).

   You may use Voice Dialogue, Focusing, Inner Child work, etc., to get in touch with some of those wounded parts and give them a voice. Explore their feelings, and discover your needs. Then work to heal and fulfill unmet love needs in healthy relationships.
2. Before healing seminars and classes:
   a. Pray for all the participants (begin a few weeks before the event).
   b. Ask for God to provide breakthrough and healing for all.
   c. Ask for protection from invading spiritual influences.
   d. Ask for wisdom, love, and guidance for the event.
   e. Pray for all the staff members.
3. After healing seminars and classes:
   a. Pray for all participants.
   b. Clean yourself off by asking God to remove any spiritual residue.
   c. Grieve as necessary.
   d. Receive healthy touch, massage, or whatever you need to take care of yourself.
   e. Take a break, get rest, and refresh your heart, mind, body, and spirit.
   f. You are not responsible FOR people, you are responsible TO them:
      Do your best to be genuine and authentic, but do not do their work for them.
4. *Compassion Fatigue—Managing Yourself,* Eric Scalise, Virginia Board of Counseling Newslink, Winter-Spring 2003, Vol. 4, Issue 1, pgs. 3-4.
   "A consistent orientation toward compassion can tax the physical, mental, and emotional resources of health care providers, often leading to a variety of lifestyle stress reactions."

"Examples include such things as:

1. Developing a preoccupation with stress-producing people or situations
2. Over-indulging in escape behaviors such as drugs, alcohol, pornography, etc.

3. Avoiding intimacy in personal relationships and seeking fantasy over reality
4. Attempting to control everything and everyone as a means of survival
5. Justifying one's actions by blaming other things and/or other people
6. Compromising ethical and professional boundaries

"High levels of stress usually result in the release of two key hormones into the bloodstream, adrenaline and cortisol. Both have the potential to produce harmful effects over time. These include an increase in the production of blood cholesterol; a narrowing of the capillaries and other blood vessels leading in and out of the heart; a decrease in the body's ability to flush excessive cholesterol out of its system; and an increase in the depositing of plaque on the walls of the arteries. Like sleep loss, the effects of stress and compassion fatigue are accumulative. Sooner or later, one's body will demand a payback and if the person cannot comply, it begins to shut down all its systems in fairly rapid succession.

"There are two major categories of stress for counselors. One is the stress 'of' the profession and the other is the stress that is "brought into' the profession. Counselors who successfully manage the second category of stress will usually handle the first category more effectively. As in sound treatment planning with clients, developing one's own preventive stress management plan could be essential in helping to ensure longevity. A few considerations include:

1. Depersonalizing the process when it is appropriate by recognizing countertransference reactions and the signs of secondary traumatic stress
2. Learning the art of the 15-minute vacation and taking time to be silent and to be still every day
3. Setting aside at least one 2-4 hour period of time each week for self-care, relaxation, play, exercise, and rest
4. Triaging daily events and prioritizing tasks to avoid the tyranny of the urgent
5. Having realistic expectations at the personal level and in terms of potential therapeutic outcomes with clients
6. Resolving those things that can be attended to easily and quickly and focusing the majority of available resources in this direction
7. Learning to manage the clock, the calendar and the appointment book by saying 'no' when necessary and without feeling guilty about it
8. Delegating to others whenever, wherever, and however it is appropriate
9. Scheduling a personal retreat at least once a year for a time of renewal, reflection, and refocusing
10. Finding two or three key people in life as part of a personal support system and as accountability partners who have permission to offer objective feedback."

In his article, Scalise references *Compassion Fatigue: Coping with Secondary Traumatic Stress Disorder in Those Who Treat the Traumatized* by Charles Figley, Brunner/Mazel, New York, 1995.

[Additions of mine below.]

1. Relationship with God: spiritual connection to the Creator, spending time in the Word, worship, fellowship.
2. Relationships with spouse, friends, mentors. Filling up your love tank, getting your needs met on a regular basis.

DAY FIVE

Continued Growth into Manhood / Womanhood

1. Exchange sessions with another therapist/coach/counselor. Take care of one another.

    Find good friends to share deeply with, taking care of each other.

2. Staff Journey Into Manhood (JIM), Adventure In Manhood (AIM), New Warrior Weekends, Women Within Weekends.

3. Attend other trainings and conferences for continued education.

4. Do your own work for continued healing and growth; if you aren't willing to continue your own healing journey, then it's time to stop assisting others.

5. We must be role models for those we work with:
    a. Proper self-care.
    b. Face your shadows/unconscious, deal with your pain, and resolve your issues.
    c. Maintain healthy relationships with others.

6. Keep a balanced diet and balanced life:
    a. Exercise.
    b. Eat healthy foods.
    c. Have fun.
    d. Enjoy your passions (check in with your inner child).
    e. Create loving, successful relationships.

7. You will be tested often. This is a labor of love, and many forces (physical and spiritual) do not want you to do this work. Maintain a healthy spiritual life and feel loved by God. Then you may give from abundance.

Political Aspects of SSA in the World

- Historical Discrimination Without Solution
- Civil Rights Movement in the '60s
- Capturing the Scientific Community in the '70s
- *After the Ball*: The Homosexual Manifesto
- Major Gay Rights Organizations
- Religion: The Great Divide
- Gay Activism's Influence on the Mental Health Profession
- Solution: What Can You Do?

Historical Discrimination Without Solution
- Failure of religions
- Failure of the governments
- Failure of the educational systems
- Failure of the scientific community
- Failure of families

Civil Rights Movement in the '60s
- Sick and tired of discrimination
- Stonewall Riots in New York City
- Organized and unified efforts
- National Gay and Lesbian Task Force
- Other organizations spring up

Capturing the Scientific Community in the '70s
- American Psychiatric Association (APA) decision to remove homosexuality from the *Diagnostic and Statistical Manual of Mental Disorders* (DSM), and in other parts of the world, eventually the International Classification of Disorders (ICD)
- "Doctors Declare Homosexuality Normal"
- From the APA to all medical and mental health organizations

After the Ball: The Homosexual Manifesto
- Strategic campaign to indoctrinate the world into the "innate, immutable" myth of homosexuality: **"Born Gay and Cannot Change"**
- Took the debate from the realm of:
   Religion and psychology to
   Human rights and social justice
- Hollywood jumped on the bandwagon
- Media and the educational system followed

[For more details, please read *Understanding Our LGBTQ+ Loved Ones*, Richard Cohen, M.A., PATH Press, 2022.]

DAY FIVE

After the Ball: How America Will Conquer Its Fear and Hatred of Gays in the 90's

By Marshall Kirk and Hunter Madsen, Plume Books, New York, 1989. Used by permission from the publisher.

Marshall Kirk (researcher in neuropsychiatry, graduated Harvard in 1980) and Hunter Madsen (expert in public persuasion tactics and social marketing, graduated Harvard 1985) are both active gay men.

This outline of *After the Ball* was created by Richard Cohen.

It paraphrases the core concepts contained in this book.

The authors used the term "homo hatred" long before the term "homophobia" was created.

Codes:

( ) = page numbers

H = homosexual or homosexuality

<u>Underline</u> and **bold** are my emphasis

SSA = Same-Sex Attractions

1. **This is a campaign of unabashed propaganda, firmly grounded in long-established principles of psychology and advertising. (xxviii)**

2. **Address hostile public opinion about homosexuality. (xxviii)**

3. **List of prejudice and harmful actions is the specific agenda for change. (4)**

4. **Distinguish between the causes and symptoms of homo-hatred. Essential for agenda and strategies. (4)**

5. **What straights think about homosexuals?**
   a. Know very little about homosexuality and would prefer to know less. (5)
   b. Info from myths, rumors, jokes, stories, Bible. (6)
   c. Avoidance of events with homosexuals. (6)
   d. Reluctance to discuss the issue in public.(7)
   e. Willful perpetuation of ignorance about homosexuality. (7)
   f. Don't care to read serious treatment of homosexual life. (8)
   g. Neglect H in mass culture. <u>Change attitude from *problem* to *condition* to be tolerated and permanently accepted.</u> (9-10)
   h. There are no H heroes. (11)
   i. There aren't many H in America—<u>spread the 10% myth</u>. If we must draw the line somewhere and pick a specific percentage for propaganda purposes, we may well stick with the solidly

conservative figure suggested by Kinsey decades ago; taking men and women together, at least 10% of the populace has demonstrated its homosexual proclivities so extensively that that proportion may reasonably be called "gay." This means that 25 million are H with 50 million parents, plus siblings, relatives, etc. (14-16)

j. <u>When it comes to fighting the charge that H is statistically abnormal hence immoral, there is strength in numbers.</u> (17)

k. Easy to recognize H, stereotype images, effeminate males, masculine females (fags and dykes). (18)

l. Signs of being H: Unusual intelligence, speaks certain way, dresses a particular way, moves specific ways, fails designated tests of manly courage, artistic (21)

m. Why are they H? <u>Promote the innate, immutable theory.</u> (26-27)

n. <u>Behind theories of H is hatred and fear (black heart). Willful ignorance that is mean spirited.</u> (28)

   (1) Caused by sinfulness – against natural law, voluntary and deliberate, unnatural, social contrariness.

   (2) Caused by mental illness – confusion over one's gender identity, fear of opposite sex, result of masturbation, pathological, against culture norms, traced to Dr. Richard von Krafft-Ebing, 1886, "Psychopathia Sexualis," case histories of H. Karl Ulrichs, Edward Carpenter, and other sexologists in late 1800s that H due to gender confusion. Due to parental influence. (33-38)

   (3) Caused by recruitment – older H recruit innocent young straights, like vampires or werewolves. Rev. Jerry Falwell said, "H do not reproduce, they recruit." Sexually depraved, mentally unstable, not to be trusted with our kids, disproportionately involved in child molestation, H and pederast interchangeable. (42) Parents beware; if recruitment is true, your kids might turn out H. Protect your kids from shameful contagion, avoid H.(44)

o. <u>Debunk theories of the causes of H, even if they are true. Purpose is to debunk such theories so straights cannot blame H as sexually deviant.</u> (45)

p. H are kinky, loathsome sex addicts. (48)

q. H are unproductive and untrustworthy members of society. Suicidal, sick, unhappy. (52)

6. **Homosexuality is portrayed as either (a) a permanent condition or (b) a temporary problem that can be fixed. This distinction between problem and condition is crucial to the way straights think about homosexuality. A problem has a solution. A condition doesn't need to be fixed. It is simply an aspect of life that must be accommodated. It requires permanent tolerance, and you must come to terms with it psychologically, practically, and morally. We must therefore change public opinion from problem to condition. (10-11)**

7. **How straights treat H: (64)**
   a. Actions that prevent H behavior.
   b. Actions that deny H their fundamental civil rights (not allowed to speak on TV, radio, newsprint). (77)
   c. Actions that vent public disapproval of H: "Though your tissues gel, and you rot in hell, don't feel gloomy friend, it will never end, happy death, faggot fool." (From death threat Christmas cards sent to H in 1987 by Iron Fist, a hate group at the University of Chicago.) (98)

8. **Our field trip concludes: An agenda for change (107-109)**
   a. H don't warrant or deserve much attention from straights.
      Preferred: H are a valuable part of American society; we should be familiar with their nature, culture, news, and heroes.
   b. H are few in number; I don't know any H.
      Preferred: H constitute a large minority of our society, and some of my friends/family are H.
   c. H are easy to spot.
      Preferred: They are not; most of them look just like anyone else.
   d. H become H because of sin, insanity, seduction.
      Preferred: Sexual feelings are not really chosen by anybody; H is just as healthy and natural for some persons as heterosexuality is for others.
   e. H are kinky sex addicts.
      Preferred: The sex and love lives of most H and straights today are both similar and conventional.
   f. H are unproductive, untrustworthy members of society.
      Preferred: H are hardworking, patriotic Americans.
   g. H are suicidally unhappy.
      Preferred: H would be as happy as anyone else, if we'd just treat them fairly.
   h. H acts, and intimate public contact, are outlawed across roughly one half of the nation.
      Preferred: All sex acts among consenting adults should be decriminalized; no discrimination is permitted between straights and H in content and application of laws.
   i. Freedoms of speech and assembly by H are impeded by public intolerance.
      Preferred: H are provided, by special law if necessary, the same opportunity to speak (including access to mass media) and gather as straights currently enjoy.
   j. Rights of H to work, shelter, and public accommodations are limited by public intolerance.
      Preferred: H are assured, by affirmative action if necessary, equal opportunity in these regards.
   k. H couples cannot legally marry, nor enjoy property rights; nor are their rights to parent natural or adoptive children secure.
      Preferred: H are permitted all the standard rights of marriage and parenthood.
   l. H are often taunted, harassed, and brutalized.
      Preferred: The public no longer sanctions this behavior, which becomes as socially incorrect, discreditable, and repugnant as overt racism or anti-Semitism.

9. **Understanding prejudice:** (112)
    a. Prejudice is not logical. It cannot be overcome by facts and logic.
    b. Prejudice is deep, automatic, prelogical, a product of emotional conditioning unassailable by any appeal to the intellect. And so homo-hatred is impervious to argument.
    c. To solve the problem, you must first understand it through and through.

10. **Tactics that won't work to overcome prejudice:**
    a. You can't inform or argue it away.
    b. It's not "evil," so burning our enemies at the stake won't work.
    c. Not an illness, so it can't be cured by therapy.
    d. Not a conspiracy by sick or wicked people.
    e. Consciousness-raising won't work.
    f. H parades where H looks extreme won't work.
    g. Learning to love and respect others won't work.
    h. Storming the barricades or picketing won't work.
    i. Having sex in public won't work. (113-114)

11. **How prejudice works:**
    a. Seat of emotion is in the limbic system, a set of six or eight organs located in the center of the brain. (115)
    b. Three specific and unmixed emotions: *(1) septal region causes pure pleasure, (2) locus ceruleus causes fear, and (3) amygdala causes anger.*
    c. Emotions serve as internal drive states that motivate a mammal to do the right thing, at the right time, in order to survive and reproduce. Appropriate emotions, appropriately timed, motivate appropriate behavior. (115)
    d. Emotions fall into two major categories: (1) *trophic emotions*—which are pleasant, feel good, induce an animal to approach that which elicits them; driven by dopamine-containing nerve fibers, pleasure circuits of the mid-brain, which activate the septal region, feels good, and (2) *countertrophic emotions*, which are unpleasant, feel bad, and induce an animal to avoid that which elicits them; driven by norepinephrine-containing nerve fibers, pain circuits of mid-brain, subdivide into two categories (located in separate brain-organs) and motivate two separate behavioral functions (both feel bad):
        (1) Anxiety/fear: activated in the *locus ceruleus* and causes flight response. Caused by situations that are dangerous (discretion is better than valor).
        (2) Anger/rage/hate: activated in the *amygdala* and induces fight response, attempt to kill enemy. It is solicited by other creatures, rather than situations, that are dangerous or weaker, and more feasibly dealt with by aggression than flight. (116)
    e. *Evolutionary function of prejudice—for survival and reproduction. Agnatic selection: "survival of the fittest."* This means that strong, clever animals survive and reproduce, passing to their

offspring the genes for strength and cleverness, thus, over time, making their species as a whole stronger and more clever. And so it goes with the strongest, cleverest tribes and societies. All baboon tribes are hostile to one another and fight viciously upon contact; the best tribe wins, gains greater land-space and food, and so reproduces in greater numbers. This process concentrates successful genes. (118)

    f. In order for agnatic selection to work, individual baboons come equipped with the ability to discriminate at a glance, or perhaps sniff, between members of their own tribe and members of other tribes and make snap judgments on the basis of superficial characteristics—knee-jerk reactions—without thinking. Here we see prejudice unfolding!

    g. Having discerned the stranger at a glance, the baboon must react immediately, so as to jump the gun on his enemy. This automatic response has two stages: (1) unpleasant emotion—countertrophic fear and/or anger, which motivates (2) a behavior, either fight or flight: "see the stranger, fear the stranger; hate the stranger, kill the stranger." (119)

    h. Humans feel similar to baboons when they experience prejudice: rewarding a sense of fear and anger when they avoid or destroy outsiders, and an equally rewarding sense of pride and self-righteousness, and the respect and approval of their own tribe (parents, family, neighbors, their "set," class, nation, race). (119)

12. How homo-hatred arises in men:
    a. Prejudice with humans: how homo-hatred arises in man, who has more intellectual abilities than other primates. Two highly developed abilities: (1) learn patterns of behavior, instead of being limited to those instinctive patterns with which one is born and (2) form mental patterns, or concepts—like little models of things inside the head. (120)

    b. <u>Therefore, what was learned can be unlearned. Connections made in the brain can be broken and new connections can be learned that will counteract and nullify the effects of the old. It's comparatively easy to train a relatively flexible human being if not to like then to feel and react neutrally to previously hated minority groups, like H!</u> (121)

    c. How the mechanism of prejudice develops in children: (1) learn to hate, (2) learn anger/fear toward H, (3) learn emotional reactions toward H by:
       (1) *Associative conditioning*: link between two things so one evokes the other (homosexuals and hatred).
       (2) *Direct emotional modeling*: learn to hate/love/fear as our parents/others do. Not through reasoning but by example we learn to hate or fear others. (122)

    d. Emotions motivate biologically necessary behaviors, including fight or flight, when social mammals, living in herds, are confronted by enemies of their own or other species. A child has learned, as a conditioned emotional reaction, to hate the things his parents hate. (124)

    e. Kinsey said one in three males has homosexual tendencies (this is a mischaracterization of Kinsey's findings), so, many will experience H feelings. (125) He will learn to hate in others what he denies in himself:

(1) Pattern One: Rage—repression and reaction formation. Horrified by his SSA, he represses it immediately. Has a subconscious need to seek out and destroy in others (through violence, murder, hurtful behaviors) what he cannot tolerate in himself (e.g., Roy Cohn, Joe McCarthy).

(2) Pattern Two: Terror. Strives to appear straight (actions and appearance). Lifelong self-hatred, avoidance of H.

(3) Pattern Three: Wretched excess. Goes overboard with exaggerated effeminate behaviors, shock tactics, etc. (126-127)

 f. *Picture-label pair: Group images and labels together in the mind (e.g., fag and specific behaviors).* (129)

13. How homo-hatred works in adults: (130)

Step 1: Bigot either sees or hears, or thinks about, an instance of the picture/label pair.

Step 2: His sighting, or thinking about, the instance evokes, from his limbic system, a conditioned response or countertrophic emotion—that is, fear and/or hate. If the emotion is sufficiently intense, he may

Step 3: Run away (by trying to ignore the instance or by crossing the street), or attack (verbally or physically)—which discharges the fear and/or hate and thus

Step 4: Rewards the behavior.

Step 5: Step 2 and, if present, Step 3 are interpreted (perhaps automatically and unconsciously) by the rest of the brain as "being like Mom and Dad"—meaning, "those from whom I get my love and respect." This notion evokes

Step 6: A conditioned response of trophic emotions—felt subjectively as "being loved," and labeled "pride and solidarity." This once again

Step 7: Rewards the whole sequence.

Step 8: Rationalization: Rationalization is learned after hatred, so you cannot persuade someone to stop being prejudiced by reason! (131)

Rationalization is the last in the above sequence, which is why rationalization doesn't work to change bigotry. Therefore, rationalization isn't fruitful in the war on homo-hatred/not useful in the campaign of propaganda to change opinions. (131)

14. Three tactics that don't work:

1. Consciousness-raising
   a. Trying to argue people out of their homo-hatred doesn't work. Prejudice is not a belief; it's a feeling. Arguments cannot change feelings, only beliefs. It's not useful in the treatment of homo-hatred. Arguments with facts is a waste of time. (136)
   b. Actions/behavior help us outgrow/overcome fear/hatred. Experience the feared thing in small increments over time; then the fear peters out. Reason won't persuade. Emotional appeal works. (137)

c. Ninety percent of people have low intelligence. Ten percent fairly high intelligence. <u>Can never alter the 90% through beliefs or arguments, only through emotions.</u> Highly intelligent can step outside themselves and analyze their feelings, the causes of their feelings, and modulate them. Sometimes arguments directed at the 10% can trickle down to the 90%. (138)

   d. Argument creates negative reaction and reinforces their prejudice (negative emotion when feel threatened). (139)

   e. Cannot disprove the Bible, validity of the Bible, or other authoritative sources of moral judgment. (139)
  2. Storming the barricades
   a. Fighting won't/doesn't work. (140)
   b. Solving problems with fists is ill advised.
   c. Acts of violence reinforce prejudice. (141)
  3. Gender bending
   a. We've been shut out of the majority culture and made to feel worthless and wicked.
   b. By demonstrating differences, it strengthens prejudice with picture/label pairing, creating hostility and anxiety. (144-145)

15. "First you get your foot in the door, by being as similar as possible; then, and only then—when your one little difference is finally accepted—can you start dragging in your other peculiarities, one by one. You hammer in the wedge narrow end first. As the saying goes, 'Allow the camel's nose beneath your tent, and his whole body will soon follow.'" (146)

16. How to halt, derail, and/or reverse the engine of prejudice, a three-step approach:
  1. *Desensitization*
   a. Prejudice = Alerting Signal. Warns tribal mammals that a potential alien mammal is in the vicinity and they should fight or flee. Two things can happen: (1) Strong or weak stimulus: Fight it or flee from it or (2) low grade stimulus: Don't take action against it, treat it as irrelevant, get used to it. (148)
   b. If H present themselves as different and threatening, then straights go on the alert and fight against them.
   c. <u>To desensitize straights, H inundate them with conscious flood of H-related advertising, presented in the least offensive fashion. If straights can't shut the shower off, they may at least eventually get used to being wet.</u> (149)
  2. *Jamming*
   a. Insertion of incompatible emotion into the pre-existing system. Like <u>sprinkling sand into a pocket watch</u>.
   b. Jamming is more active and aggressive than desensitization.
   c. Jamming uses the rules of <u>associative conditioning</u> (<u>when two things are repeatedly juxtaposed, one's feelings about one thing are transferred to the other</u>) and <u>direct emotional</u>

modeling (<u>the inborn tendency of human beings to feel what they perceive others to be feeling</u>). (150)

d. Consequent internal confusion has two effects: *Unpleasant/emotional dissonance* will tend to result in an alteration of previous beliefs and feelings so as to resolve the internal conflict. And second, the *internal dissonance* will tend to inhibit over-expression of the prejudicial emotion—which is, in itself, useful and relieving. (151)

e. <u>All normal people feel shame when they perceive that they are not thinking, feeling, or acting like one of the pack. The trick is to get the bigot into the position of feeling a conflicting twinge of shame, along with his reward, whenever his homo-hatred surfaces, so that his reward will be diluted or spoiled</u>. (151)

f. Propagandistic advertising can depict homophobic and homo-hating bigots as crude loudmouths and assholes—people who say not only "faggot" but "nigger," "kike," and other shameful epithets—who are "not Christian." It can show them being criticized, hated, shunned. <u>It can depict H experiencing horrific suffering as the direct result of homo-hatred—suffering of which even most bigots would be ashamed to be the cause. It can, in short, link homo-hating bigotry with all sorts of attributes the bigot would be ashamed to possess, and with social consequences he would find unpleasant and scary. The attack, therefore, is on self-image and on the pleasure in hating.</u> (151-152)

g. When our ads show a bigot—just like the members of the target audience—being criticized, hated, and shunned, we make use of <u>direct emotional modeling</u> as well. Remember, a bigot seeks approval and liking from "his crowd." When he sees someone like himself being disapproved of and disliked by ordinary Joes, <u>direct emotional modeling</u> ensures that he will feel just what they feel—and transfer it to himself. This wrinkle effectively elicits shame and doubt, jamming any pleasure he might normally feel. In a very real sense, every time a bigot sees such a thing, he is unlearning a little bit of the lesson of prejudice taught him by his parents and peers. (152)

h. <u>*Effect of jamming is achieved without reference to facts, logic, or proof.* Through repeated infralogical emotional conditioning, his bigotry can be alloyed in exactly the same way, whether he is conscious of the attack or not.</u> Indeed, the more he is distracted by any incidental, even specious, surface arguments, the less conscious he'll be of the true nature of the process—which is all to the good. (153)

i. <u>In short, jamming succeeds insofar as it inserts even a slight frisson of doubt and shame into the previously unalloyed, self-righteous pleasure. Need massive public exposure of the message to succeed</u>. (153)

3. ***Conversion***
   a. Desensitization aims at lowering the intensity of anti-H emotional reactions to a level approximating sheer indifference. Jamming attempts to blockade or counteract the rewarding "pride in prejudice" by attaching to homo-hatred a pre-existing, and punishing,

sense of shame in being a bigot, a horse's ass, and a beater and murderer. Both of these techniques are preludes to our highest—though necessarily very long-range—goal, which is conversion. (153)

b. <u>Conversion of the average American's emotions, mind, and will, through a planned psychological attack, in the form of propaganda fed to the nation via the media.</u> We mean "subverting" the mechanism of prejudice to our own ends—using the very process that made America hate us to turn their hatred into warm regard—whether they like it or not. (153-154)

c. ***If desensitization lets the watch run down, and jamming throws sand in the works, conversion reverses the spring so that the hands run backward.*** (154)

d. In conversion, the bigot, who holds a very negative stereotypic picture, is repeatedly exposed to literal picture/label pairs, in magazines, and on billboards and TV, of H— explicitly labeled as such – who not only don't look like his picture of H, but are carefully selected to look either like the bigot and his friends, or like any one of his other stereotypes of all-right guys—the kind of people he already likes and admires. This image must, of necessity, be carefully tailored to be free of absolutely every element of the widely held stereotypes of how "faggots" look, dress, and sound. He or she must not be too well or fashionably dressed; must not be too handsome; that is, mustn't look like a model or well groomed. The image must be that of an icon or normality—a good beginning would be to take a long look at Coors beer and Three Musketeers candy commercials. Subsequent ads can branch out from that solid basis to include really adorable, athletic teenagers, kindly grandmothers, avuncular policemen, ad infinitem. (154)

e. <u>But it makes no difference that the ads are lies; not to us, because we're using them to ethically good effect, to counter negative stereotypes that are every bit as much lies, and far more wicked ones; not be bigots, because the ads will have their effect on them whether they believe them or not.</u> (154)

f. When a bigot is presented with an image of the sort of person of whom he already has a positive stereotype, he experiences an involuntary rush of positive emotion, of good feeling; he's been conditioned to experience it. But here, the good picture has the bad label—H! (The ad may say something rather like "Beauregard Smith, beer drinker, Good Ole Boy, pillar of the community, 100% American, and H as a mongoose.") The bigot will feel two incompatible emotions: a good response to the picture, a bad response to the label. At worst, the two will cancel one another, and we will have successfully jammed, as above. At best, associative conditioning will, to however small an extent, transfer the positive emotion associated with the picture to the label itself, not immediately replacing the negative response, but definitely weakening it. (155)

g. You may wonder why the transfer wouldn't proceed in the opposite direction. The reason is simple: <u>Pictures are stronger than words and evoke emotional responses more</u>

powerfully. The bigot is presented with an actual picture; its label will evoke in his mind his own stereotypic picture; but what he sees in his mind's eye will be weaker than what he actually sees in front of him with the eyes in his face. <u>The more carefully selected the advertised image is to reflect his ideal of the sort of person who just couldn't be H, the more effective it will be</u>. Moreover, he will, by virtue of logical necessity, see the positive picture in the ad before it can arouse his negative picture, and first impressions have an advantage over second. (155)

    h. <u>In conversion, we mimic the natural process of stereotype-learning, with the following effect: We take the bigot's good feelings about all-right guys and attach them to the label "gay," either weakening or, eventually, replacing his bad feelings toward the label and the prior stereotype</u>. (155)

    i. Understanding direct emotional modeling, you'll readily foresee its application to conversion: Whereas in jamming the target is shown a bigot being rejected by his crowd for his prejudice against H, <u>in conversion the target is shown his crowd actually associating with H in good fellowship</u>. Once again, it's very difficult for the average person, who, by nature and training, almost invariably feels what he sees his fellows feeling, not to respond in this knee-jerk fashion to a sufficiently calculated advertisement. In a way, most advertisement is founded upon an answer of "Yes, definitely!" to Mother's sarcastic question: I suppose if all the other kids jumped off a bridge and killed themselves, you would too? (155-156)

17. **Success depends on flooding the media, and that, in turn means money, man hours, and unifying the H community for a concerted effort.** (157)

18. **Learn from Madison Avenue to roll out the big guns! H must launch a large-scale campaign—we've called it the <u>Waging Peace Campaign</u>—to reach straights through the mainstream media. We're talking about propaganda.** (161)

19. **The term *propaganda* applies to any deliberate attempt to persuade the masses via public communications media.** Its function is not to perpetrate but to propagate; that is, to spread new ideas and feelings (or reinforce old ones) which may themselves be either evil or good depending on their purpose and effect. The purpose and effect of pro-gay propaganda is to promote a climate of increased tolerance for H. (162)

20. **Three characteristics distinguish propaganda from other modes of communication and contribute to its sinister reputation:** *(1) Relies on emotional manipulation—through desensitization, jamming and conversion; (2) Uses lies; and (3) It's subjective and one-sided. Tell our side of the story as movingly as possible. In the battle for hearts and minds, effective propaganda knows enough to put its best foot forward. This is what our own media campaign must do. (162-163)*

21. **Must train leaders through national workshops for full acceptance in America.** Begin a national "Positive Images Campaign." Recognition is dawning that anti-gay discrimination begins, like war, in the minds of men and must be stopped there with the help of propaganda. (163)

22. **Principle goal of the campaign is to gain tolerance and acceptance by the straight community. (165)**

23. **Show, in the media, that H community lives by an ethical code in order to achieve our goal of tolerance and acceptance. (166)**

24. **Publicly "Come Out" to desensitize, jam, and convert straight America.** Jamming means interrupting the smooth workings of bigotry by inducing inconsistent feelings in the bigot. Extreme bigots become less confident that their incitements will generate applause and are further inhibited by the majority of "mild bigots," who now become uneasy that a fag slur might provoke an unpleasant scene. Once these dynamics get going, displays of homo-hatred suddenly become off-color and boorish. Thus, when H come out, they help transform the social climate from one that supports prejudice to one that shuts homo-haters up. Coming out is a critical catalyst for the all-important "conversion" process, to make straights actually like and accept H as a group, enabling straights to identify with them. Coming out is the key to sociopolitical empowerment, the ability of the gay community to control its own destiny. (167-168)

25. <u>**Coming out process is too slow, so we also need a national media campaign**</u>. After meeting enough likeable H on TV, Jane Doe may begin to feel she knows H as a group, even if none has ever introduced himself to her personally. Thwart bigotry. (169)

26. **Carefully crafted, repeatedly displayed mass-media images of H could conceivably do even more to reverse negative stereotypes than could the incremental coming out of one person to another**. (169)

27. **The wide range of favorably sanitized images that might be shown in the media could eventually have a more positive impact on the H stereotype than could exposure to H friends, since straights will otherwise generalize a suboptimal impression of gays from the idiosyncratic admixture of good and bad traits possessed by their one or two H acquaintances. Portray only the most favorable side of gays, thereby counterbalancing the already unfairly negative stereotype in the public's mind.** (170)

28. **The media campaign will work well in tandem with the Everyone Comes Out strategy because it is actually a catalyst to coming out.** (170)

29. **Two different avenues to gay liberation: education (i.e., propaganda) and politics.** (170) Politicians must be responsive to public sentiment on sensational issues if they value their careers. (171) But this often happens in politics, especially on the H issue where. As Yeats would say, "The

best lack all conviction, while the worst are full of passionate intensity." Our political success could be greatly advanced by media campaign conducted prior to, or simultaneously with, political initiatives. (172)

30. Waging Peace Campaign:
   a. "Those who have supreme skill use Strategy to bond others without coming to conflict." (Sun Tzu, *The Art of War*)
   b. Three points of effective *propaganda*:
      (1) Employ images that desensitize, jam, and/or convert bigots on an emotional level. This is, by far, the most important task.
      (2) Challenge homo-hating beliefs and actions on a (not too) intellectual level. Remember, the rational message serves to camouflage our underlying emotional appeal, even as it pares away the surrounding latticework of beliefs that rationalize bigotry.
      (3) Gain access to the kinds of public media that would automatically confer legitimacy upon these messages and, therefore, upon their gay sponsors. To be accepted by the most prestigious media, such as network TV, the messages themselves will have to be—at least initially—both subtle in purpose and crafty in construction. (173)
   c. Waging Peace Campaign: 8 Practical Principles for the persuasion of straights:

Principle 1: Don't just express yourself, communicate!
   a. Genuine public outreach requires careful communication. Key: Put yourself in the listener's shoes. "If I were straight and felt the hostility most straights feel toward gays, what would it take to get me to change my anti-gay feelings?" (174)
   b. Don't start by deciding what you most ardently wish to tell straights: Start by determining what they most need to hear from you. (174)
   c. Straights must be helped to believe that you and they speak the same language. (174)
   d. Dress and speak like them. (175)

Principle 2: Seek ye not the saved or the damned; appeal to the skeptics.
   a. Intransigents (core) 30-35%, ambivalent skeptics (swing) 35-45%, friends (pansexual) 25-30%. (175)
   b. Silence those who oppose homosexuality (intransigents) because of their religious beliefs.
   c. Ambivalent skeptics are our most promising targets. (176)
   d. Ambivalent skeptics are more or less passively negative toward H. (176)
   e. Focus the media campaign on the ambivalent skeptics: Desensitize/jam/convert them.
   f. Silence the intransigents (core).
   g. Mobilize the friends (pansexuals). (177)

Principle 3: Keep talking.

a. Help straights view homosexuality with neutrality rather than keen hostility. In the beginning, seek desensitization and nothing more. (177)
b. "You can forget about trying right up front to persuade folks that homosexuality is a good thing. But if you can get them to think it is just another thing—meriting no more than a shrug of the shoulders—then your battle for legal and social rights is virtually won." (177)
c. "Application of the keep-talking principle can get people to the shoulder-shrug stage. The free and frequent discussion of gay rights by a variety of persons in a variety of places gives the impression that homosexuality is commonplace. That impression is essential, because, as noted in the previous chapter, the acceptability of any new behavior ultimately hinges on the proportion of one's fellows accepting or doing it." (177)
d. "The fastest way to convince straights that homosexuality is commonplace is to get a lot of people taking about the subject in a neutral or supportive way." (178)
e. "Talk about gayness until the issue becomes thoroughly tiresome." (178)
f. "In the early stages of the campaign, the public should not be shocked and repelled by premature exposure to homosexual behavior itself. Instead, the imagery of sex per se should be downplayed, and the issue of gay rights reduced, as far as possible, to an abstract social question." (178)
g. "As it happens, the AIDS epidemic—ever a course and boon for the gay movement—provides ample opportunity to emphasize the civil rights/discrimination side of things, but unfortunately it also permits our enemies to draw attention to gay sex habits that provoke revulsion." (178)
h. **Accuse religious people: "Gays can use talk to muddy the moral waters, that is, to undercut the rationalizations that 'justify' religious bigotry and to jam some of its psychic rewards." "Portray such institutions as antiquated backwaters, badly out of step with the times and with the latest findings of psychology." (179)**
i. "Where we talk is critical." TV, films, magazines—most powerful image makers in the Western civilization. (179) Marshall McLuhan said, "Where desensitization is concerned, the medium *is* the message ... of normalcy." (179)

Principle 4: Keep the message focused: You're a homosexual, not a whale.

a. Talk about gay rights issues and nothing more: be single-minded. (180)
b. Michael Denneny said, "We have no natural allies and therefore cannot rely on the assistance of any group; we have only tactical allies—people who do not want barbarous things done to us because they fear the same thing may someday be done to them." (181)
c. Be focused in your efforts to reach the public via mass media. Talk, talk, talk about gay rights, and leave it at that. (182)

Principle 5: Portray gays as victims, not as aggressive challengers.

a. "Gays must be portrayed as victims in need of protection so that straights will be inclined by reflex to adopt the role of protector. If gays present themselves instead as a strong and arrogant tribe promoting a defiantly nonconformist lifestyle, they are most likely to be seen as a public menace that warrants resistance and oppression." (183)

b. **KEY:** *"The purpose of victim imagery is to make straights feel very uncomfortable; that is, to jam with shame the self-righteous pride that would ordinarily accompany and reward their anti-gay belligerence, and to lay groundwork for the process of conversion by helping straights identify with gays and sympathize with their underdog status."* (183)

c. <u>"Persons featured in the media campaign should be wholesome and admirable by straight standards, and completely unexceptional in appearance; in a word, they should be indistinguishable from the straights we'd like to reach."</u> (183)

d. "Conventional young people, middle-aged women, and older folks of all races would be featured, not to mention the parents and straight friends of gays. One could also argue that lesbians should be featured more prominently than gay men in the early stages of the media campaign." (183-184)

e. Two different messages about gay victims:
   (1) Public persuaded that gays are victims of circumstance, that they no more chose their sexual orientation than they did, say, their height, skin color, talents, or limitations. *"To suggest in public that homosexuality might be chosen is to open the can of worms labeled 'moral choice' and 'sin' and give the religious intransigents a stick to beat us with. Straights must be taught that it is as natural for some persons to be homosexual as it is for others to be heterosexual: wickedness and seduction have nothing to do with it. And since no choice is involved, gayness can be no more blameworthy than straightness. In fact, it is simply a matter of the odds—one in ten—as to who turns out gay, and who straight. Each heterosexual must be led to realize that he might easily have been born homosexual himself."* (184)
   (2) <u>Gays should be portrayed as VICTIMS OF PREJUDICE. Straights don't fully realize the suffering they bring upon gays and must be shown: graphic pictures of brutalized gays, dramatizations of job and housing insecurity, loss of child custody, public humiliation, etc.</u> (184)

f. *Help straights become homosexual protectors.* (185)

g. <u>Play for sympathy and tolerance.</u> (186)

h. March if you must, but don't parade (look good for the camera/newspaper). Look ordinary, not like disenfranchised drag queens, bull dykes, exotic elements of the gay community. (186)

i. **Desensitization works gradually or not at all.** (186)

Principle 6: Give potential protectors a just cause.

a. <u>Use anti-discrimination as the campaign, not homosexual behavior.</u> (187)

b. **"Our campaign should not demand explicit support for homosexual practices, but should instead take *antidiscrimination* as its theme. Fundamental freedoms, constitutional rights, due process and equal protection of laws, basic fairness and decency toward all of humanity—these should be the concerns brought to mind by our campaign."** (187)

Principle 7: Make gays look good.
a. In order to make a gay victim sympathetic to straights, you have to portray him as an Everyman. (187)
b. Paint gay men and lesbians as superior, veritable pillars of society. (188)
c. Use famous historical homosexual figures.
d. Use celebrity endorsements of homosexuals because people like celebrities, so they will like homosexuals. (188-189)

Principle 8: Make victimizers look bad.
a. *"The objective is to make homo-hating beliefs and actions look so nasty that average Americans will want to dissociate themselves from them."* (189)
b. "The best way to make homo-hatred look bad is to vilify those who victimize gays. The public should be shown images of ranting homo-haters whose associated traits and attitudes appall and anger Middle America." (189)
c. In TV and print, images of victimizers can be combined with those of their gay victims by a method propagandists call the "bracket technique" (e.g., Rev. Fred Phelps picketing at Matthew Shepard's funeral saying, "God hates gays." Then people are disgusted by him, so they dissociate from him and his hateful attitude.). (189)
d. "Every time a viewer runs through this comparative self-appraisal, he reinforces a self-definition that consciously rejects homo-hatred and validates sympathy for gay victims. Exactly what we want." (190)

31. Tactics for eating the media alive:
    a. Three main ways: (1) public relations, (2) news reporting, and (3) advertising. (193)
    b. Make a big noise. People love scandals, gossip. Cultivate liaisons with broadcast companies and newsrooms in hopes of seeing issues important to the gay community receive some coverage. (194)
    c. Public disturbances: (1) Look like a mass event. (2) Behavior must be nonviolent. (3) Disobedient acts must be portrayed as a last resort. (4) Viewing public must be helped to understand that gay protestors expect and accept arrest; they're not just out to break laws. (5) Public must understand the logical connection between gay rights issue and the particular act of civil disobedience adopted. (196-197)
    d. Public relations tactics:
        (1) Creative formatting: need fresh angle, way to make gay rights argument more topical.

(2) Use news to make news—gay persons can respond to a new law, court case, death, or scandal.

(3) Human interest—people more interested in the human, personal side of your story.

(4) Celebrity spokespersons—a celebrity does not simply make news—she is news—she can get on the air and tout the gay cause relatively easily, without further pretext. (198)

a. TV is OK, but advertising campaign is necessary to be successful, in order to desensitize, jam, and convert people. (199)

b. Advertising tactics/five big media outlets:

(1) TV best because it teaches the widest amount of people. It's the most intrusive medium. Changing picture/label pair best on TV.

(2) Radio: reaches millions daily, intimate medium.

(3) Magazines: good vehicle for the gay message. More affordable than TV blitz, less intrusive, and packs less punch.

(4) Newspapers: do even less to build legitimacy than magazines.

(5) Outdoors: billboards, display ads in public areas, subway placards, etc. Excellent job of reaching a broad audience over and over again. Message must be simple and benefit from being seen over and over again. **Goal is to desensitize straights to homosexuality.** (204)

c. Over long term, TV and magazines are probably the two media of choice. TV is more persuasive, and magazines are the most affordable. (204)

d. Fairness doctrine by FCC to get on shows, etc. Personal Attack Rule by FCC, get on shows. Equal Time Rule of FCC—equal time for each office. (206)

e. How to get on TV, radio, newsprint:

(1) Make ads like white bread; completely unobjectionable. Go after middlebrow or upper-middlebrow publications and then work your way down.

(2) Use free access—Public Service Announcements (PSA).

(3) Run symbolic gay candidates for every high political office. (212) Through such political campaigns, mainstream America would get over the initial shock of seeing gay ads.

(4) Waging Peace Campaign: Launch media messages of open <u>support for the civil rights of gay people in ads that work directly to jam homo-hatred and convert straights to feelings of greater tolerance</u>. (213)

32. **Create one unified national gay organization for tactical purposes.** (249)

a. <u>*"We're more willing to attack one another than to go after our common enemy."*</u> (Jeff Levi, executive director of National Gay and Lesbian Task Force).

b. *AFL-CIO learned many years ago there is tremendous strength in unification under a single-run organization.* (249)

c. Fundraising in two phases:

PHASE ONE: Name, mission, tax-deductibility, good ladder (continue all tactics after campaign is launched):

(1) Trademark name of the campaign.

(2) Statement of mission: prioritize objectives, make measurable milestone goals, working plan.

(3) Funding: Government grants, foundation grants, business contributions, individual contributions. (265)

(4) The more directly personal your contact with donors, the more funds you will raise. (266) Fundraisers ladder chart.

(5) Lion's share of individual donations usually come from a few wealthy individuals and business executives who must be wooed in person. (267)

(6) List of fundraising ideas for Phase One (268-269):
   a. Cultivate gay upper class.
   b. Conduct direct mail appeals.
   c. Place fundraising ads in the gay press.
   d. Develop dedicated fundraising events.
   e. Introduce an affinity credit card for the campaign.

(7) Exposed-root appeals (269):
   a. Let other gay organizations contribute directly to the campaign.
   b. Persuade gay bars and other gay-patronized businesses to donate regularly to the campaign.

PHASE TWO: Solicit additional funds from gays and straights via straight media, through ads themselves.

33. **Motivation over the long haul is to sustain emotional steam that comes from rage, not love:**

"You may discount what the pious tell you, because it is actually rage, not love, that lay behind all those progressive events."

"Like all emotions, rage has its purpose. And its time and place. When a situation becomes intolerable, an oppression unbearable, when millions do not even dare to cry out beneath the heel of injustice, rage is the appropriate response." (382)

Major Gay Rights Organizations

1. HRC: Human Rights Campaign: political action committee (www.hrc.org)
   a. Fighting for gay rights on the federal, state and local levels of politics.
2. Lambda Legal: Legislative organization (lambdalegal.org)
   a. Lawsuits promoting gay rights in the realm of politics, education, and public policy.
3. GLSEN: Gay, Lesbian, Straight Educational Network (www.glsen.org)
   a. Gay Straight Alliances (GSA) in public schools.
4. GLAAD: Gays and Lesbians Alliance Against Defamation (www.glaad.org)
   a. Media watchdogs.
5. NGLTF: National Gay and Lesbian Task Force (www.thetaskforce.org)
   a. Social activism for gay rights nationwide.

Religion: The great divide

1. One side: Endorses homosexual behavior (Affirming Churches)
2. One side: "Homosexuality is sin"; rejects SSA persons (Rejecting Churches)
3. Godly response: Embrace SSA people without endorsing the behavior (Receiving Churches)
4. All religions of the world must take a stand:
   a. Ordain active SSA men and women or not?
   b. Bless same-sex ceremonies/marriages or not?

Gay activism's influence on the mental health profession

1. All main stream mental health organizations promote "gay affirmative therapy."
2. If the client doesn't accept his SSA, he is diagnosed with "internalized homophobia."
3. If parents don't accept their child's SSA, they have "internalized homophobia" and are considered the problem.
4. The American Psychological Association and American Psychiatric Association have powerful LBGTQ+ committees and organizations.
5. For those who are licensed therapists, you may use other *DSM* diagnoses for insurance purposes: Generalized Anxiety Disorder, Dysthymic Disorder, Posttraumatic Stress Disorder, Sexual Disorder NOS, etc.

DAY FIVE

Solution

Understanding Our LGBTQ+ Loved Ones, Richard Cohen, M.A., PATH Press, 2022.

1. **Apologize for wrong speaking and/or doing. Words matter!**

2. **Spread the truth in love:**
   - No one is essentially born with SSA
   - No one chooses to have SSA
   - *Change is Possible*

3. **Love those who experience SSA the right way—Listen, Love, Last:**
   - Listen: Good communication and listening skills
   - Love: Heterosexual men mentor SSA men, and Heterosexual women mentor SSA women
   - Last: Most homosexual relationships don't last
     Be the last one standing
     Whoever loves the most and the longest wins!

4. **One individual and/or one family love one SSA person, whether they wish to change or not.**

COUNSELOR TRAINING PROGRAM MANUAL

How to Meet the Press: A Survival Guide

(by Jack Hilton, Sagamore Publishing, Inc., 1990. Used by permission from the publisher.)

CHAPTER 1
MARSHALING SUPPORT

1. Finally, what I found very disconcerting was the indifference in the eyes of the interviewers. Most of them managed to be professionally curious—they looked curious—but when I looked into their eyes, they weren't there. They were distracted.
2. I learned the truth that being interviewed is a lot easier than interviewing if you know what you are talking about. It's far easier than standing up and making a speech.

You realize they didn't read the book when they will ask you what you want to be asked.

3. **Know what you want to say and use whatever questions you are asked to say it—briefly, along the way, you may actually address the question put to you, or not, as you choose.**
4. You can flatter the host by saying things like, "That's a really interesting question," or "Now, I think that's the nub of the whole thing." Just don't get so fixated by the questions you are asked that you forget to make your points, assuming you have some. Practice helps: The fifth time is a lot better than the first time.
5. It is on the local TV news that a person interviewed needs to be wary. Few news interviews are done "live." Mostly just a sound "bite" is taken out of a long scene. The selected sound bite may or may not represent the thrust of what the person interviewed intended to say. That makes people feel they have been quoted "out of context."
6. Cultivate relationships with newsmen.
7. Businesses would be wise to practice what politicians have done for years. They cultivate and befriend TV newsmen when there are no crises. It is not a question of "buying" the journalist, but educating him in the concerns and the realities of whatever the business is. When there is a crisis or a hot news story, that newsman will at the very least be more receptive to your point of view. In fact, I don't share the widespread impression that television is out stalking business executives to make fools of them. Television newsmen line their studies with congratulatory plaques from business associations, not the scalps of company officers.
8. Prepare 15-second sound bursts or 43 words.
9. Well-turned statements in 15-second bursts to utter at the conference. It greatly improves the chances that CBS or other networks would excerpt it intact.

    One key to success is brevity; making sensible points in a hurry and succinctly requires forethought and practice.
10. One hundred seventy-two (172) words per minute uninterrupted, two minutes of 344 spoken words.

CHAPTER 2
NEWSPAPERS [These are 1990 stats and information.]

1. We are a "visually-biased society." **Seeing is believing.**
   83% of what we learn comes from what we see.
   11% of what we learn comes from what we hear.
   50% of what we remember is both seen and heard, which is television's forte.

CHAPTER 3
SIX TYPES OF INTERVIEWS

1. Inquisition: So-called inquisitorial interviews are where the guests start off and remain guilty until proven innocent, which rarely happened on *Night Beat*, the show this was first introduced in. I did an experiment, all to teach several lessons, which are applicable today:

Lesson 1: All of us occasionally say things extemporaneously that we don't really mean.

Lesson 2: Never underestimate your opposite number in an interview. Some of them do their homework.

Lesson 3: Avoid inquisitorial interviews unless subpoenaed.

2. Hard news: Easiest to follow.
3. In-depth interview or called informational: To probe deeper and reveal more.
4. Entertaining interview.
5. Nitwit interview: You are in the presence of a nitwit when the interviewer hasn't done any homework and doesn't listen to the answers either. Reporters who always ask how everyone feels are among the worst in listening to the answers – never mind the nodding.
6. Ambush interview: when reporter and cameraman surprise you "in the dark alley."

CHAPTER 4
BE PREPARED

Know what you want to say and use whatever questions you are asked to say it. Along the way you can actually address the questions put to you or not, as you choose. Just don't get so fixated by the questions you are asked that you forget to make your points, assuming you have some.

1. First comes a defensive game plan. Anticipate the questions that you may be asked. Decide beforehand how you'll answer. Ad-libbing in public on matters of importance is a no-no, but don't use a script either. Just get your salient points on each topic lined up in order of their importance and rehearse out loud.
2. Offense: Ask yourself, "What in the world compelled me in the first place to accept this invitation to boil slowly under TV's hot lights? What do I want to accomplish for alma mater?" Remember this is a conversation. Be prepared to take the initiative when the opportunities arise.

3. Bridges: Once the game commences, time of possession is important, too. Getting from defense to offense requires an exchange: A kick-off, punt, fumble, interception, or (I hope for you) a touchdown! In conversational dynamics an exchange occurs when one participant bridges another and seizes the initiative. A bridge gets you from where you are in a discussion to where you want to be, which is presumably on the safer ground of topics or points of your choosing (based on your previous decisions concerning the offensive game plan). Successful bridging requires a smooth connecting phrase, clause, or sentence as a preface. "Let me put that matter in a slightly different perspective," or, "Let's consider the larger issue here." If you're asked about a problem at your school, don't dwell on it unless it's the problem that you're aiming to discuss. Talk about the solution. If the past tense of an issue is awkward for you, bridge to the present tense or the future tense. Getting from the former to the latter is up to you; six or eight words of bridging should be sufficient to do the job. Don't be fixated by the question(s); don't be confined or impaled by the specific or limited thrust of your interrogator's query; and be alert for chances to go on offense, to take the initiative.
4. Wrong prep: "What questions will I be asked?" and, "How will I answer?" Be honest. That's what you are thinking, isn't it? If so (not that those questions are irrelevant), you are on a loser's track. You are preparing yourself (with sizable doses of trepidation) solely to respond, which immediately puts you in a reactive, or passive, mode. (In other words, you're probably doomed on Sunday, and NBC doesn't supply cigarettes or blindfolds.)
5. Never ad-lib. Prepare your lines well—rehearse.
6. Express exasperation over an erroneous charge. "There you go again!" (long pause) Remember Reagan, when accused about Medicare. He prepared 23 words on a legal pad and flawlessly spoke them.
7. To anticipate an interviewer's questions beforehand doesn't necessitate an advanced degree in prescience. Just subscribe to about 6 of the 1,688 newspapers: *The New York Times, The Washington Post, The Wall Street Journal, The Los Angeles Times, Time,* and *Newsweek*, the crème de la crème of American journalism.
8. Write down the 25 likeliest questions that you can expect to be asked.
9. Repetition is OK on TV.
10. It is even advised—preferably creative repetition, which is different from redundancy. The oldest rule of education and/or advertising applies here: Tell them what you're going to tell them. Tell them. Then tell them what you told them.
11. CHOOSE WORDS, PRACTICE, PAUSES, PLAIN ENGLISH, SINGLE SENTENCES, SHORT: 43 WORDS GOOD FOR TV NEWS – 15 seconds.
12. Pause after "and" and put central message in the second sentence. Attack the word "if."
13. Qualities to have: Enthusiasm, conviction, specific, correct, anecdotal, and cool.
14. When you are in the right, you can afford to keep your temper. When you are in the wrong, you can't afford to lose it.

15. **EXERCISE: HOW TO WRITE YOUR RESPONSE AND THEN BRIDGE.** Write down three things you definitely want to say. Simple, declarative sentences will suffice for now. Write the same points a second time expressed another way. Now a third time, again differently.
16. Now you have nine different statements or assertions on three separate themes. Next write down experts who agree with you on each point, and write down their credentials. Write down statistics and data in your favor. Keep doing this until you have nine different, supportive dissertations, attaching one to each of your declarations.
17. Then, with the teeniest amount of bridging and oral dexterity, and in the total absence of fixation, can't you respond to the 25 likely questions with any or parts of these nine recitations? If not, start over, because if you're doing this correctly the answer will always be yes. As previously noted, the route from defense (questions) to offense (statements and support) is called bridging.
18. If you watch television attentively, you will see demonstrations of the bridging technique on virtually every program. Great bridge is: "I can't tell you that, but I can tell you this …"
19. It works for two reasons: The guest is willing to take the initiative by volunteering new information about a topic, hopefully more interesting or provocative information than the question seemed to elicit.
20. Bridging is a basic trick in this trade, which was adapted from debating techniques. It springs from the ground of commonsense and basically boils down to a single premise: Never let the host or other participants control your contribution to the program; reserve that privilege for yourself.
21. Don't evade the difficult question. An accomplished interviewee knows that it is possible to restructure a question before answering it and in so doing to remove the worst dangers. If it is done skillfully enough, it may be possible not to answer the question at all without looking evasive.
22. An accomplished guest volunteers much more than the required information when he or she likes a question. When a question is too delicate, or tangential, or petty, the same guest volunteers nothing. No question is sacred, and none need be answered slavishly. That's how amateurs get caught. You are entitled to say everything you choose to say about all the topics that are raised, whether the initiative was somebody else's or your own. You do not need to answer specific questions. Through this tactic, as I said, it is possible, even likely, for an interviewee to actually control the conversational exchanges.

Summary:
1. The interviewee takes initiative by offering more interesting information.
2. Never let the host or other participants control your contributions—reserve that privilege for yourself.
3. Don't avoid difficult questions. Restructure the question before answering and remove the worst dangers.
4. Volunteer much more in answering good questions.
5. Volunteer little in answering bad questions.
6. You need not answer specific questions; restructure and bridge.

CHAPTER 5
STYLE VERSUS SUBSTANCE

1. Wardrobe and makeup are important on TV.
2. Impressions outweigh substance on TV.
3. Manner has more impact than matter on TV.
4. In books, magazines, and newspapers, WHAT is said is usually more important than HOW it is said.
5. On TV, just the opposite is true. People remember the emotional content and keep the impression for years, not the content of the interview. DON'T LOOSE YOUR TEMPER ON TV.
6. Be yourself and be liked.
7. There are three ways to be liked:
    a. Well prepared and back up your statements with crisp examples.
    b. Show humor or composure in the face of adversity.
    c. Or you become an underdog at the mercy of a bullying host.
8. You can fail to state any of your objectives and still win as long as the viewer at home feels admiration or sympathy for you. But your attitude can work against you too.
9. Keys to intimacy with the audience:
    a. Eye contact with the camera's lens, which is tantamount to eye contact with the audience.
    b. Camera awareness.
    c. Speak to "one," and glance their way at times.

So that the camera in front of you isn't five million people anymore. It's me. It's your spouse, your next-door neighbor, your best friend, any one of us. I'm across the room in my den, not your TV studio. Just talk to me with that in mind, even glance my way when you think it's appropriate. I'll like you better.

10. What viewers notice:
    a. Posture: Sit up straight, cross your legs, lean slightly forward, and keep your hands in front of you above your waist. Be natural and comfortable. Remember that the picture people see at home is most of the time the top of your head to your sternum, maybe your waist.
    b. Wardrobe: Not too flashy, wear blues, grays and browns. KNEE-LENGTH SOCKS. Keep jacket buttoned. Wear no new clothes, or else test them sitting down in front of a mirror. Wear a quiet pattern. Find out color of chairs at studio. Don't overdress or underdress (bank vice president).
    c. Gestures: Use small ones on TV. People will particularly notice if any of these strike them as odd or somehow wrong. If they are, at worst, they'll think less of you. At best, they'll be distracted from what you are saying. Don't let that happen.
    d. Jewelry: Only wedding band and watch, nothing that will interfere with microphone.
    e. Makeup: Touch of pancake makeup will absorb the light, giving you a smoother, more natural look. Buy also an applicator sponge and removing cream, unless it is water based. Put on all

exposed skin, also back of hands, also down to your neck and jaw. Lipstick that lasts through the whole show.

    f. Haircut: Avoid the wet look; go to the barber several days before. Neatness counts! Coif your own hair; don't put your glasses on in the last moment.

CHAPTER 6
BASIC TRAINING

1. Reporters are trained to ask everyone WHO, WHAT, WHEN, WHERE, WHY and HOW? Your job is to answer them succinctly and truthfully, which is a job made appreciably easier in a crisis if reporters already know from past contact WHO you are, WHAT you do, and WHERE and WHY. This makes for a more level playing field in moments of stress when the press is hurried and you are harassed.
2. Inform news assignment desk at local TV stations.
3. If you are promoting a worthy cause with a hot-air balloon race, all you have to do is alert the assignment desks at the local stations and there will be a cavalry charge of reporters and crews to get there early for the best camera positions.
4. TV likes visual stories to break the monotony of talking heads. If you want visual aspect, start with news department of TV station. Call local talk show producers.
5. You must have something new to say.
6. Worthy cause is not enough in itself. You must have something new to say, something you have discovered yourself, contrived yourself, or dramatized in a newsworthy fashion.
7. Style—how to say it:
   a. Ultimately the importance of your cause is less important than the style in which you sell it.
   b. Is there a way to demonstrate a perceived benefit to many people from your cause?
   c. Is there a way to package your cause that makes it seem new, even if it's old?
   d. Is there a dramatic way to illustrate your cause, even if your message is decades old?
   e. Can you demonstrate a particular expertise in talking about a subject of continuing public interest?
8. How to get on the air:
   There's always the simplest procedure: You call the host on the phone and ask if you can be on the show. If the host won't talk to you, speak to a producer. They are sometimes called bookers. Most programs are booked by someone other than the star, and the bigger the show the more bookers there are. Broadcasters are schooled to pre-interview prospective guests to determine their air-worthiness. Be honest about why you want to get on the show, what you have to offer, and what you cannot supply. Do not, however, ask the host to recommend another show or approach for you.
9. Express things differently and be innovative.

"Dare to be different. If you have something to say, find a way to make it interesting. Don't approach things in a given way just because you've always seen it done that way on *Donahue* or *Meet the Press*. Do your homework. Think things through. And then find a way to express your thoughts in a manner that is meaningful and innovative. If you can get my attention, chances are I'll hear you. If not, chances are I'll assume that I already have—at least a hundred times!"

10. Best guests:

Host: "I want interesting people with strongly held views."

CHAPTER 7
THE IRRELEVANT QUESTION

1. Do not ad lib; you are quotable (out of context).
2. You can discuss anything you choose with the press and on TV, as long as you remember that you are quotable, and that you will not necessarily be quoted in context.
3. Sincerely chuckle and repeat the question or express amazement that you were asked that question, like: "You're asking the president of Youth Services if I think marijuana should be legalized!" Then more soberly go on and bridge by saying what the issue really is.
4. Speak as a representative of an organization, not as an individual.
5. It helps in such situations to think of yourself as the personification of your title and affiliation. What might be an issue of great interest and firm feeling for you, the person, may not be an issue on which someone of your title should comment. Before you answer an irrelevant question, think how it will look attributed to your organization tomorrow in the papers or tonight on the TV news.
6. You can steer the conversation. Watch for irrelevant topics.
7. That leads to my second reminder: Matters of relevance and irrelevancy are shared decisions between you and interviewer. You are not a puppy on a leash to be jerked hither and yon against your will from topic to topic. You can, should, and must participate in deciding the conversation.
8. It's useful to fix a definition of relevant in your head at the outset. Mine is the following: If it's extraneous in my representative capacity, it is irrelevant, and usually I'll dodge it. I hope gracefully and graciously. If it's extraneous to my purpose in the interview, ditto. If it's dangerous, I will avoid it like the plague, even gracelessly.

CHAPTER 9
THE INCONSISTENCY TRAP

1. Admit inconsistency—it shows growth.
2. When faced with a charge of inconsistency, admit it. You are allowed to change your mind. In fact, it shows growth and flexibility. If you once felt that way but no longer do, just say so: "Yes, it's true I made that statement in 1980. But I've changed my mind," or, "When I said that, my first-hand investigation of the situation wasn't complete. I've subsequently finished it, and it's made a difference in my opinion."

3. The worst thing you can do in a broadcast situation is to leave an audience with the impression that your old view still prevails. When you change your mind about an important issue on which you've taken a strong stand in the past, you should say so publicly and without equivocation.

CHAPTER 10
BOTTOM LINE COHEN

(This has nothing to do with me, Richard Cohen. This is truly the name of the chapter!)

1. Short news interviews want short, no-nonsense answers.
2. A or B dilemma: In broadcast news especially, interviewers and tape editors seek short, no-nonsense replies, sparing audiences long, complicated explanations. They want to keep their programs moving at a brisk pace.
3. Keep in subject position—no matter what.
4. When a person who is expected to answer impossible questions actually tries to do so, the level of the program as a medium of information drops precipitously. It does so not only because the answer is usually as inane as the question, but because the interviewee has surrendered his autonomy. From there on, the reporter or host becomes the authority figure. He has proved to be the manipulator. If you, the guest, lose control of a question, you lose control of the interview. And if the host has a particular dislike for you or your cause, it's an entrée to squash you like a grape underfoot.
5. All the conviction, preparation, and determination you can possibly muster for a given situation will do no good if you suffer an attack of blind panic, or worse, surrender your independence to the host.
6. Host and guests are equal. You can challenge host's questions! This is not the U.S. Army. The host is not the general, and the guests are not privates. They are equals. It is not only permissible, but frequently necessary, for a guest to challenge a host's statements, and even to refuse to answer a question as presented.
7. You must be your own defense lawyer. In a broadcast interview, the interviewee must be his own defense lawyer. And if he doesn't assume that role, he's in trouble. The witness stand is not a good model for a broadcast interview, and some questions dare not be answered as they're framed. An alert guest must remember that.
8. Don't give YES or NO answers: There are four options: A, B, BOTH, or NEITHER. It is folly to let the pressure of the moment force you into an either/or, yes/no, true/false quiz when neither of the choices really serves your purpose or conveys your position. In responding to an A or B question, there are four options available, not merely two. The others are both and neither: STAY IN CHARGE!!!

CHAPTER 12
THE ABSENT PARTY QUESTION

1. Say anything you like about your opponent's position, his illogical assumptions, his useless conclusions, his insubstantial arguments. But never question your opponent's motives, his sincerity, or his devotion to a cause, especially when he or she isn't present.
2. Don't speak negatively about your opponent, or the audience won't trust you! Don't attribute ugly motives to your opponent. It makes the audience question your motives and consequently distrust your position.
3. There are all kinds of ways to sidestep such situations. You can make a mitigating remark: "I find it hard to believe that he said this, but if he did, I certainly can't agree because …" Or you can simply address the issue and ignore the personal aspersions. Or you can take the hard line: Defer the answer until you have seen the exact quote, context and all, for yourself. Don't be suckered into making a remark you'll later regret.

CHAPTER 13
THE LOADED PREFACE

1. Key is preparation:
    a. Have your own story and clear facts.
    b. Anticipate arguments and contentions of host and opposition.
2. Preparation doesn't mean just getting your side of the story straight. It also means anticipating the arguments and contentions of the opposition.
4. Expect the worst and unexpected, and have an answer prepared. If there is one question you dread being asked, rest assured that it will be asked. And woe to the man or woman who does not have an answer prepared.
5. If the opponent is not polite, let him interrupt you two or three times. Then lean forward, smile, touch his forearm, and say, "Just a moment please. I wonder if I can finish this point." Then smile graciously.

DAY FIVE

Media Prep

Rich Wyler, Principal, Wyler Public Communication. / www.brothersroad.org
Used by permission from the author.

Before the Interview

1. When a reporter calls, be sure to ask:
   a. The reporter's name.
   b. The publication or program.
   c. Its audience (readers, viewers, listeners).
   d. "What types of guests have you had recently?"
   e. The interview format (live, taped, point-counterpoint, printed Q&A, etc.).
   f. Location.
   g. Number of listeners.
2. Never give an interview immediately. At a minimum, arrange to call back in 10 minutes so you have time to gather your thoughts and review your notes.
3. Have a goal for each interview:
   a. What do I hope to accomplish? What would the ideal headline be?
   b. What are the main points I wish to share?
4. Bring your own agenda to the interview.
   a. Don't just answer questions.
   b. Have your "key message points" or "single over-riding communications objective" (SOCO) in front of you (or memorized).
5. Anticipate questions—both the easy ones and the hard ones.
6. Plan possible "bridges" from the reporter's questions to your key messages.
   a. **"You asked about homophobia. You know, tolerance is a two-way street …" (bridge to tolerance, right to know, personal choice)**
   b. *"Who has questions for my answers?"* (Henry Kissenger to White House staff)
7. Plan "escape routes."
   a. "I don't want to guess on that. Let me check and call you back."
   b. "I'm not familiar with that particular issue. Let me see if I can find someone who is better equipped to answer that."
   c. "You're missing the point. The point is …"
   d. "That's not an issue that I'd like to discuss. What I would like to say is …"
8. Identify flags.
   a. "… but the real story is …"
   b. "The key issue here is …"
   c. "There are three important points to keep in mind here …"
9. Practice with a colleague who can play reporter.
10. Consider taping yourself, so you can learn from yourself. You are your own best teacher!

During the Interview

1. It doesn't really matter what they ask. Give the answers you are prepared to give (especially your key messages).
   a. Don't ignore the question, but don't be a slave to it either.
   b. Touch on the question and BRIDGE to your main points.
2. Demeanor is half the interview.
   a. Sound pleasant and assured, non-threatened and non-threatening.
   b. Be engaging and likable.
   c. Get tough when called for (but not until "provoked," and then only deliberately and for effect).
3. Think before you answer. Don't rush.
   To give yourself time to think, repeat the question first.
4. Give the conclusion first, then supporting points. Speak in headlines.
5. Be quotable but not sarcastic. It's okay to be provocative if it's deliberate and thought out in advance. ("That's absurd!" or "So who says the APA knows anything about ethics? Politics, sure. Political correctness, definitely. But ethics?")
6. Don't over-answer. Short answers are better than long.
7. Don't repeat negative statements. (e.g., "No, I don't think I'm homophobic.") Frame your answer as a positive statement. (Reporters will set you up.)
8. Don't fall for hypothetical situations or a false "A or B" dichotomy. Restate the answer in your own way. (Ignore and bridge ...)
9. Don't use jargon.
10. Speak from personal experience with the issue:
    a. "What we've found in our program ..."
    b. "The background of the people I've worked with is ..."
    c. "We're not saying everyone should or has to change. It's a choice for those who wish to change...."
11. Never lie, exaggerate, or deliberately give the wrong impression.
12. It is okay to say: "I don't have an opinion on that," or "I'd prefer not to discuss that issue." Don't say: "No comment."
13. Keep to an absolute minimum any spiritually oriented or religious statements you make to a secular reporter.
14. When you've made your key messages a few times, find a polite reason to end the interview.

Additional Tips (by Richard Cohen):

1. Command the space. Make it yours.
2. Stay on message. Don't allow the interviewer or opponent to suck you into their game. Keep repeating your main points. If you don't like the conversation, change it. Redirect and share your main speaking points.
3. People only remember a few things, so stick to your main points and share from the heart.
4. Stories move people. Don't just give theory. Share either your story or those of others (with their consent).

DAY FIVE

Family Healing Session (FHS) Protocol Manual
(Companion with the FHS Film Series)

Richard Cohen, M.A.
Facilitator

www.pathinfo.org
www.TimeTouchandTalk.com
Email: pathinfo@pathinfo.org

© 2023 Richard Cohen, M.A.

All rights reserved. Reproduction or translation of any part of this work beyond that permitted by Section 107 or 108 of the 1976 United States Copyright Act without the permission of the copyright owner is unlawful. Requests for permission or further information should be addressed to the Permissions Department, PATH Press, P.O. Box 2315, Bowie, MD 20718 / pathinfo@pathinfo.org

This publication is designed to provide accurate and authoritative information in regard to the subject matter covered. It is sold with the understanding that the publisher is not engaged in rendering psychological or other professional services.

No part of this publication may be reproduced, stored in or introduced into a retrieval system, or transmitted, in any form or by any means (electronic, mechanical, photocopying, recording or otherwise) without the prior written permission of the publisher of this book.

Dedication

I dedicate this Family Healing Session (FHS) Protocol Manual to my teacher, mentor, and supervisor Martha Welch, M.D., who taught me, trained me, and gave her life to the improvement of parent-child relationships throughout the world.

I wish to thank Hildegard Reinold-Wiemann for assisting in the further development of this protocol over the past thirty-five years. Our collaboration took Dr. Welch's work to a new level and has helped families throughout the world.

Disclaimer

The facilitation of the Family Healing Session (FHS) is reserved for mental health professionals, i.e., counselors, social workers, marriage and family therapists, certified coaches, psychologists, and certified sexual orientation coaches through Positive Approaches To Healthy Sexuality (PATH). The correct use of the FHS protocol is the sole responsibility of the facilitator. S/he is responsible for maintaining the safety and confidentiality of all participants. By using this manual, facilitators agree to take full responsibility to protect and provide a safe environment for all families in their care. Facilitators and their families agree to hold harmless PATH, its staff, and board members, in the unlikely event that a client is harmed in any way by any of the processes described in this manual.

ISBN 978-1-7338469-4-3
Cohen, Richard, 1952–

PATH Press, P.O. Box 2315, Bowie, MD 20718
Tel. 301-805-5155 / Email: pathinfo@pathinfo.org / Web: www.pathinfo.org

DAY FIVE

Family Healing Session (FHS) Protocol Manual

Richard Cohen, M.A., © 2023 / www.pathinfo.org / www.TimeTouchandTalk.com

[Release form must be signed: You are 100% responsible for using the FHS protocol, and hold harmless Richard Cohen and PATH staff, board members, and volunteers.]

[Credentials: In order to practice this FHS protocol, you must be a licensed therapist, counselor, or certified coach.]

Comments regarding the film series:

- The filming of the FHS Protocol Training took place in Mexico City in October 2017. You will hear everything in both English and Spanish. The excellent translator is Andreina del Villar. We worked together for many years, traveling throughout Mexico and training thousands of professional therapists, physicians, and ministry leaders. For this reason, the translation is seamless, as we developed our own rhythm and connection after working together for many years.
- Throughout the filming of this training, I refer to a couple who shared their remarkable experience during a FHS in October 2014. Even though they gave me permission to include their story in this training film series, I felt it was much too personal to make public. I removed it to maintain their confidentiality and that of their children.
- During the FHS Protocol Training film series, I mention the International Healing Foundation (IHF) which I founded in 1990 and dissolved in December 2015. From January 2016 I became the President and Executive Director of Positive Approaches To Healthy Sexuality (PATH), which I co-founded it 2003. Also, throughout the filming, I use the acronym AMS which means Attracion al Mismo Sexo in Spanish, and SSA which means Same-Sex Attraction in English.
- It is my opinion and suggestion that the therapist/coach/counselor is at least middle-aged with teenagers or adult children, otherwise the professional has no personal life experience and credibility to assist the families.
- A final suggestion: we recommend that you learn a variety of Process Training Protocols.

Table of Contents

1 – Introduction and Information from Dr. Martha Welch
2 – Informed Consent Agreement
3 – Family History Questionnaire for Parents
4 – Family Healing Session Protocol for Therapists/Coaches
5 – Charts and Communication Skills

1 - Introduction

I learned about the Family Healing Sessions (FHS) in June 1995 from Dr. Martha Welch, former associate professor of clinical psychiatry at Columbia University (https://nurturescienceprogram.org/nsp-team/martha-welch/). I read her book, *Holding Time* (Simon & Schuster, 1988), contacted her, and asked if she would train me. Through our sharing, she suggested that the quickest way to learn her method was by having a Family Session with my wife and three children. So off to Connecticut we went.

On the first day, we had an eight-hour session. It was an unforgettable day full of profound sharing, tears, bonding, and attachment. On day two we participated in Dr. Welch's group with other parents and their children who experienced attachment disorders (many of whom were either adopted or had characteristics of autism). The group lasted for four hours, followed by our final three-hour family session with Dr. Welch. In those two days, our family was transformed. We resolved longstanding issues, experienced greater intimacy, released pent-up emotions, and acquired practical skills to help us resolve past and present-day conflicts.

After our two-day session with Dr. Welch, I began to facilitate Family Healing Sessions (FHS) with many of my clients and their families. I called Dr. Welch with questions, seeking her wise counsel and supervision. She was a wonderful mentor with helpful insights, always willing to supervise my work.

Over the past thirty-five years, I further developed the Family Healing Session protocol together with my former assistant Hilde Reinold-Wiemann, who is a certified relationship and parenting coach.

I anticipate that you too, with your unique training, expertise, and personality, will make this protocol your own. The most important thing to remember is to follow the client's lead. We are here to help them resolve personal and relational issues, while giving all family members the skills to create greater intimacy and love for a lifetime.

Cautionary Note:

Dr. Welch learned, after five years of facilitating family sessions with mothers and their children, that it is essential and more effective for both the father and mother to participate in the FHS with all their children. If only one parent is present, the results will be compromised and limited.

Initially, this type of treatment was called Attachment Therapy. However, in the USA, several therapists made mistakes with their clients, and the term "Attachment Therapy" became frowned upon by the mental health profession. Dr. Welch was different from those types of therapists, always practicing and promoting that only the parents should hold their children and not the therapist. Dr. Welch renamed the therapy Direct Synchronous Bonding (DSB). While conducting research at Columbia University, she renamed the approach Family Nurture Intervention.

For more information about Dr. Welch, please read her book, *Holding Time* and visit the websites 1) https://nurturescienceprogram.org/martha-g-welch-md-honored-by-american-psychiatric-association/ and 2) http://nurturescienceprogram.org

The following information is from: The Welch Method *Direct Synchronous Bonding* Manual, ©1999, Martha Welch, M.D.

1. Barriers to Attachment (page 6)
   - Emotional Hurt
   - Fear
   - Anger
   - Unmet Needs
2. Emotions are bottled up (in the child or children) and the parent needs to pop the cork using Direct Synchronous Bonding (DSB) (pages 6-7)
3. What Parents Can Do: (p. 13)
   - Help child express feelings
   - Accept the child's feelings
   - Maintain eye contact
   - Express your feelings
   - Insist on hugging
   - Insist on getting hugged back
   - Spend time: talk, read, cuddle, touch, and play
   - Set limits
4. Logic & Reasoning fail because the attachment disordered child is (p. 19):
   - Deregulated: distracted by own conditioned inner alarm stimuli
   - Shut off from feelings: has stopped seeking response from others
   - Too stressed: can't respond to others

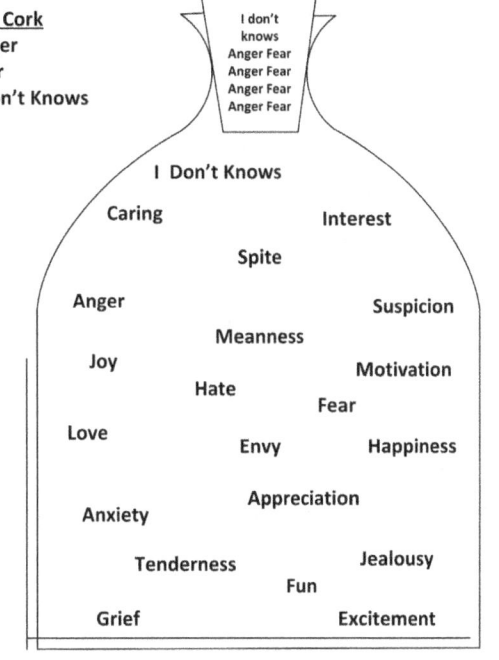

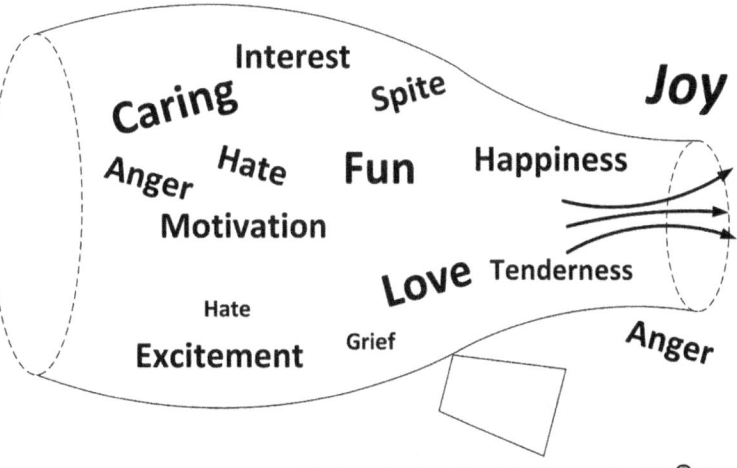

- Therefore, talking and logic do not change the child's inner deregulation.
- Only DSB, which is high-intensity communication, will help re-regulate the child.

5. Welch's 1st Law of Child Attachment (p. 21):
    - If a child has bad or symptomatic behavior, then the attachment between mother and child is disturbed.
    - The causes of disturbance is not of primary importance.
    - If attachment is disturbed, then the needs of the child as well as the mother are not being met.
    - Only when the needs of both mother and child are met will the child's behavior improve.

6. Welch's 2nd Law of Child Attachment (p. 21):
    - A child's primary attachment is to the mother.
    - A broken or insecure primary mother attachment will result in negative behavior until the attachment is created or repaired.
    - To create or repair a primary maternal attachment, both physical and emotional synchrony must be achieved between mother and child.
    - Synchrony can only be achieved when mother and child interrelate with direct physical contact.

7. Welch's 3rd Law of Child Attachment (p. 21):

    The Way the Child Adapts to:
    - Physical and mental stress
    - Attachment to mother

    The Way the Mother Responds Determines How the Child Will:
    - Learn
    - Behave and Interact
    - Love, Fear, and Live

8. Stages of Direct Synchronous Bonding (p. 26):

    Stage 1: Confrontation
    - Often a short period of good feeling
    - Hugging
    - Prodding or appeasement
    - Avoidance

    Stage 2: Conflict
    - Anger
    - Fear
    - Negative feelings
    - Aversion to real closeness
    - Aversion to physical contact, eye contact, smell

    Stage 3: Resolution
    - Mutual gaze, touch, caress, kiss
    - Both feeling better

- Breathing in synchrony
- Molding to each other's bodies
- Includes eye contact, reciprocity

9. Conclusion: State of Synchrony (p. 27)
- Calm arousal
- Able to give and receive help, learn, feel, and play
- Tolerate other's feelings
- Tolerate frustration
- Emotional hurt disappears
- Fears dissolve
- Anger dissipates
- Reciprocity becomes possible
  Willing and able to have needs met and meet other's needs

[As you have read, Dr. Welch stressed mother-child attachment and bonding. My experience as a husband and father over the past 43 years, and as a psychotherapist for 35 years, is that the father is equally important in the parent-child bonding process. Of course, nothing will take the place of the mother-child bonding in the first years of life. Additionally, fathers are always important for the healthy development of their children. When father and mother are united, children feel safe and loved.]

2 – Contract

This is an example of my contract with each family. Make sure to check with an attorney and adhere to state and federal laws governing counseling/coaching in your country. You must protect yourself, your practice, and your organization.

**Informed Consent and Liability Release Form
for the Family Healing Session (FHS)**

This contract is made by and between **Therapist Name**, hereafter referred to as "Therapist," and **Name of Family or Parents,** hereafter referred to as "Family," mutually agree to the following:

The Family hereby engages the Therapist to facilitate a two-day Family Healing Session (FHS) on the terms and under the conditions stated herein:

1. VENUE: Location of the FHS.

2. DATES: List the dates.

3. HOURS OF ENGAGEMENT: List the days and hours or approximate times.

4. TOTAL CONTRACT FEE: $_____, (½ due upon signing of the contract; ½ **before the FHS begins** (bank account, PayPal account, check, etc.).

5. The Family agrees to provide at no expense to the Therapist the following:
   a. Round-trip airfare to and from the _____ Airport.
   b. Hotel and food the day before, days during, and one day after the Family Healing Session.
   c. Transportation from the airport to the hotel, and return trip to the airport.

6. The Family understands that the Therapist will make every reasonable effort to safeguard its communications and treat them as confidential and privileged information. The Family further understands that the Therapist will comply with any applicable federal or state laws regarding the maintenance and safekeeping of its records pertaining to the FHS. Notwithstanding the foregoing, I understand that the Therapist may need to share my confidential information with the appropriate authorities if:
   a. If the Therapist suspects that a child, or other person, has been physically abused, neglected, and/or sexually abused;
   b. If the Therapist suspects that a family member may have a condition or is engaging in a behavior that may require restraint and/or hospitalization to protect a family member and/or others;
   c. If the Therapist suspects that a family member has committed or is about to commit a crime or other violation of the law and the Therapist is required or permitted to report it;

d. If the Therapist is required by a court of law or was issued a legal subpoena for the Therapist's records; and/or if the Family provides written consent to release information about a family member(s).

If the circumstances described above arise, I will not require the Therapist to obtain a release-of-information form from me designating each person to whom they will be communicating.

7. The use of touch in the Family Healing Session is strictly at the discretion of the Family and for the sole purpose of healing. We adhere to the Code of Ethics of The United States Association for Body Psychotherapy (https://usabp.org/USABP-Code-of-Ethics).

8. The Family understands that all clients experience healing in different ways and may have varying degrees of success, and that change is determined by each individual.

9. The Family understands that they may email several times after the FHS with questions. One preparation session and a follow-up session are part of this original fee. Subsequent sessions will be charged at $_____ per session.

10. If the Family wishes to cancel four weeks before the Family Healing Session, the Family agrees to pay the Therapist $_____. If the Family wishes to cancel less than four weeks before the family healing session, the Family agrees to pay the Therapist $_____.

11. This Informed Consent represents the entire agreement between us regarding the FHS that our Family will be receiving from the Therapist and shall not be modified unless done so in writing and signed by both the Therapist and the Family for the duration of the services provided. There are no other promises, representations, or warranties of any kind not included in this Informed Consent. If any provision is declared void or unenforceable, it shall not affect the validity or enforceability of any other provisions.

12. By signing this Informed Consent, the Family hereby releases, acquits, discharges, indemnifies, and holds harmless the Therapist from any and all actions, claims, demands, damages, and expenses, including attorney's fees or other legal expenses, arising from and/or in connection with the Family Healing Session provided by the Therapist.

13. The Therapist shall not be bound by any term or condition contained herein, until the agreement between the parties hereto, has been signed by all parties.

14. The Therapist is an Independent Contractor and this agreement does not create an employee/employer relationship. The Family will not withhold any taxes or other deductions from monies due Therapist.

15. This constitutes the entire agreement between the Therapist and the Family.

16. The persons signing below warrant that they have the authority to bind the two parties.

The signatures below confirm that the parties have read and agree to all terms and conditions contained herein.

Family Name: _____   Therapist Name: _____

Family Representative Signature: _____

Date: _____

Therapist's signature: _____

Date: _____

DAY FIVE

3 – Family History Questionnaire for Parents

I email this Family History Questionnaire to the parents several months (minimum four weeks) prior to the FHS. I ask both the father and mother to respond to all the questions, no longer than eight (8) pages each. They must email me their answers one month to two weeks before the FHS so that I have time to review everything, create genograms, and write notes.

Section One helps you to construct the genogram for both the father and mother.

Sections Two and Three help you describe the type and quality of generational relationships.

Family History Questionnaire

Please answer all the questions, a maximum of eight typed pages (12 font size).

Section One:

1. Name your father's parents (your paternal grandfather and grandmother) and name your father's siblings in birth order from oldest to youngest, including your father. Include the year that each person was born (grandparents and siblings). Identify who is/was married to whom, and who might have passed away. Also include if there were any miscarriages, still born, abortion, or if a child died.

2. Name your mother's parents (your maternal grandfather and grandmother) and name your mother's siblings in birth order from oldest to youngest, including your mother. Include the year that each person was born (grandparents and siblings). Identify who is/was married to whom, and who might have passed away. Also include if there were any miscarriages, stillbirths, abortions, or if a child died.

3. Names, birth years, and children that your parents had (your siblings and you). List if your siblings are married, and their spouses' name(s), and number of children.

4. Include the age, name, and gender of each of your children (if you are married). If there was a miscarriage, stillbirths, abortions, or child died, please include each of them as well. List their birth order, year they were born, or passed away.

Section Two:

1. Describe the relationship between your father and his father, your father and his mother, your father and his siblings (if he had any), and your father and any other significant people in his life while he was growing up. Include the names and birth order of all your father's siblings.

2. Describe the relationship between your father's parents—past to present.

3. Where did your father's family live? Where did he grow up?

4. What was their ethnic background? What was their religious background?

5. Describe the relationship between your mother and her father, your mother and her mother, your mother and her siblings, and any other significant people in her life growing up. Include the names and birth order of all your mother's siblings.

6. Describe the relationship between your mother's parents—past to present.

7. Where did your mother's family live? Where did she grow up?

8. What was their ethnic background? Religious background?

9. Be sure to describe any major issues or events on both the paternal and maternal sides of the family, such as war experiences, immigration, sexual abuse, physical abuse, emotional-mental abuse, drug/alcohol/sexual addictions, gambling addictions, eating disorders, sexual problems, major depressions, divorce, suicide, rape, murder, theft, autism, abortions, homosexuality, adoption, moving, etc.

Section Three:

1. Describe your relationship with your father—past (from your earliest memories) to the present (current-day relationship).

2. Describe your father's personality—past to present.

3. Describe your father's education, employment history, and religious history.

4. Describe your relationship with your mother—past to present.

5. Describe your mother's personality—past to present.

6. Describe your mother's education, employment history, and religious history.

7. Describe the relationship between your father and mother—past to present.

8. Describe your relationship with your siblings (if you have any)—past to present.

9. Describe your siblings' personalities.

10. Describe your relationship with any other significant people in or out of your family system (e.g., grandmother, grandfather, uncle, cousin, neighbor, stepparent).

11. What was your role in the family system (e.g., hero, pleaser, clown, rebel, substitute spouse, golden child, caretaker, loner, scapegoat, peacemaker)?

12. Describe your school history—academically and socially, past to present.

13. Describe your sexual history—from your earliest memories to the present. Include all references to sex and sexuality, in or outside of the family. Have you or your spouse had any affairs or sex outside your relationship?

14. Describe your spouse, and his/her personality. Succinctly describe your relationship—from the past to the present.

15. Describe your children and their personalities. What issues are they experiencing?

16. Describe your religious history—past to present.

17. Describe yourself—how you see yourself today.

18. List any other significant issues about your life or your family that were not covered in these questions, such as health issues, marriage issues, extramarital affairs, career issues, money issues, and previous treatment or therapy.

19. How do you feel about your body? Are you pleased with how you look? Has this changed over time?

20. List your current and past employment history, and your age.

21. Please list your goals for the FHS.

4 – Protocol

Before the Family Healing Session:

1. Prepare copies of the following for each family member:
   a. The Feelings Wheel
   b. Layers of Our Personality chart
   c. Causes of Wounding in Men & Women chart
   d. Communication Skills (sharing and listening)

2. Instruct all family members to wear comfortable clothes. Women should wear pants (no dresses or skirts).

3. If you meet in the morning, tell them to eat a light breakfast. Recommend they not drink caffeinated drinks or eat sweets (sugar) for the two days of the FHS. Ask them to prepare plenty of water for everyone (unless the FHS takes place in your office; then you need to prepare water, lunch, and healthy snacks for the breaks).

4. Have them prepare lunch in advance so they don't need to leave the house or to cook.

5. Tell the parents to enroll their children into the FHS by saying something like, "This is for all of us to get closer. It is not about you, it's about us. We want to take responsibility for our past mistakes and shortcomings as parents. This will be a wonderful opportunity for family healing. Please do it for us." In this way, the designated "problem child" will not feel like it's about him or her. The real purpose is for the entire family to resolve issues/conflicts and create greater love and intimacy.

6. I recommend to the parents: "You will receive the maximum benefit from the Family Healing Session if all your children participate." It is also fine if any of their children's spouses wish to attend. Everyone is a part of the family system and will grow significantly from the FHS. If a woman is pregnant, it is fine for her to attend. When a family member is expressing strong emotions, instruct her to tell the unborn child, "This is not about you. It's about ____ (person's name). She or he is expressing how she or he feels, and that is a good thing. I love you, and you are safe." I have had children from 10+ years attending the FHS.

During the Family Healing Session:

- Take breaks throughout the day as necessary.
- Have lots of water available.
- Cell phones are turned off during the FHS and placed in a box or bowl. The phones are not returned until the end of each day. Strongly suggest that no one use their cell phone during lunch or breaks.

The amount of time for a FHS will depend upon several variables: 1) the number of family members, 2) how many unresolved issues there are, and 3) the willingness of each family member to share honestly his or her thoughts, feelings, and needs. Over the past thirty-five years, a FHS is generally two eight-hour days; sometimes we go over the eight-hour day if necessary. If you or the family doesn't have that much time, sometimes a mini-one-day family session may work.

FHS Protocol for Facilitators

Richard Cohen, M.A., © 2023

As the therapist/coach/counselor, bring your computer, or some paper, and take notes throughout the day. This will help you remember what occurred, and what each family member needs. This is important for the conclusion of the FHS when you will give each person, and the entire family, homework assignments.

[If we are doing the FHS in their family home, I have already instructed the things that the parents need to prepare in advance, i.e., water, healthy snacks, lunch, pounding pillows, sheets to wrap around the chair, tennis racquet, exercise gloves, etc.]

1. I fly to the city one day before the FHS and give myself time to get settled and prepare. Later in my career, I had the families fly to my area and did the FHS in my office.

2. First day of the FHS we begin at 9 am. I arrive 30 minutes early (if it's in the family's home) to prepare the room—make sure that everyone has a chair or sofa to sit on. We remove tables so there is a circle of chairs/sofas with no furniture in the center.

3. Lead therapist shares (for example), "I have been a psychotherapist/coach with 35 years' experience. The Family Healing Session is a wonderful opportunity to resolve personal and relational issues, and to create greater love and intimacy within the family."

[If a child or another family member experiences a particular (sexual) issue, I never discuss or address this. It is all about healing, intimacy, and love.]

"This is a safe space for everyone. Your feelings, thoughts, and needs are the most important things during this FHS. Everything that is shared, expressed, and experienced during the FHS is completely confidential."

[If there is a co-facilitator, then s/he introduces themselves.]

[Additionally, all the following items and exercises are divided—sometimes the lead therapist guides, other times the co-facilitator leads. This will be discussed and prepared well before the FHS.]

4. Introduce a no Cell Phone policy. Collect all mobile phones and place them in a bowl. Explain that they will get their phones back at the end of the day (unless someone has an emergency or childcare issue to deal with during a break; generally no one uses their phones until the end of the day).

5. Ask if there are any questions.

6. Hand out The Feelings Wheel to each family member and ask:
   - "Please share two feeling words, how you are feeling right now. Then describe what is behind your feelings. After that, please express your hopes, desires, and expectations for the Family Healing Session."
   - Then we go around the circle and each person shares.

7. I do the following exercise if I think it may be helpful. Many times I will introduce this exercise later (on day two), or not at all. It depends upon how open and ready the family is for healing.
   - I hand out the Layers of Our Personality chart for each person.
   - After explaining the chart (you may read an explanation of this chart on pages 48-51 of *Healing Humanity: Time, Touch and Talk*), I ask all the family members to put a circle around each issue that she or he has resolved. Then he or she puts a rectangle around issues that he or she is still dealing with. [Put beautiful music on while they do this…perhaps about 10 minutes.]
   - After they are finished I say, "We need to be real, and feel, in order to heal. This is a safe place. All of your thoughts, feelings, and needs are welcome here. It is a judgment-free zone, and everything is strictly confidential."
   - Then begin: go around the room, starting from Mom, Dad, oldest to youngest child. Each one shares their realizations and reflections based on the chart.

8. After finishing this exercise, we move the chairs from a circle to form a half circle.

9. Once again I repeat, "All of your thoughts, feelings, and needs are welcome here. I will help protect each one of you to make it safe for you to share your truth. This is a precious opportunity to resolve unspoken issues and experience greater love and intimacy."

10. [Facilitator or co-facilitator leads.] The mother sits in front of the family (half circle with her children and husband facing her). Ask her to tell her life story, what she shared in the family history questionnaire (focus on what the children DO NOT know). If she is stuck, I ask about her about the relationships with her grandparents, parents, siblings, etc. This helps the children understand her belief system and why she is like she is.

During the process of her sharing, if she experiences powerful feelings (grief, sadness, pain, anger, etc.), then you may assist her in expressing these feelings more deeply, using different therapeutic techniques, i.e., Bioenergetics (you can simply put a sofa pillow on a chair for her to hit), Role Play (have her husband play the role of her father, mother, etc.), Inner Child (she can speak to her inner child), etc.

[I always prepare the parents well in advance of the FHS: "The more open and vulnerable you are, the easier it will be for your children to share their truth."]

After she finishes, if any of the children have questions for her, then she may answer. Then ask the children how they experienced her sharing? "Was there anything that you learned, any new insights?" Go around the circle and let the husband and children share how that was for them.

11. Then the father changes chairs with his wife and he tells his story.
    Follow the same protocol as you did with the mother…

12. Usually this may take us up to lunch. Take a one-hour (or 45 minute) break for lunch. It should be prepared in advance. We have lunch in the family's house, or in my home office (ordered and prepared). Never go out for lunch. This breaks the safe container. [Once again, no cell phone use during the lunch break.]

After Lunch

We start with the amended Welch protocol below.
[If there is limited time for the FHS, I omit the mother and father sharing their life stories and begin with this protocol.]

13. We always start with the mother and father sharing with each other. Have them stand up, look into each other's eyes, and put their arms around each other. The father's arms are above and the mother's arms are below his. They stand chest-to-chest, to establish a heart-to-heart connection.

If at any time the couple, or parent and child (when it's their turn), gets tired from standing, then we switch to having them sit across from each other holding hands, looking into each other's eyes, and with their knees touching.

When it's time for the parents to share with their children, the parents' arms are on top and their child's arms below; this establishes the natural parent-child relationship whereby the parent is giving and taking care of the child, and the child is receiving.

First, we start with the mother sharing with her husband standing (or sitting) across from each other, arms around each other (or holding hands), and looking into each other's eyes. Once again, if they are standing (I always begin in this position unless someone has a physical disability), the father's arms are always around his wife on top, and the mother's arms are always below his.

The children are sitting in the half-circle of chairs or on the sofa(s), watching their parents. During the parents sharing, keep an eye on the children to understand their reaction(s). If any of them disengage, begins to fall asleep, or checks out, gently put your hand on their shoulder and ask him or her to give his or her parents their full attention. Dr. Welch would have the children by the side of the parents and connect through some form of healthy touch, i.e. their hands supporting Mom and/or Dad. However, we don't follow that protocol these days. We have them sit around their parents and make sure that the children are attentive and engaged.

14. Instruct the mother to begin:
    a. "The first time I saw you…"
        She begins by sharing how she felt and thought when she first met her husband.
        She shares things that she liked/loved about her husband at the beginning of their relationship.
        If she has no specific positive memories, have her close her eyes, feel his touch, and remember the wonderful times before and at the beginning of their marriage.
        Then have her share things that she appreciates, likes, and loves about her husband.
    b. "The things that hurt/irritate me are…"
        Now she begins to share things that he did/does that hurt her.
        Make sure she continues to look into his eyes (of course, when someone is processing deeper thoughts and feelings, she may look away in order to get in touch with what she is thinking or feeling).
    c. If she gets stuck in her head, and/or her sharing is shallow or superficial, have her close her eyes and begin to repeat her husband's name, e.g., "Sam," "Sam," "Sam." Have her take a deep breath before she speaks his name each time.
        This allows her to go deeper into her psyche and get in touch with suppressed or repressed thoughts and feelings.
        If this approach doesn't work, you can step in, take her place (role-playing the wife), and speak from your heart (to the husband) so that she can see what honest sharing looks like, e.g., "I feel hurt when I don't get your attention. I feel so small and hurt by your harsh words. It reminds me of earlier times when my father would scream. I have a real need for your kindness and loving words. As things are now, I feel empty and afraid." Demonstrate sharing from the heart. Then have her step back into her place.
        When she starts to feel her feelings, you can gently tell her just to express them, without reservation, and if necessary, without words, just let the feelings out while she is holding her husband.
        [Other times, rather than standing in for the mother, ask the children to stand and put their hands on their mother, and tell her to get real. For example, "We know how hurt you are by Dad. You have told us so many times. You cried a lot. Tell him your truth! Be real."]
        You can always shift the parents, from sitting to standing or standing to sitting if that seems most helpful to resolve issues and create greater intimacy.
        After she finishes with the hurtful thoughts and feelings, then she expresses her needs: "I would feel so much better if I heard you say, 'I really love you.' Criticism drives a wedge between you and me. Also, I would love to go out on dates."
    d. After she finishes with the hurtful thoughts and feelings, then she apologizes for things that she feels bad about: "Would you please forgive me for…" Her husband does not respond now. He will have a chance to share next.

e. Finally, she concludes with:

   "I love and appreciate you for…"

   Have her once again thank him for his love and all the good things that he has done, is doing, and what he means to her.

   They finish with a long kiss (if the couple is capable of this; some are too distant and detached from each other.)

15. Next it is the husband's turn … he follows the same protocol as the mother.

    Some parents take me aside and ask, "If I really say how much I don't like my wife/husband, won't this hurt them?" I respond, "First of all, your children already know this. You don't have to say it in words. Within the family, everyone is connected on a very deep emotional and psychic level. Secondly, it will allow your children to breathe and feel relieved. They always feel responsible when their parents (who are in the position of Mr. & Mrs. God—the masculine and feminine nature of God) fight and argue. This will bless them. So, feel free to share your genuine thoughts and feelings. It will also give your children permission to express their truth with you. You lead by example. If you want them to be real, feel, and heal, demonstrate what it looks like."

16. When both mother and father are finished sharing, they turn their chairs and face their children. Then I ask each child to share how that was for him or her: "How was that for you? Is there anything that you learned and didn't know before?"

    After the children share, take a (short) break. There should be healthy snacks prepared in advance, i.e., fruit, nuts (no sugary foods, no caffeine during the FHS). Make sure there is lots of water for everyone to drink throughout the FHS. Once again, no caffeinated drinks. Water is best.

17. Now we begin with the parents sharing with their children, and children sharing with their parents, starting from the oldest to the youngest child.

    a. Mother shares with the oldest child:

       They are standing face-to-face with their arms around each other (always the parent's arms above and the child's arms below; this establishes the natural parent-child relationship whereby the parent is giving and taking care of the child, and the child is receiving), or if they insist on, or have a physical problem, sit across from each other, hold hands, and look into each other's eyes.

       Throughout the mother's sharing with her child, the father is standing by their side with one arm around his wife, and one arm around his child. This creates a connection between all three of them and demonstrates the father's support of his wife and child. If the mother and child are sitting, the father sits by their side and puts his arm around each one.

       ○ The mother starts by telling her son or daughter how she felt and thought about him or her from the time of conception, until today, sharing about her memories throughout his or her youth until the present time. "I remember when I got pregnant. I was the happiest woman alive! We wanted a child so much…" "When I had you, you were the most wonderful baby…" She continues sharing about him/her from birth to the present day. [If time is limited, you may need to ask her to hit the highlights. If she shares very little, ask her to go deeper and remember beautiful things about her child.]

- ○ Next the mother shares about things she likes and loves about him/her. "You are such a gifted young man. I admire how tenacious you are about everything you set your mind to do…"
- ○ Then she shares about things that she doesn't like about him/her. "It really hurts me when you say such sorrowful things about yourself and put yourself down. It breaks my heart…" "I don't like it when you shout at me and then walk out and shut your door. I really wish you would stay and engage in meaningful conversation so we can work things out," etc.
- ○ Then she apologizes for her mistakes, things that she regrets she did or didn't do. *[I forgot to mention this during the filming. Please be sure to include this in the protocol—when parents or children apologize to one another.]* "I am so sorry that I wasn't there for you when you were hurting each time Dad and I were arguing. I can't imagine how it made you feel. Would you please forgive me? I apologize from the bottom of my heart." It's important for the parents to show their feelings. It gives their children permission to share their deeper thoughts and feelings. We, as parents, lead by example.
- ○ Afterwards, she concludes by saying how much she loves and appreciates him/her. "I love you with all my heart. You are the most amazing son a mother could hope for…"

NOTE: Make sure the mother stays in her adult self and doesn't speak from her wounded inner child (gets into her "poor me" mode); otherwise, the son or daughter will feel insecure and will be unable to receive her sharing. Many times I have had to bring the parent back into their adult-self.

Finish with a hug, kiss, and the mother saying, "I love you."

18. The oldest child now shares with his/her mother:
    - S/he follows the same protocol, starting from the earliest memories until the present day.
    - S/he says things that s/he likes and loves about his/her mother.
    - Next s/he shared about things that s/he is upset about.
    - This is followed by apologies for things that s/he did that may have hurt her/his mother. If s/he has any regrets, let him/her apologize and ask for forgiveness. *[Once again, I forgot to mention this during the filming. Please be sure to include this in the protocol.]*
    - Finally share about gratitudes and appreciation.
    - Finish with "I love you," a hug and a kiss.
      [During the process, if the child has a lot of anger, let him separate from his mother, and do some bioenergetics, pounding out his anger into the pillow. Direct him to be specific with things that hurt him.]

19. Father now shares with the oldest child:

   They are standing face-to-face with their arms around each other (always the parent's arms above and the child's arms below; this establishes the natural parent-child relationship whereby the parent is giving and taking care of the child, and the child is receiving), or if they insist or have a physical problem, sit across from each other, hold hands, and look into each other's eyes.

   Throughout the father's sharing with his child, the mother is standing by their side with one arm around her husband, and one arm around her child. This creates a connection between all three of them, and demonstrates the mother's support of her husband and child. If the father and child are sitting, the mother sits by their side and puts her arm around each one.

   - The father starts by telling his son or daughter how he felt and thought about him or her from the time of conception, until today, sharing about his memories throughout his or her youth until the present time.
   "I remember when mom got pregnant. I was the happiest man alive! We wanted a child so much…" "When we had you, you were the most wonderful baby…" He continues sharing about him/her from birth to the present day. [If time is limited, you may need to ask him to hit the highlights. If he shares very little, ask him to go deeper and remember beautiful things about his child.]
   - Next he shares about things he likes and loves about him/her. "You are such a gifted young man. I admire how tenacious you are about everything you set your mind to do…"
   - Then he shares about things that he doesn't like about him/her. "It really hurts me when you say such sorrowful things about yourself, and put yourself down. It breaks my heart…" "I don't like it when you shout at me and then walk out and shut your door. I really wish you would stay and engage in meaningful conversation so we can work things out," etc.
   - Then he apologizes for his mistakes, things that he regrets he did or didn't do. *[I forgot to mention this during the filming. Please be sure to include this in the protocol—when parents or children apologize to one another.]* "I am so sorry that I wasn't there for you when you were hurting each time Mom and I were arguing. I can't imagine how it made you feel. Please forgive me. I apologize from the bottom of my heart." It's important for the parents to show their feelings. It gives their children permission to share their deeper thoughts and feelings. We, as parents, lead by example.
   - Afterwards, he concludes by saying how much he loves and appreciates him/her. "I love you with all my heart. You are the most amazing son a father could hope for. I am committed to supporting you. I will do my best to make changes so you feel loved and supported."
   NOTE: Make sure the father stays in his adult self and doesn't speak from his wounded inner child; otherwise, the son or daughter will feel insecure and will be unable to receive his sharing. Many times I have had to bring the parent back into their adult-self.
   - Finish with a hug, kiss, and the father saying, "I love you."

20. Oldest child shares with father:
    Now it is time for the son/daughter to share with his/her father.
    Follow the same protocol as the child shared with his/her mother.

21. Group sharing when the mother-child & father-child are finished:
    After each sharing is finished (mother-child / father-child), they turn their chairs (or sit in the chairs), face the family and everyone shares about it—how the sharing/processing impacted them. Many wonderful things occur when everyone is involved, speaking their truth.

    The same the protocol continues with each parent-child, the next oldest until the youngest. The mother shares first, then the child, and then the father shares, followed by the child.

    Group sharing follows when each parent-child pair is finished (mother-child & father-child), if you sense there is enough time. If there are too many children, then you may omit the group sharing in between each parent-child pair.

    Take breaks as necessary, but don't let the breaks last too long or the healing energy/atmosphere will dissipate. Often during the breaks, they may wish to use their mobile phones. DO NOT allow this...

    The parent-child sharing usually finishes on the first day. If you didn't finish with the parent-child sharing on the first day, then continue with this the next morning.

    At the close of day one, you may suggest that the children not go out socializing that evening, as they may drink, stay out late, and therefore be unfocused for day two. Ask them to refrain from nighttime social activities until the FHS is finished the next day. Recommend that they all stay home in the evening and share more deeply, or just stay quiet in their own space. Forewarn them that having a headache after such healing work is normal. Their emotional system was stirred up—feelings buried alive never die. It's OK if someone needs to take Aspirin or Tylenol or something for their headache during the evening (on rare occasions, if someone's headache is too much to tolerate, I let them take an Aspirin or Tylenol during the session).

Day Two

1. Start with a check-in: Everyone shares two feeling word check-in, what's behind their feelings, and any issues that came up for him or her during the nighttime. Go around the circle, either oldest to youngest, or youngest to oldest.

2. Are there any questions, comments, or needs?

3. Continue with parent-child sharing if that was not completed the day before. Use the same protocol as listed above.

4. Next you will begin the same process of sharing, this time with the children, starting from the oldest child, who will share with each sibling, from the next-to-oldest sibling, to the youngest.

a. Generally, I have them stand in a circle (sometimes sit in a circle). They are all holding hands and looking into each other's eyes when they share.

   The oldest shares first with the next-to-the-oldest child.
   - S/he shares wonderful and fun memories from the earliest memories to the present day. If time is limited, have her/him share highlights of childhood fun memories. This is generally an enjoyable experience with laughter and joy.
   - Next, s/he shares things that hurt her/him.
   - After that, s/her expresses regrets and apologizes for mistakes made.
   - Finish with "I love you," a hug, and a kiss (if that's culturally appropriate and/or a family tradition).

b. Then that next-to-the-oldest child responds to the oldest sibling…in the same manner, using the same protocol:
   - Fun memories…
   - Hurtful things…
   - Regrets/apologies/Forgiveness, etc.
   - Love and appreciation…hug and a kiss (if that's appropriate to this family)

c. Next, the oldest child shares with the third child using the exact same protocol as above. And the third child shares with the oldest.

d. If there are more children, the oldest continues, and the others respond.

e. Once the eldest child has shared with each of his/her younger siblings, then the next-to-the-eldest child begins sharing with each of his/her younger siblings, one at a time, following the same protocol. If there are more than 3 children, then the 3rd child will share with each younger sibling, following the same protocol. This process continues until each sibling has shared with the others.

f. If there is not enough time for all the children to do this entire protocol, I have each one just share one fun memory from childhood, one hurtful memory, share what they don't like about the other, ask forgiveness for mistakes that s/he made, and finish with "I love you" and a hug (and a kiss).

g. If one of the children's spouse (or spouses) is (are) present, then s/he has an opportunity to share with her/his in-laws any unresolved issues. [I have seen this to be most beautiful.]

h. While the children are sharing with each other, the parents are sitting by each other, supporting each other, and witnessing their children's sharing.

i. When all the children have finished, ask them to sit in a circle, look into each other's eyes, and silently thank each other (with their eyes) for what was shared, and the healing that occurred. Then go around the circle and each child (from oldest to the youngest) expresses two feeling words and one sentence about what their feelings are about.

   Note: If there is or are major issue(s) between any of the kids that need to be addressed, then pull them out of the circle, and allow them to process this with both Mom and Dad standing by their sides supporting them. This, of course, will take more time. As always you must be mindful of how much time is remaining. Never leave out the rest of the children. If the issue is too much to handle during this session, you will need to make arrangements for a follow-up session, or more in-depth therapy for them.

Take a break after all the children have shared.

Be sure to leave at least 1½ hours at the end of the FHS for homework and the check-out process.

5. Teach Communication Skills:
Give each family member the Communication Skills handout (sharing and listening). Teach them how to share and listen effectively. Have them practice with each other in dyads. Choose key skills for them to practice. After they finish, have them all come back into the circle, and ask how it went. Field questions and explain further if necessary.

6. Homework (play beautiful music in the background):
Give homework assignments: What's next for personal and relational growth and healing. You may recommend specific books for homework.
[You as the therapist/counselor/coach need to have been preparing the homework assignments throughout the FHS, based on each person's wounds and unmet needs. I often do this in the evening after Day One, and update throughout Day Two.]

7. Example of homework assignments:
   a. Parents go on weekly dates. Be specific. One week he chooses what they'll do. The next week she decides what they will do.
   b. Use The Feelings Wheel daily. Parents and children share with each other, perhaps during the family meal, while driving in the car to school, before bedtime, etc.
   c. Everyone practices communication skills ___ number of times per week.
   d. Father becomes head of the family (if he abdicated parenting to mom).
   e. Father spends specific times per week with the neglected child, sharing, holding, etc., and the mother spends time with another child(ren), etc.
   f. Set love in order: if the mother is too close to her son, the father will now become closer to his son, etc.
   g. Do the exercises in *Recovery of Your Inner Child* first, *Self-Parenting* second, and then *Ten Days to Self-Esteem*. Share their homework with each other one day per week. (Books and authors are listed below.)
   h. Everyone gets together weekly, or bi-weekly, and shares their thoughts, feelings, and needs. (If some children live in different cities/countries, they can meet via Skype, Zoom, Google Hangout, FaceTime, etc.). Have them schedule a specific day and time, otherwise, it most likely will not happen. Take advantage of the momentum. Set up a regular family time to share.

    i. Give each child homework assignments based on their wounds and unmet love needs.

8. Check-out:
Each one shares two feeling words, and how they experienced the FHS: "How do you feel now as opposed to when we first started?" Each one shares 2-5 minutes (again, be sensitive to finishing on time—always respect your own time and their schedule. No messiah's required!).

9. Schedule a follow-up session (part of the same fee) with all the family members one month after the FHS (in-person or video conferencing).
During the follow-up session, check in with everyone and see how they are doing with their homework assignments. You may need to modify their homework based on circumstances and their schedules, i.e. work, school, travel, etc. I start the follow-up session with a two feeling words check-in, what's behind their feelings, and if they have any requests/needs for this session.

After the follow-up session, you may set up individual sessions with the parents to continue counseling them (then you may begin to charge for these sessions). Additionally, some may desire to have follow-up family sessions.

<u>Suggested Books:</u>
Real Love in Marriage or *Real Love*, Greg Baer
Recovery of Your Inner Child, Lucia Capacchione
Self-Parenting, John Pollard
Ten Days to Self-Esteem, David Burns
Mind Over Mood, Dennis Greenberger and Christine Padesky
Boundaries, Henry Cloud

<u>Preparing children for dating:</u>
Conscious Dating, David Steele

COUNSELOR TRAINING PROGRAM MANUAL

Feelings Wheel

Feelings when your needs are not met

Feelings when your needs are met

Outer ring (needs not met): Aggravated, Upset, Resentful, Irritated, Jealous, Animosity, Enraged, Furious, Reluctant, Uninterested, Bored, Sickened, Nauseous, Scorn, Hateful, Suspicious, Apprehensive, Concerned, Worried, Helpless, Susceptible, Frightened, Terrified, Shocked, Amazed, Preoccupied, Hesitant, Stunned, Stressed, Confused, Puzzled, Hopeless, Fatigued/Tired, Miserable, Despair, Heartbroken, Devastated, Discouraged, Disappointed, Self-conscious, Uncomfortable, Regretful, Remorseful, Mortified, Horrified, Chagrined, Flustered

Middle ring (needs not met): Frustrated, Annoyed, Envious, Mad, Averse, Apathetic, Repulsive, Contempt, Insecure, Anxious, Vulnerable, Scared, Astonished, Distracted, Startled, Overwhelmed, Depressed, Pain & Hurt, Grief & Sorrow, Unhappy, Awkward, Guilty, Embarrassed, Humiliation

Inner ring (needs not met): Angry (judgment), Disgusted (repulsion), Afraid (threatened), Surprised (caught off guard), Sad (loss), Ashamed (self-judgment)

Inner ring (needs met): Proud (self-acceptance), Joyful (gain), Intrigued (attentive), Trusting (security), Loving (attraction), Peaceful (acceptance)

Middle ring (needs met): Self-Confident, Self-Esteem, Encouraged, Powerful, Happy, Ecstatic, Excited, Grateful, Engaged, Fascinated, Entranced, Energetic, Assured, Hopeful, Secure, Confident, Affectionate, Adoration, Connected, Caring, Content, Relaxed, Tranquil, Harmonious

Outer ring (needs met): Poised, Self-Assured, Fulfilled, Pleased, Brave, Courageous, Empowered, Effectual, Delighted, Glad-Pleased, Elated, Thrilled, Enthusiastic, Passionate, Appreciation, Thankful, Absorbed, Engrossed, Interested, Curious, Captivated, Mesmerized, Animated, Refreshed, Positive, Relieved, Optimistic, Expectant, Safe, Comforted, Certain, Convinced, Friendly, Fondness, Admiration, Reverence, Close, Intimate, Compassionate, Tenderness, Satisfied, Comfortable, Serene, Calm, Quiet, Centered, Congruous, Balanced

Based on Nonviolent Communication by Marshall Rosenberg, Ph.D. May be duplicated for personal use and for teaching Nonviolent Communication. Graphics and organization of feelings and needs wheels by Bret Stein. artisantf@hotmail.com Revised 1/1/11

Feelings are <u>internal</u> emotions. Words mistaken for emotions, but that are actually thoughts in the form of evaluations and judgments of others, are any words that follow "I feel like ... " or "I feel that ..." or "I feel as if ... " or "I feel you ...", such as:

Abandoned	Attacked	Abused	Betrayed	Blamed	Bullied	Cheated
Coerced	Criticized	Dismissed	Disrespected	Excluded	Ignored	Intimidated
Insulted	Let Down	Manipulated	Misunderstood	Neglected	Put down	Rejected
Unappreciated	Unloved	Unheard	Unwanted	Used	Violated	Wronged

DAY FIVE

LAYERS OF OUR PERSONALITY

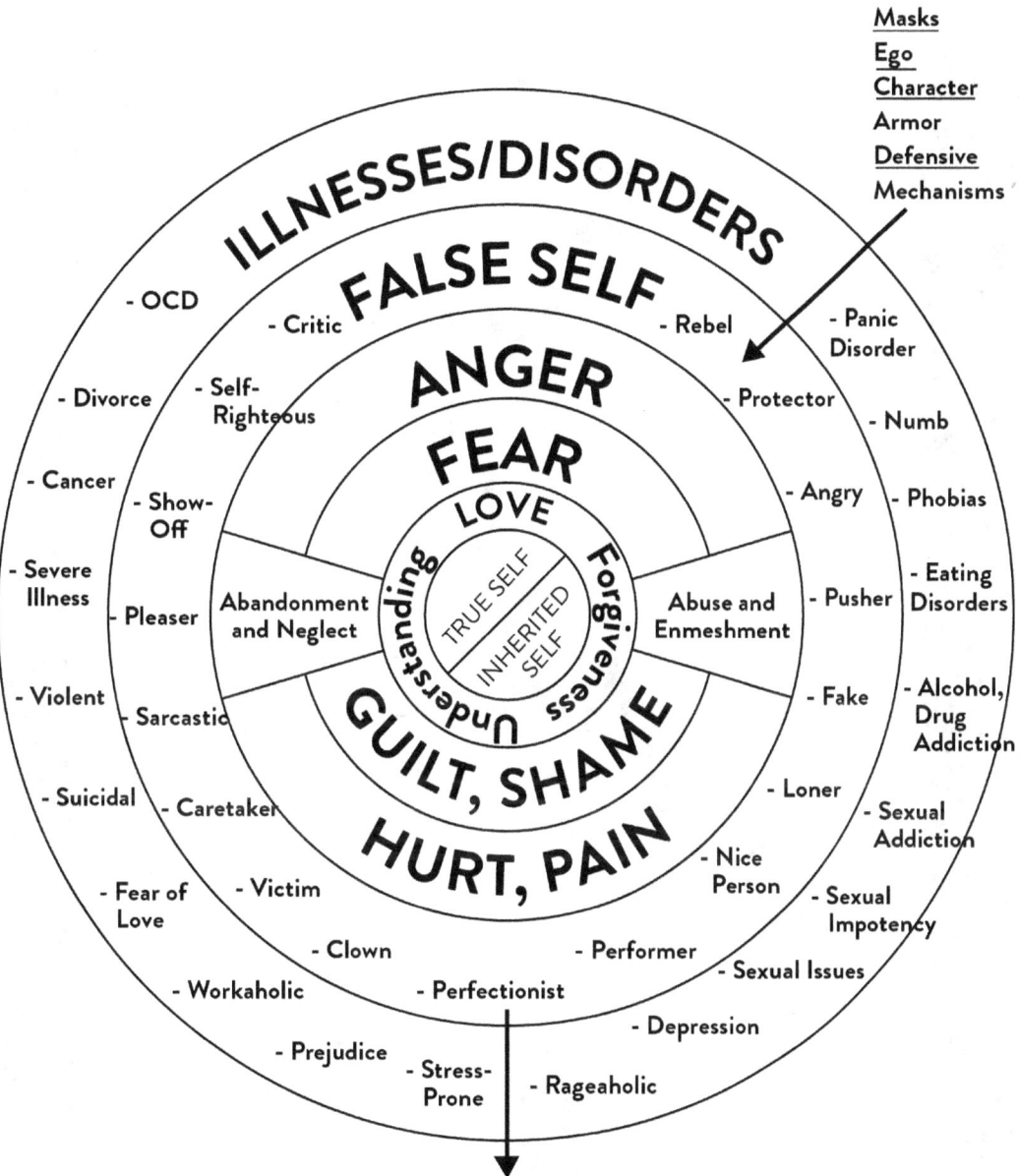

Affection, Affirmation, Acceptance

Richard Cohen, M.A. © 2023

Potential Causes of Wounding in Men & Women

Heredity	Temperament	Hetero-Emotional Wounds	Homo-Emotional Wounds	Sibling Wounds/ Family Dynamics	Body Image Wounds	Sexual Abuse	Social or Peer Wounds	Cultural Influences	Others Factors
Generational blessings and curses	Hypersensitive	Over-attachment to opposite-sex parent	Over-attachment to same-sex parent	Abuse: mental, emotional, physical, and/or sexual	Late bloomer	Premature sexualization	Name-calling	Internet porn	Divorce
Unresolved family issues	Artistic	Lack of attachment to opposite-sex parent	Lack of attachment to same-sex parent	Don't fit in	Physical disabilities	Heterosexual or homosexual imprinting	Put-downs	Media/Entertainment Industry promoting sex	Death
Men resenting women, women resenting men	Four temperaments: Sanguine Choleric Melancholic Phlegmatic	Abuse: mental, emotional, physical, and/or sexual	Abuse: mental, emotional, physical, and/or sexual	Don't belong	Shorter / Taller	Learned/ reinforced behavior	Teacher's pet	Sexualizing legitimate needs for love	Suicide
Addictions: substances, sex, gambling	Enneagram	Parentified child: role reversal between parent and child	Parentified child: role reversal between parent and child	Different from others	Heavier / Thinner	Sex used as a substitute for love	Goody-goody		Addictions: alcohol, drugs, sex, gambling, etc.
Medical/Mental health issues	Extrovert / Introvert			Bullying / verbal abuse	Skin color issues		Nerd		Intra-uterine experience: insecure attachment
Financial problems							Non-athletic		Adoption
Predilection for rejection							Lack of gender identification and/or gender non-conforming behaviors		War/genocide
Racial, religious, ethnic prejudice									Religion: toxic beliefs

The severity of wounding in each category will have a direct impact on the amount of time and effort it will take to heal.

© Richard Cohen, M.A., 2019

DAY FIVE

Communication Skills – Effective Listening

1. **Maintain eye contact:** When standing or sitting across from another person, be sure to look her straight in the eyes. This creates your first connection, and lets her know that you are attentive to what she is saying.
2. **Join together.** Rather than give advice or your opinion, stand in her shoes. As you listen, seek to understand her viewpoint. This will take practice as you need to quiet your own thoughts and opinions. Join in her world.
3. **Observe.** Take note of her body language, tone, and words. Research has shown that body language and tone generally say more than the spoken word. Observe her posture, her gestures, and her facial expressions. Are her arms crossed around her chest, or relaxed at her side? Is her face joyful or upset? Listen to the tone of her voice. Is she saying one thing and yet speaking another message through her tone and with her body language? Listen with your eyes, your mind, and your heart.
4. **Practicing reflective listening:**

As suggested by Dr. Harville Hendrix, here is a threefold technique to teach the art of reflective listening:

First: Mirror or paraphrase his communication. After listening to a few sentences, you may say,
"If I heard you correctly, you said that you were upset that I do not greet you with a hug and a kiss when you come home from work. Did I get it? Is there more?"

Continue to listen and paraphrase, listen and paraphrase every few sentences. If he goes on for too long, gently interrupt and say, "Dear, if I heard you correctly, you said…" If you get something wrong, or forget something, don't worry, he will correct you. After his sharing is complete, then summarize all that he spoke:

"In summary, what I heard you say was that you get upset if I don't hug and kiss you when you come home from work. You really need that each night because you work very hard to provide for our family. All you need is for me to honor you in this way. Then you will feel so much better and loved. Is that the essence? Did I get it right?"

If he says, "Yes, but you forgot …" Then after he finishes, paraphrase this thought and say, "Is that it?" When he says, "Yes," then you move to the next phase.

Please do not put your thoughts, feelings, or inflection into the communication when you paraphrase. It is fine to 100% disagree with the speaker. However, you need to *join* with him and reflect what you heard. In this way, he will feel understood and respected.

Second: Validate his thoughts. Here you imagine how he is thinking based upon what you just heard. It is difficult to separate thoughts and feelings; do your best.

"You make sense to me because you worked hard all day to take care of us and simply want me to validate you with affection. Is that it? Did I get it?"

Here you have to imagine how he *thinks*. You are validating his thoughts. After you finish say, "Is that right?" If it's wrong, don't worry; he will correct you. Then paraphrase what he says and ask, "Is that right?"

If he affirms your understanding of his thinking, then you finish with:

Third: Empathize with his feelings, using simple feeling words (you may refer to the Feelings Wheel).

"Given all that, I imagine you feel hurt, frustrated, and sad. Are those your feelings?"

Wait for him to confirm or amend your suggested simple feeling words.

"Yes, but I also felt upset and mad."

Finish with validating his new feeling words. "I see, you also felt upset and mad. Is that it?"
"Yes, thank you for listening and understanding me. I appreciate you very much." You have successfully heard what he was saying.

During reflective listening, you do not have to agree with what the speaker is saying. The important thing is to hear and validate him. Most of the time, we do not need advice; we just need to be heard. When you are paraphrasing, make sure *not* to interject with a sarcastic tone. As best as you can, use the same tone as the speaker. If you use a sarcastic tone, this will invalidate everything he shared. Remember, you don't need to agree, just listen and paraphrase. This takes a lot of practice and patience. As one of my clients brilliantly stated, "I would rather be in relationship than be right."

Reflective listening is learning to walk in the other person's shoes, seeing life through his eyes. And, if you wish to respond to what he just shared, you must ask his permission when you finish the three-step reflective listening process. "Would you like to hear my thoughts?" If he says "Yes," proceed. If he says, "No," then that's it. The communication loop is complete.

5. **Use the magic words**: "Thank you, (person's name), tell me more." If you are too upset by his words, and you cannot paraphrase what he is saying, then simply say, "Thank you (his name), tell me more." This is such a simple, yet effective listening skill. Try it and you will see how great it works with family, friends, co-workers, and your boss.

6. **If all else fails, KYMS**: Keep Your Mouth Shut and just listen without comment. Be a silent witness. You can always add, "Thank you, tell me more." Use KYMS when temperatures are hot, especially yours!

7. **Silence is golden**: Silence is one of the greatest gifts you can give another person. You do not need to fill the empty moments with words or questions. Just "be" with her. It will allow her to know that you are "there" for her, and it gives her the opportunity to go deeper.

8. **Don't look at your watch while she is talking**: Do it when you are speaking.

DAY FIVE

Communication Skills – Effective Sharing

1. **Use "I" statements, not "You" statements:**
   Own your thoughts, feelings, and needs.
   Do not say: "You shouldn't speak to me that way."
   Say: "I don't like it when you speak to me that way."
   Speak in the first person…
   Do not say: "You upset me when you did…"
   Say: "I get upset when you…"

   Important use of "I" statements: In the USA, we are taught from elementary school to speak in the second person, that it is selfish to begin sentences with "I think…" or "I believe…" or "I feel…" We are also taught to write in a similar manner.

   Each time you use an "I" statement instead of "You" statements when referring to your own experience, you step into your personal power and begin to know thyself more intimately. Begin to listen to yourself when you are sharing with others. Soon you will become aware of when you are speaking in the second person, "You" instead of "I." Slowly change and own your thoughts, feelings, and needs. "I think…" "I feel…" I need…" This is not selfish, but self-full. You are becoming a more powerful man or woman.

2. **Practice optimum effective communication:**
   a. Eye contact.
   b. Physical touch—with family, friends, and other close relationships.
   c. Responsible language—"I" statements, not "You" statements.

3. **Encourage conflict resolution:**
   Here is a five-step protocol to express your thoughts, feelings, and needs when you are upset about what someone said or did (modified from *Nonviolent Communication* by Marshall B. Rosenberg, Ph.D., and Mankind Project clearing protocol):

   First: Present the facts—what he said or did that caused you to have a strong reaction. Make it specific to this one event. Please do *not* say "You always…" or "You never…" or "Everybody says…" or "Everybody thinks…" Keep it focused on this one-time event, what he said or did. Example: "This morning before you left for work, you got angry and yelled at me."

   Second: Acknowledge your feelings—use simple feeling words (sad, mad, glad, afraid, etc.). Example: "When you raised your voice to me this morning, I felt scared, mad, and upset."

   Third: Identify the judgments and beliefs that you have about what he said or did. Here you own your projections and personal issues, how what he said or did reminds you of past issues.

Example: "When you raise your voice with me, it reminds me of my father's angry outbursts. I become like a naughty little girl."

Fourth: State your needs, desires, or wishes. Example: "I do not deserve to be spoken to in such a manner. When you are upset, would you please speak to me in a civil tone, or ask me to hold you so that I may comfort you. I appreciate that very much."

Fifth: State what you are willing to give to make the relationship work. Example: "I know that I can get upset and lose my temper as well. Therefore, let's both commit to not taking our feelings out on each other. I will ask you to hold me when I'm upset, or I will withdraw from the room to calm down. Please agree to do the same. Thank you."

Be mindful *not* to preach in the third step. No sermons on the sofa. Own your reactions to what he said or did. Make simple requests and offer the same. This conflict resolution protocol works in all personal and professional relationships. Like all communication skills, it takes lots of practice. Try using this and the other skills when things are going well, so when tempers are hot, you will be able to use it more easily.

For those who believe in Christ, he spoke of another conflict resolution protocol written about in Matthew 18:15-18. If you feel hurt by another…

1) Go to him and express your concerns (using good communication skills). If he listens and responds well, great, it's finished. However, if he is defensive and unresponsive…

2) Go to him once again, this time with one or two witnesses so that every matter may be testified as fact. If he apologizes, the matter is settled. If he still remains intractable…

3) Bring the matter to the "church," or a respected body of elders. If he listens and apologizes, finished. If he remains obstinate and unrepentant, then he is to be ignored. Wipe the dust off your feet and move on. You cannot make another person do anything that he is unwilling to do. You can only change yourself.

4. **Learn the 'Sandwich Technique':**

First: State how you feel about the relationship.

"I really care about you."

"I love you."

"I value our relationship."

Second: State the difficulty that you have with the individual. State what outcome you would like to see.

"Recently, you have been screaming at me a lot. That hurts me deeply. I feel unloved, unimportant, and rejected. I think you are under a lot of pressure, and I'm taking the blame for your frustrations. Please deal with your feelings more responsibly. Do not take them out on me. I am willing to help you in a positive way, but not be your punching bag."

Third: State once again how you feel about the relationship.

"I love you and I am committed to our relationship."

In this way, you sandwich the problem (meat of the sandwich) in between your real feelings of love (the bread). It makes it easier for the other person to receive your sharing. Again, please be responsible in all communication, using "I" statements instead of "You" statements. "I" statements mean that I take responsibility for how I think, feel, and what I need. "You" statements try to make others responsible for your wellbeing.

5. **Use "And" as a conjunction instead of "But:"**
"I think what you said is important, *and* I have a different opinion."
Now feel the difference between these two sentiments:
"I love you *but*…"
"I love you *and*…"
What a difference the "and" makes! When you use "but" as a conjunction in most sentences, you annihilate all the good that you shared previous to the "but." After hearing "but," the listener will shut down and their walls will come up. Be sure to use "and" as a conjunction in all your personal and professional communications. This includes texting and emails.
"You're a great man, but your temper scares me."
"You're a great man, and your temper scares me."

6. **Make a Reality Check:**
If you think someone is thinking something about you or another person, then ask them if this is correct or not. For example, "Are you upset with me?" "Did you mean (such and such) when you said (such and such)?"
Do not make assumptions. When I assume anything, I make an "ass" out of "u" and "me." Instead use a "reality check" if you think someone is upset with you. Here is an example of a reality check: "Were you angry with me when I saw you in the kitchen this morning?" A reality check is a litmus test about a belief or judgment that you have about another person. It helps objectify perceptions.

7. **Remember - Expectations Kill:**
Do not expect others to know what you need. It is important to learn to express your needs, rather than expect others to know what you want (expecting them to mind-read). Infants and toddlers expect us to know what they need because they are totally dependent upon the parent or caregiver for survival. As adults, we must learn to express that which we need rather than assume or expect others to know what we want, need, or desire.

8. **Ask "How" and "What" questions, not "Why" questions:**
"Why" questions send a person into her or his head, intellect. A "How" or "What" question helps her share more deeply, that which is in her heart. For example, "How was that like for you?" If you ask, "Why did you do that?" She immediately becomes more intellectual. "What did you go through?" "How did that make you feel?"

9. **Recognize Triangulation:**

   If someone is upset with another person and shares with you about it, that is called triangulation. A is upset with B. Instead of A sharing directly with B about his grievance, he goes to C and shares about his consternation about B. Now C is triangulated between A & B, put in an impossible lose-lose situation. Here is a simple solution to this conundrum. When A shares with you about his being upset with B, simply say, "I know that you are upset with B, I hear you, I understand. Honestly this issue is between the two of you. Please share directly with B about your thoughts, feelings, and needs. Thank you very much." Finished. It is not your job to save anyone else. It is not healthy or appropriate for you to be involved in their communication. Saviors not wanted!

About the Author

Richard Cohen, M.A., is a psychotherapist, educator, and author who travels throughout the United States, Europe, Latin America and the Middle East teaching about marital relations, parenting skills, healing from sexual abuse, and understanding gender identity and sexual orientation issues. Over the past 35 years, he has helped hundreds in therapy and thousands through healing seminars, as well as trained over 6,000 physicians, therapists and ministry leaders how to assist those dealing with gender identity and sexual orientation concerns.

Cohen is the author of 1) *Being Gay: Nature, Nurture or Both?*, 2) *Gay Children Straight Parents: A Plan for Family Healing*, 3) *Understanding Our LGBTQ+ Loved Ones*, 4) *Healing Humanity: Time, Touch, and Talk*, 5) *A Therapist's Guide: Assisting Those with Same-Sex Attraction and Their Loved Ones*, 6) *Rich's Home*, and 7) *Counselor Training Program Manual*. His books are published in twelve languages.

He founded the International Healing Foundation (IHF) in 1990, and is currently the president and co-founder of Positive Approaches To Healthy Sexuality (PATH). Based in the Washington, D.C. metropolitan area, PATH offers consultations, family healing sessions, resource materials and speaking engagements. Cohen is a frequent guest lecturer on college and university campuses, and at therapeutic and religious conferences.

Cohen holds a Bachelor's degree from Boston University and a Master of Arts degree in counseling psychology from Antioch University. For three years, he worked as an HIV/AIDS educator for the Seattle, Washington chapter of the American Red Cross where he authored a statewide curriculum for foster parents and health care providers dealing with HIV infected children.

Cohen has been interviewed by newspaper, radio and television media including appearances on *20/20, Jimmy Kimmel Live, Rachel Maddow, Howard Stern,* ABC, NBC, CBS, CNN and other news outlets throughout the world. He lives in the Washington, D.C., metropolitan area with his wife of forty-three years and has three adult children.

Positive Approaches To Healthy Sexuality (PATH)
P.O. Box 2315, Bowie, MD 20718 / Tel. (301) 805-5155
Email: pathinfo@pathinfo.org
www.pathinfo.org
www.TimeTouchandTalk.com

www.ingramcontent.com/pod-product-compliance
Lightning Source LLC
LaVergne TN
LVHW061933070526
838199LV00060B/3830